WONDERFUL,
DANISH

A DOUBLE COOKBOOK
OF 500 DANISH RECIPES

by
Ingeborg Dahl Jensen

With an Introduction by
VICTOR BORGE

SIMON AND SCHUSTER
NEW YORK

WONDERFUL
COOKING

BAKING
from Coffee Cakes to Pastries to Torten

DINING
from Soups to Smorgasbord to Sweets

Drawings by Edward Kasper

In Memory of My Mother
Maria Kristen Dahl

*The publisher wishes to thank
the Danish Information Office
and Georg Jensen, Inc.,
for their interest and cooperation.*

CONTENTS

PART ONE: DANISH BAKING

PART TWO: DANISH DINING

INTRODUCTION

M UCH AS I enjoy American food, or, in fact, good food of any nationality, my tastebuds are predominantly, nostalgically, and fundamentally Danish. Imagine my pleasure, then, when I was asked to say a few words about Ingeborg Dahl Jensen's *Wonderful, Wonderful Danish Cooking*. Here's a cookbook with hundreds of superb recipes that promise good eating until I'm ninety without repeating once — and best of all, they're Danish!

What memories of the land of my birth Mrs. Jensen's book has stirred! Here are the delicious pastries Denmark is famous for, and the open-faced sandwiches — smørrebrød, we call them — piled high with tempting ingredients. Here are boiled beef with horseradish, and lamb with dill, and all those good Danish desserts . . . from the feather-light apple dumplings called Æbleskiver . . . to fruit soups . . . to torten . . .

My dear wife, who is devoted to my best interests, says she likes the arrangement of the book into one cookbook of Danish Baking and one of Danish Dining. Regarding the dining specialties, it is clear to her that I have to eat dinner. So that is one half of the reason she turns to Mrs. Jensen. But I'm having a little trouble with the other half. My wife has the temerity to say she will indulge my fondness for the baking

9

specialties only on one condition: I must curb my appetite for these good things sufficiently to allow me to get into my concert apparel for one more year.

But that's my problem, not yours. All you have to worry about is which one of Mrs. Jensen's wonderful, wonderful recipes to try first.

— VICTOR BORGE

"SKAAL" AND "VELKOMMEN"

TO DANISH COOKING

V ELKOMMEN is a word you often hear in friendly Denmark, and I would like to use it to welcome fellow cooks to this book, one I hope you will enjoy. For me it is a dream come true to be able to preserve and share with you this wonderful old heritage collection of recipes. Most of them have been handed down from one generation to another in my mother's family. Although I have lived in America for many years I was born in Denmark and trained in Danish ways from the time I was big enough to hold a wooden spoon. My American friends enjoy these Danish dishes, and it seems to me that Americans and Danes have many tastes in common.

First of all, we both love good baking. "Coffee and Danish" is a favorite custom in both our countries, and I think you'll find these real Danish coffee cakes and sweet breads and pastry morsels especially good. And what a feeling of accomplishment to make delicious and unusual cakes that will have your guests begging for the recipe – I often have that experience with my One-Hundred-Year-Old Recipe for Brandy Cake and with the Beer Cake from Kolding, Denmark (my birthplace). There are wonderful Christmas cakes and Christmas cookies, too (plus Christmas drinks to serve with them). In fact the

11

whole first half of the book is devoted to baking, and it starts off with the most basic baking of all — breads of every variety, from famous Danish Sourdough Bread that takes about ten days to make to all the flavorful breads made from a variety of whole grain flours.

These are the breads Danes use to make their famous open-faced sandwiches, or smørrebrød, and since Americans are enthusiastic sandwich eaters I hope you will find inspiration in the great variety of sandwich combinations on these pages.

Another thing Americans and Danes both like is the buffet style of entertaining. And so our smørgåsbord of many varied dishes has made a big hit in the United States. The second half of the book — Danish Dining — starts off with some recipes that are special favorites at my smørgasbord dinner parties, but there are dozens of other suitable ones in the chapters on fish, meats, salads and vegetables. The idea with smørgasbord as with buffet dinners is — use your imagination!

Of course simple family meals are just as much a part of Danish life as they are here, and it's nice to have some new ideas for everyday lunches and suppers. I hope you'll find inspiration here, too — in the recipes for hearty Danish soups, roasts and stews and meat loaf, dumplings and fritters, and old-fashioned puddings.

I like to think these tried and true Danish recipes will add to the friendly feelings Americans and Danes have for each other — even if you never visit wonderful, wonderful Copenhagen and taste these dishes in their native surroundings. As one who loves both countries, I wish you good results and good appetite when you cook them. *Skaal* — to your health — *skaal* to your family and guests!

— INGEBORG DAHL JENSEN

A NOTE ON
INGREDIENTS AND EQUIPMENT

SOME OF THE RECIPES in this book call for flours, grains, nuts and cooking utensils which are not available throughout the year on store shelves all over the country.

The following merchants (and for the research on many of these I am indebted to Beatrice Trum Hunter, author of *The Natural Foods Cookbook*) will send catalogues and price lists and will fill mail orders:

FLOURS AND GRAINS

Mr. Joseph Carsten, Deer Valley Farms, Guilford, New York
Mr. Ernest Halbleib, Halbleib Orchards, NcNabb, Illinois
Mrs. R. Towle, Maple Bend Farm, Box 8, Rindge, New Hampshire
Rodger Grain Company, Hereford, Texas
Vitamin Products Company
    2023 West Wisconsin Avenue, Milwaukee 1, Wisconsin
    612 North Vermont Avenue, Los Angeles 4, California
    Maryland Avenue, St. Louis 8, Missouri
Mr. Paul Keene, Walnut Acres, Penns Creek, Pennsylvania

Mr. Walter Bushman, Wholewheat Products, Box 100, Sugar Loaf, New York

Brumwell Milling Company, Solon, Iowa

Trinacria Importing Company, 415 Third Avenue, New York, N.Y. (also ships nuts of various kinds)

NUTS

James Pecan Farm, Highway 24, Brunswick, Missouri

Sullivan Pecan Co., Crest View, Florida
(Both of these firms are prepared to supply a variety of nuts, in addition to pecans.)

GRINDING MILLS FOR NUTS

Magic Mill, House of Health, Croton-on-Hudson, New York

Mitey-Mill, Sture-Dee, 238 Livingston Street, Brooklyn 1, New York

Speedmaster (Mrs. Mildred Hatch, Agent; 8 Pine Street, St. Johnsbury, Vermont)

BAKING UTENSILS AND EQUIPMENT

(Thanks to Paula Peck of *The Art of Fine Baking* fame for help in this department.)

Lekvar by the Barrel (formerly H. Roth & Son), 1577 First Avenue, New York, N.Y.

Maid of Scandinavia, 3245 Raleigh Avenue, Minneapolis, Minnesota

Williams-Sonoma, 576 Sutter Street, San Francisco, California

Casual Living, Inc., 108 Chatsworth Avenue, Larchmont, New York (springerle rolling pins and molds)

Griswold Manufacturing Co., Sidney, Ohio (Danish cake pans)

Iron Art Gift Shop, Copenhagen Square, Solvang, California (Æbleskiver pans)

Marshall Field & Co., State and Lake Streets, Chicago, Illinois (Æbleskiver pans)

Health food stores often carry flours and grains which are not in sufficient demand for grocery stores to stock. If you have a good one near you, by all means try it before you start ordering by mail.

PART ONE

DANISH BAKING

· 1 ·

BREADS, ROLLS,

MUFFINS AND RUSKS

ASK WHY Danish breads are so good and you get two simple answers: one – Denmark's varied and abundant grain and her bountiful yield of fresh, sweet butter bless bread inside and out; two – Danish cooks have a talent for breadmaking that goes back hundreds of years. Long ago, before the common people used dishes, the Danes were baking big rounds of crusty *fladbrød* to serve food on, and every one but the elite ate his plate.

As soon as a little girl in Denmark can bend her elbows over a floured board and stir with a wooden spoon, she becomes a full-fledged apprentice to a breadmaker – her mother. She learns patience enough to let her dough rest as long as necessary, to cream sugar and butter with her hands, to mix eggs one at a time, and to beat well after each egg is added.

There is still another reason why Danish breads of whole meal, rye, sweet potato, rice or wheat flour, with their spicy and golden crusts, are so delicious. They reflect the influence of French finesse on Danish cooking. For centuries the Danish people were settled around a royal court heavily influenced by French dress and cuisine. Chefs imported from France reigned over the big, luxurious royal kitchens. To learn the fine art of baking, young Danish bakers went to France. To this day in Denmark white bread is *Franskbrød* or "French bread."

Some of the recipes herein have been handed down from mother to daughter for as many as four centuries. From them one can make hospitality breads to slice and serve to say "*Velkommen*" to friends and neighbors. Slice and serve warm, or let your bread cool and wrap it in foil for storage in the freezer to have on hand for holidays or special family celebrations. These are breads to butter generously with fresh, sweet butter, to savor with freshly ground, lovingly brewed coffee, with iced aquavit or vintage wine, or with a mug of steaming drink or a glass of cold Danish beer.

Danish breads make wonderfully acceptable gifts. In Denmark miniature loaves baked before the holidays are wrapped, pan and all, on small individual breadboards, in shiny paper of many colors interwoven like a girl's braids.

Breads can be the backbone of lunch or dinner, turning the simplest meal into an occasion. They may be used *smørrebrød* fashion to make holiday party fare more exciting. *Smørrebrød* literally means "spread or buttered bread," but the word has also come to mean an open-faced sandwich on which a creative cook expresses her versatility with meats, sea foods and spreads.

The Danes have a wide choice of bread, ranging from light to dark, from sour to sweet, from soft to crisp. These are the Dane's staff of life and the thing which he misses most of all if and when he goes abroad to live in one of the many countries where such breads are not baked.

GENERAL INFORMATION ON BREAD BAKING

About Yeast

The recipes using yeast call for either cakes of fresh, compressed yeast or their equivalent in packages of dry, granular yeast. Fresh yeast is not as universally obtainable as dry, but do buy it if you can find it. Experienced bakers consider it superior to granular yeast for breadmaking.

If you must use dry yeast, dissolve it in liquid *a little warmer* than the lukewarm temperature mentioned in most of these recipes. The liquid should be 110 to 115 degrees. If you don't have a thermometer, flip a drop on the inside of your wrist. It should feel comfortably warm.

In some areas of the country a 4-ounce jar which contains the equivalent of 16 envelopes of dry yeast is being marketed. One tablespoon of this yeast equals one package of granulated yeast or one cake of compressed yeast. The jar can be resealed after use and kept for months in the refrigerator.

About Milk

Make sure you scald milk which is to be used in bread dough. Unscalded milk seems to have an undesirable softening effect and occasionally slows down the action of the yeast.

About Kneading

"Rock and roll" is the best method. Pull the dough toward you. Then push it away with the heels of your hands. Give it a quarter turn. Continue until the dough is smooth and elastic, working in only enough flour from the board you're working on so that the dough no longer sticks to the board.

The ball of dough should look smooth, tight and satiny and feel springy to the touch when it has been sufficiently kneaded. It generally takes 8 to 10 minutes to get the dough to this consistency. If you're in doubt, cut a gash in the ball with a very sharp knife. If the air bubbles in the dough are small and even, you're ready to go on to the next step. If there are large air holes in the dough, knead longer.

About Rising

Dough needs a temperature of 80 to 85 degrees to rise properly. This may be over a pilot light on a gas stove, in a cold oven with a pan of hot water placed on a rack below the pan, on a kitchen counter covered with a warm, clean cloth. Assess your own kitchen for a spot where the temperature is likely to be consistently correct and which is away from drafts.

About Baking Times

Regardless of what recipes say about time required for baking, bread isn't done until it's nicely browned on top. Watch for this. If you haven't baked bread before, try this as a test: Before the filled pans go in the ovens, turn one upside down and tap the bottom of the pan. Note the quality of the sound — a sharp ring. When you think the bread is properly baked, take a pan out of the oven and again tap it on the bottom. If the bread is done, the pan will sound hollow.

QUICK OATMEAL BREAD

•

KNÆKKEBRØD

¾ cup butter
1½ cups sour milk
3 cups flour

3 cups finely ground oatmeal
1 teaspoon baking soda
1 teaspoon salt

Melt the butter and add the sour milk. (To turn sweet milk sour, add 2¼ tablespoonfuls of lemon juice or 2 tablespoonfuls of vinegar to the above amount of lukewarm milk. Allow to stand a few moments before combining with other ingredients.) Add other ingredients. (If you can't buy finely ground oatmeal, put regular packaged oatmeal through a food grinder, using the finest blade you have, or an electric blender.)

Roll out to a thickness of ¼ inch on a floured board. Make a long roll about 1½ inches thick. Cut off small pieces and roll out into round shapes about the size of a small dinner plate, ½ inch thick. Bake on a preheated greased griddle until light golden brown on one side. Turn only once, and bake until brown on other side.

FLAT BREAD

•

FLADBRØD

4 cups white flour
1 cup graham flour
1 cup bran flour
1 cup buttermilk
1 cup hot water

½ cup melted butter
¼ cup sugar
2 teaspoons baking powder
1 teaspoon salt
1 teaspoon baking soda

Stir all ingredients together. Beat well.

Roll out into very thin circles on a floured board.

These may be cooked in either of two ways: Bake on a greased griddle on top of the stove over a hot fire until brown and crisp at the edges like pancakes. Or, if you're doubling or tripling this recipe, bake each thin sheet of dough on a greased griddle on top of the stove over a moderately hot flame for a few moments, then put on baking sheet and slip them into a preheated 400° oven to finish browning while you're starting the next sheet on the griddle.

EGG CRACKERS

•

ÆGGECRAKERS

2 eggs
½ teaspoon salt

1¼ cups flour
½ teaspoon baking powder

Mix all ingredients to a doughy consistency.

Knead on a floured board until firm. Roll thin and cut into large diamond shapes. Sprinkle with sugar and prick with a fork.

Bake on an ungreased, floured baking sheet in a preheated 450° oven for 5 minutes. Turn off heat. If edges of crackers need more browning, leave the baking sheet in the oven for a few seconds after the fire is off.

ALMOND BREAD

•

MANDELBRØD

3 eggs, beaten
½ cup sugar
2 teaspoons baking powder

1½ cups flour, sifted
½ cup chopped almonds,
  blanched

Add sugar to the beaten eggs and beat until very thick. Add sifted flour with the baking powder. Blend in the chopped almonds and mix well.

Place in a greased loaf pan and bake 45 minutes in a preheated moderate oven (375°). Frost with a powdered-sugar glaze (*pages 134-35*) if so desired.

ANISE LOAF

•

ANISBRØD

2¼ cups flour, sifted
2 teaspoons baking powder
½ teaspoon salt
½ cup soft butter
1 cup sugar
1 teaspoon anise seed

½ teaspoon almond extract
5 eggs
¾ cup almonds, ground or
  chopped and toasted briefly in
  a hot oven

Sift together twice the flour, baking powder and salt.

Cream the butter and sugar together until soft. Add the anise seed and the almond extract and blend well. Add the unbeaten eggs, one at a time, beating well after each addition. Add the sifted dry ingredients, mixing thoroughly. Fold in the ground or chopped almonds.

Bake in a preheated 350° oven for 1 hour, in a greased and lightly floured loaf pan (9 x 5 x 3).

BUTTERMILK NUT BREAD

•

KÆRNEMÆLKSBRØD MED NØDDER

5 teaspoons baking powder	3 cups whole wheat flour
2 teaspoons baking soda	1½ cups brown sugar
¾ teaspoon salt	2 eggs
1 teaspoon cinnamon	3 cups buttermilk
½ teaspoon nutmeg	2 tablespoons melted butter
1½ cups white flour	1½ cups nut meats, chopped

Sift baking powder, soda, salt and spices together with the white flour. Add the whole wheat flour, sift again. Add the sugar.

Beat the eggs until light and frothy and add the buttermilk and the butter, mixing well. Stir in the nuts.

Pour into 2 buttered and floured loaf pans (9 x 5 x 3) and bake in a preheated 325° oven for 1 hour.

HICKORY BREAD

•

VALNØDDEBRØD

1 cup milk, scalded	1 cup white flour
½ cake compressed yeast or	1 cup whole wheat flour
½ package dry yeast	¼ pound shelled hickory nuts,
2 tablespoons brown sugar	ground
½ teaspoon salt	

When scalded milk has cooled add the yeast, sugar, salt and flours, and beat well.

When beaten light, add the ground nut meats. The dough should be stiff; add more flour if necessary.

Place in a greased loaf pan (9 x 5 x 3) and let rise in a warm place until doubled in size. Bake in a preheated 375° oven for 1 hour.

BEER BREAD

·

ØLLEBRØD

2 cups water	1 tablespoon warm water
1½ cups beer	2 teaspoons salt
⅔ cup molasses, lukewarm	5 cups rye flour
1 cake compressed yeast or	5 cups white flour
1 package dry yeast	

Mix the water, beer and molasses. Add the yeast, softened in the 1 tablespoon of warm water. Add the rest of the ingredients, mixing well. Let rise in a warm place until doubled in bulk.

Knead on a floured board. If necessary, use more white flour to make a good stiff dough.

This recipe can be made into 1 loaf or into 3 small ones. If you prefer one, place the dough in a floured cloth in a large bowl and let it rise again until doubled in bulk. For 3 loaves, divide the dough into 3 equal parts and put each portion into its own floured cloth to rise.

Turn the dough upside down into a well-greased 11 x 7 x 2 pan, or 3 pans measuring 7¾ x 3⅝ x 2½.

Bake the single loaf in a preheated 400° oven for 10 minutes, then reduce the temperature to 325° and bake for 50 minutes more. If you are making 3 small loaves, bake them for 10 minutes at 400°, reduce heat to 325° and bake for an additional 35 to 40 minutes.

BLACKBREAD

·

SURBRØD

2 cakes compressed yeast or	2 tablespoons salt, scant
2 packages dry yeast	10 cups rye flour
1 tablespoon water	8 cups white flour
1 teaspoon sugar	1 teaspoon caraway seeds
4½ cups water	

Mix the yeast, 1 tablespoon water and sugar in a large bowl. Add the rest of the ingredients in the order given. Beat well.

Put the dough on a floured board and knead well. Let rise on the board in a warm place until doubled in bulk. Knead well again and shape into loaves. (5 small loaves are better than 3 standard-sized ones if you have pans smaller than 9 x 5 x 3.)

Put in greased pans and return to warm place to rise until again doubled in size.

Bake 10 minutes in a preheated 450° oven, then lower the heat to 325° and bake 1 hour more. Slice very thin.

OLD DANISH BLACKBREAD
·
GAMMELSURBRØD

½ cake compressed yeast or	1 cup rye meal, sifted
½ package dry yeast	1 cup wheat flour, sifted
2 cups lukewarm water	¼ + cup rye meal
2 cups rye meal, sifted	¼ + cup wheat flour
1 teaspoon salt	

Dissolve yeast in the lukewarm water. Add the 2 cups sifted rye meal and mix well by beating with a spoon for 2 minutes. Cover and set in a warm place to rise and fall.

This "sponge" can be mixed the night before to rise. This was the old Danish method. In the morning it will have risen and fallen, or "soured."

Beat it well, adding the salt, the 1 cup of rye meal and 1 cup of wheat flour. Beat again for 3 minutes. Cover and let rise until light and spongy. Punch down and turn onto a board sprinkled with equal parts of rye and wheat flour — about ¼ cup of each.

Knead for 10 minutes, working in as much more meal and flour as necessary for a stiff dough. As a rule, ½ cup of each is plenty.

When the dough no longer sticks to the hands and is light in texture, shape into 2 small loaves. Place in greased pans (9 x 5 x 3) and cover with slightly dampened tea towels. Let rise until light and the surface starts to crack.

Bake 1¼ hours in a preheated 300° oven. Place a shallow pan about ¼ full of warm water under the pans in the oven to prevent the loaves from becoming hard and crusted on the bottom. Brush tops with melted butter while warm. This firm bread should be sliced very thin.

HURRY-UP BLACKBREAD

•

SURBRØD

2 cakes compressed yeast or	1½ tablespoons salt
2 packages dry yeast	10 cups rye flour
1 tablespoon lukewarm water	8 cups white flour
1 teaspoon sugar	1 tablespoon caraway seeds
4½ cups water	Melted butter

Mix the first 3 ingredients, then add the remaining ones in the order given.

Knead well and let rise in a warm place until doubled in bulk.

Knead again on a lightly floured board. Shape into loaves of desired size. Let rise in greased pans until doubled in size.

Bake in a preheated 425° oven for 10 minutes. Reduce temperature to 350° and bake about 1 hour. Brush tops lightly with melted butter while still warm.

CARAWAY BREAD

•

KOMMENBRØD

½ cup brown sugar	9 cups rye flour
½ teaspoon salt	1 tablespoon caraway seeds
4 cups milk, scalded	2 tablespoons white sugar
1 cake compressed yeast or	
1 package dry yeast	

Put brown sugar and salt in a bowl and pour over them all but 2 tablespoons of the hot milk.

When cool, add the yeast which has been dissolved in the reserved milk, cooled somewhat. Stir in the flour, caraway seeds and white sugar. Beat hard with a wooden spoon for 5 minutes. Cover and put in a warm place to rise until doubled in bulk.

Knead the dough down on a lightly floured board. Shape into 2 loaves and fill greased pans (9 x 5 x 3) half full with dough. Let rise to top of pans.

Bake in a preheated 350° oven 1 hour or until the crusts are brown.

CHEESE BREAD

•

OSTEBRØD

1 cup milk, hot
¼ cup sugar
1 teaspoon salt
2 cakes compressed yeast or
   2 packages dry yeast

½ cup warm water
5 cups flour
2 cups sharp cheese, grated

Stir sugar and salt into the hot milk and let cool to lukewarm.

Soften the yeast in the warm water until dissolved. Combine the 2 mixtures and blend well. Add 2½ cups flour and stir until smooth. Add the grated cheese. Mix well. Add enough of the rest of the flour to make a stiff dough.

Put dough on a floured board and knead it for about 10 minutes. Place it in a greased bowl and let it rise in a warm place until doubled in bulk. Put it back on the board and shape into 2 loaves.

Bake in greased loaf pans (9 x 5 x 3) about 35 minutes in a preheated 375° oven.

LENTEN BREAD

•

FASTELAVNSBRØD

1 cup milk, scalded
1 cup butter
½ cup sugar
1 cake compressed yeast or
   1 package dry yeast
2 tablespoons lukewarm water

2 beaten eggs + 1 egg yolk, beaten
½ teaspoon salt
1 teaspoon cinnamon
5 cups flour
1 egg white, beaten until frothy
Ground almonds (optional)

Add the butter and sugar to the scalded milk. Cool. Mix the yeast with the water and add. Add the rest of the ingredients in the order given. Blend well and let rise in a warm place until doubled in bulk.

Flatten out with the hands on a shallow, greased baking pan. Brush with the beaten egg white. Sprinkle with sugar and additional cinnamon. To make the loaf tastier, sprinkle with ground almonds. Let rise until doubled in size.

Bake in a preheated 325° oven 50 to 60 minutes.

SOUR-MILK GRAHAM BREAD

·

SURBRØD

1 egg	2 tablespoons hot water
2 tablespoons sugar	2 cups sour milk
2 tablespoons melted butter	1½ cups graham flour
1 teaspoon baking soda	1½ cups white flour

Beat the egg with the sugar. Add the melted butter.

Dissolve the soda in hot water, and add the sour milk to the mixture. Stir in the flour, mixing well.

Combine all ingredients and blend thoroughly.

Bake in a buttered loaf pan (9 x 5 x 3) in a preheated 350° oven for 1 hour.

OATMEAL BREAD

·

HAVREMELSBRØD

1 cake compressed yeast or	½ cup molasses
1 package dry yeast	½ teaspoon salt
¼ cup lukewarm water	10 to 11 cups flour
4 cups skim milk, boiled	Soft butter
2 cups oatmeal	Oatmeal
2 tablespoons butter	

Dissolve the yeast in the lukewarm water.

To the boiled milk add the oatmeal and the butter and let stand 30 minutes. Add the molasses and beat well. Add yeast mixture.

Add 10 cups of flour sifted with salt to make a soft dough. If the dough seems too soft, add a little more flour.

Turn it out on a lightly floured board and knead the dough until smooth, about 10 or 12 minutes.

Place the dough in a greased bowl and let it rise in a warm place until doubled in bulk, about 2 hours, or until an impression remains when you press a finger deep into the dough.

Place on a floured board and let rest for 10 minutes. Divide dough into 4 parts and form into loaves. Flatten each loaf with your hands until the dough is as long as your bread pans and twice as wide. Fold from both sides to the center and place loaves in greased pans to rise in a warm place about 1 hour or until doubled in size.

Brush the tops of the loaves with soft butter and sprinkle with dry oatmeal. Bake 40 to 50 minutes in a preheated 400° oven. Remove from pans at once and allow to cool.

SWEET POTATO BREAD

·

SØDT KARTOFFELBRØD

1 cake compressed yeast or	3 tablespoons melted butter
1 package dry yeast	1 cup milk, scalded
¼ cup lukewarm water	1 teaspoon salt
1 cup mashed sweet potatoes	½ cup sugar
(canned, if you prefer)	4½ to 5 cups flour, sifted

In a large bowl soften yeast in the lukewarm water.

Blend mashed sweet potatoes with melted butter until light and fluffy. Add with milk, salt, and sugar to yeast. Beat until light.

Stir in with a wooden spoon enough of the flour to make a soft dough.

Put in a greased bowl and cover with a towel. Set in a warm place until doubled in bulk.

Shape into 3 loaves and place in greased pans (9 x 5 x 3). Let rise to top of pans.

Bake 20 to 25 minutes in a preheated 350° oven until golden brown.

POTATO BREAD

·

KARTOFFELBRØD

1 cup mashed potatoes	2 cakes compressed yeast or
(½ pound raw potatoes)	1 package dry yeast
½ cup soft butter	1 teaspoon salt
½ cup sugar	1 cup milk
3 eggs	8 cups flour
½ cup lukewarm potato water	Melted butter

Peel potatoes and boil until tender. Drain and reserve potato water. Mash potatoes.

Cream butter and sugar until well blended. Beat in the eggs one at a time, beating well after each addition.

Dissolve yeast in ½ cup of the potato water and add with the mashed potatoes to first mixture. Beat well. Add salt, milk and half of the flour. Beat until smooth. Add enough more flour, a little at a time, to make a stiff dough. Cover and let stand in a warm place until doubled in bulk.

Place on a floured board and divide dough in half. Knead well. Shape into 2 loaves and put into greased bread pans (9 x 5 x 3). Cover with a towel and let rise for about 1 hour in a warm place until the loaves are nicely rounded.

Bake 50 minutes in a preheated 375° oven. As soon as you take the pans out of the oven, brush the tops of the loaves with melted butter.

PUMPERNICKEL BREAD

•

SURBRØD

¾ cup corn meal	2 cups mashed potatoes
1½ cups cold water	1 cake compressed yeast or
1½ cups boiling water	1 package dry yeast
1½ teaspoons salt	¼ cup lukewarm water
2 tablespoons sugar	4 cups rye meal
2 tablespoons butter	4½ cups white flour
1 tablespoon caraway seeds	Corn meal

Stir cold water into corn meal. Add boiling water and cook, stirring constantly, for 2 minutes. Add salt, sugar, butter and caraway seeds. Turn off heat and let stand until lukewarm.

Add potatoes and yeast mixed with the lukewarm water. Add the rye meal and flour. Knead until smooth on a board dusted with corn meal. Place in a greased bowl and let rise in a warm place until doubled in bulk.

Divide dough into 3 equal parts. Put in greased loaf pans (9 x 5 x 3) and bake for 10 minutes in a preheated 400° oven. Lower heat to 300° and bake for 50 minutes more.

PUMPERNICKEL BREAD

•

RUGBRØD

1½ cups lukewarm water	2 cakes compressed yeast or
½ cup molasses	2 packages dry yeast
2 tablespoons caraway seeds	2 cups rye meal (not rye flour)
1 teaspoon salt	4 cups white flour
3 tablespoons butter	Corn meal

(If dry yeast is used, follow directions on package, subtracting amount of water used to dissolve yeast from amount of water called for in recipe.)

Pour the lukewarm water over the mixture of molasses, caraway seeds, salt and butter, and mix gently. Add dissolved dry yeast mixture or fresh yeast cakes crumbled into very small pieces. Add the rye meal and beat well. Sift white flour and add enough to make a stiff dough. Turn dough onto a floured board. Knead 10 to 12 minutes until smooth and elastic, adding more white flour if necessary.

Place in greased bowl, cover and let rise in a warm place (70 to 82 degrees, free from drafts) until doubled in bulk — about 2 hours.

Turn onto a floured board, cover and let rest about 10 minutes. Divide dough into 2 equal parts, shape into loaves. Place in greased baking pans (9 x 5 x 3 loaf pans, or round pans 9 inches in diameter). Sprinkle tops with corn meal.

Let rise in a warm place until again doubled in size, about 1 hour. Brush tops with cold water. Bake in a preheated 400° oven for 10 minutes. Reduce temperature to 350° and bake 35 to 40 minutes more.

RICE BREAD

•

RISBRØD

1¼ cups raw rice	3 teaspoons sugar
16 cups flour	½ cake compressed yeast or
1 teaspoon salt	½ package dry yeast
	2 cups warm milk

Wash the rice and put it in a saucepan. Add enough boiling water to barely cover the rice. Bring to a boil and cook until the grains are soft. Drain, and while rice is still warm, force it through a sieve. Rub it into the flour immediately before it cools. Use your finger tips and make sure the rice is well distributed through the flour.

Add salt and sugar.

Soften (or dissolve) yeast in 2 tablespoons of the warm milk. Add yeast mixture and remaining milk to other ingredients. Mix well. The dough should be just soft enough to handle.

Knead well on a lightly floured board and place in a greased, floured shallow pan (11 x 7 x 2).

Bake in a preheated hot oven (400°) for 1 hour, or until the edges shrink from the sides of the pan.

RYE BREAD

•

SIGTEBRØD

1 cake compressed yeast or
  1 package dry yeast
½ cup lukewarm water
2 cups rye flour, sifted
¾ cup molasses

⅓ cup butter
1 teaspoon salt
2 cups boiling water
6½ cups white flour

Soften the yeast in the warm water.

Combine the rye flour, molasses, butter and salt. Add the boiling water and blend well. Cool to lukewarm. Add the softened yeast mixture. Gradually stir in the white flour to make a soft dough, mixing well.

Turn onto a floured board and cover with a towel. Let rest 10 minutes on the board. Knead the dough until smooth and satiny, about 10 or 15 minutes. Place it in a greased bowl, turning once to grease both top and bottom. Cover with a thin towel again and put in a warm place to rise until doubled in bulk, about 1½ hours.

Punch down in the bowl, turn and let rise until again doubled in bulk, about 30 minutes.

Turn out on the floured board and divide into 3 portions; shape roughly into loaves. Cover them on the board with the towel and let them rest again for 15 minutes.

Shape the 3 loaves more precisely and put them in greased pans (9 x 5 x 3). Cover with the towel and let rise about 1 hour. Brush the loaves with lightly beaten egg and bake 35 to 45 minutes in a preheated 350° oven.

RYE BREAD

•

RUGBRØD

2 cakes compressed yeast or	11 cups rye flour
2 packages dry yeast	2 tablespoons salt
1 quart lukewarm water	1 teaspoon caraway seeds

Dissolve yeast in water. Add 4 cups flour. Beat into smooth dough. Let rise in the bowl in a warm place until doubled in bulk.

Add salt, caraway seeds, and remaining flour. Knead about 15 minutes on a lightly floured board.

Divide dough into four equal parts. Shape into loaves, and place in greased pans (9 x 5 x 3) to rise in a warm place until doubled in size.

Brush tops with cold water.

Bake 1 hour in a preheated 350° oven.

DANISH SOURDOUGH BREAD

•

DANSK SURDEJG

Genuine sourdough bread, leavened with a "sour starter," played an important role in the lives of the forefathers of most Scandinavian people. Days before the bread was made, flour and water were mixed together in a stone crock or jar, which was placed on the back of the wood- or coal-burning stove. On cold winter nights when fires got low, especially in the kitchen, my mother wrapped her woolen shawl around the crock. Every day for about ten days the mixture was inspected, and when it began to ferment, a small amount of the clear liquid which formed on the top was removed. This was combined with an identical quantity of flour and water (mixed together first in equal parts) and returned to the crock to make the "sour starter."

You can make a starter at room temperature in today's well-heated homes as well as over Grandmother's stove and with the following recipe turn out sourdough bread which tastes just as good as hers.

STEP ONE

Put 1 cup of flour and 1 cup of warm water into a stone crock or earthenware bowl or glass jar and let stand at room temperature. Take a look at the mixture every day to check for the bubbling which means that fermentation has begun. This usually takes about ten days but may happen faster if your kitchen is very warm.

When fermentation is well under way, take off a small amount of the clear liquid which has formed on top. Measure the quantity of liquid you have. Mix an equal quantity of half flour and half water. Combine with starter liquid and return to crock.

STEP TWO

When you have completed Step One, make a dough as follows:

2 cups flour	*½ teaspoon salt*
1 cup warm water	*1 tablespoon sugar*
1 cake compressed yeast or	
1 package dry yeast	

Add all the above ingredients to the starter in the crock and let stand for at least 12 hours, or until it begins to bubble again.

Let stand, covered, for 18 hours more. There should be a faint sour odor from the crock.

STEP THREE

10 hours before you want to have fresh loaves of bread on the table, take ⅔ of the dough from the crock and put into a large mixing bowl.

Have ready the following ingredients:

Generous pinch of salt	*2 eggs*
¼ teaspoon baking soda	*Flour*

Add the salt and soda to the starter right out of the crock. Beat. Add the eggs and beat very well. (Taste the dough now. You don't want it *too* sour. This is a hard term to define, but your own taste buds are probably your best guide. If it's unpleasantly sour, add a small pinch more of soda and beat well.)

Add enough flour to make a stiff dough. Fold over and over, kneading as it is turned and folded. If the dough gets too stiff, add a little syrup or a small amount of melted butter. The dough should be so stiff you can hardly stir it before you shape it.

Mold into shapes and put in greased small bread pans. Cover and let rise.

Turn loaves onto a floured board and knead well. Shape again into loaves and fill the same pans, no more than half full this time. Let rise again, until pans are full.

Bake in a preheated hot oven (400°) for about 1 hour. When loaves slip from the sides of the pan the bread is done.

Remove from the oven and tip out on the board. Brush tops with melted butter. Slice *very* thin and try it with fresh sweet butter and homemade jam for a special treat.

If you like sourdough bread and rolls (always best when they're very fresh), you'll find this superior to the finest commercial French and Italian sourdough bread available. Making the starter takes time and patience, but remember that you only have to do this once. Put aside one-third of your starter dough after every baking. Start again with Step Three when you want to make bread again. If you bake every week, the starter dough can be kept at room temperature. Otherwise, store it in your refrigerator and remove it a day before you want to use it.

SOURDOUGH BREAD

·

SURBRØD

Make a *starter* as follows that you will keep in the refrigerator for making sourdough bread:

½ cup lukewarm water	1 tablespoon sugar
1 cake compressed yeast or	1 tablespoon salt
1 package dry yeast	2 cups flour, sifted
2 cups lukewarm water	

Put the ½ cup of lukewarm water in a bowl. Add yeast and let stand until dissolved, about 10 minutes. Stir.

Add the balance of the ingredients to the first mixture and stir well. Cover and let stand for 3 days in a warm place — ideally, one with a constant temperature of about 78 degrees. Stir the mixture daily.

BREAD

1 cup starter, *at least 3 days old*	1 tablespoon butter
½ cup milk, scalded	3¼ cups flour, sifted
2 tablespoons sugar	Melted butter

Measure out the starter in a bowl. Stir sugar and butter into the milk. Cool to lukewarm, and add this mixture to the starter.

Stir in the amount of flour specified or enough more to make a soft dough. Turn it out on a floured board. Knead it well for a minute or two. Place the dough in a buttered bowl and brush it lightly with melted butter. Cover the bowl with a towel and let the dough rise in a warm place, free from drafts, until doubled in bulk, about 1½ hours.

Punch dough down and let rise again for about 30 minutes, or until doubled in bulk.

Punch down once more and shape into a round ball. Let rest for 10 minutes. Shape the dough into a loaf, place in a greased 9 x 5 x 3 pan. Cover with the towel, and again let rise in a warm place until doubled in bulk, about 55 minutes.

Bake in a preheated 400° oven about 50 minutes, or until the crust is crisp and well browned.

To continue the starter, add to the remainder of it 1 cup lukewarm water, ½ cup sifted flour and 1 teaspoon sugar. Cover the mixture and refrigerate until you need it to make sourdough bread again.

WHITE BREAD

•

FRANSKBRØD

2 cakes compressed yeast or	2 tablespoons butter
2 packages dry yeast	2 cups milk scalded
1 cup lukewarm milk	2 eggs, beaten
2 tablespoons sugar	6½ cups flour, sifted
1 tablespoon salt, scant	Melted butter

Soften the yeast in the lukewarm milk.

Into a large bowl put the sugar, salt and butter. Pour in the scalded milk and let cool to lukewarm. Add the eggs and the yeast mixture. Beat well.

With a wooden spoon stir in 2 cups of flour and beat well. Gradually add enough more flour to make a dough which will pull away from the sides of the bowl. Beat smooth and until no flour pockets remain.

Cover the bowl with a thin towel and let rise in a warm place until doubled in bulk, about 1½ hours.

Put the dough on a lightly floured board and knead *very* well. Divide into 2 parts. Mold into loaves, kneading as you work to eliminate all bubbles and get a light, smooth dough.

Fill buttered 9 x 5 x 3 pans ¾ full. Cover and let rise in a warm place until risen to tops of the pans and well rounded in the center.

Bake 10 minutes in a preheated 425° oven, then 40 minutes at 350°. Cool on racks and then brush with melted butter.

WHOLE WHEAT BREAD

•

FULDKORNSBRØD

1½ cups scalded milk	1 cake compressed yeast or
2 teaspoons salt	1 package dry yeast
2 tablespoons honey	¼ cup lukewarm water
2 tablespoons molasses	4¼ cups whole wheat flour
3 tablespoons butter	

Pour the scalded milk over the salt, honey, molasses and butter. Cool to lukewarm, then add the yeast which has been dissolved in the luke-warm water.

Add 2 cups of flour and beat well for 2 minutes. Add the remaining flour.

Turn dough onto a floured board and knead for 10 minutes. While it is still a little sticky and light, place it in a buttered bowl. Let rise in a warm place for 1½ hours.

Return dough to floured board and knead for 2 minutes. Shape into a loaf and place in a greased pan (9 x 5 x 3) and let rise in a warm place for 1 hour.

Bake 15 minutes in a preheated 450° oven, then lower heat to 375° and finish baking for 45 minutes. Let cool before slicing.

BUTTER ROLLS

•

SMØRDEJGSSNITTER

¼ cup boiling water	2 cakes compressed yeast or
½ cup butter	1 package dry yeast
¼ cup cream	1 tablespoon sugar
½ teaspoon salt	3 cups flour
3 eggs, beaten	1 cup nut meats, ground
1 teaspoon vanilla	½ cup sugar

Pour the water over the butter. Cool. Add cream, salt, eggs, vanilla and the yeast mixed with the tablespoon of sugar. Let stand 10 minutes. Add the flour. The dough will be stiff but not sticky.

Let rise in a warm place until doubled in bulk. Punch down. Cut off pieces of dough with a spoon and roll in the ground nuts mixed with the sugar. Twist each piece into a figure 8. Place on greased baking sheets and let rest 10 minutes.

Bake in a preheated 450° oven 10 or 15 minutes.

Makes 1½ dozen rolls.

MOTHER'S ONE-HOUR ROLLS

•

MORS TVEBAKKER

½ cup milk, scalded	3 cakes compressed yeast or
4 tablespoons butter	3 packages dry yeast
½ cup water	⅓ cup water
1 tablespoon sugar	6 cups flour, scant
¾ teaspoon salt	

Add the butter, ½ cup of water, sugar and salt to the milk. Let cool.

Soften the yeast in the ⅓ cup of water and add to the first mixture. Add the sifted flour.

Knead to form a good firm dough. Knead 5 minutes more. Put in a warm place, out in the hot sun or at the back of your stove when the oven has been on. (For this recipe the yeast itself needs to be at a temperature of 88 degrees.) After 15 minutes have elapsed, punch down the dough and form into rolls.

Place on a shallow, greased baking pan and let rise in the same warm spot as before until the rolls have doubled in size.

Bake in a preheated 400° oven 15 to 20 minutes.

DROP BISCUITS

•

TEBOLLER

6 teaspoons baking powder, scant	2 tablespoons soft butter
½ teaspoon salt	1½ cups milk
3 cups flour	

Sift baking powder, salt and flour together. Mix in butter with the tips of your fingers. Add the milk and beat to a soft dough. Drop by tablespoonfuls about 1 inch apart onto a greased baking sheet.

Bake for 12 to 15 minutes in a preheated 450° oven.

SALTY RYE ROLLS

•

SIGTEBOLLER

1 cake compressed yeast or	1¾ cups white flour
1 package dry yeast	2¼ cups rye flour
¼ cup lukewarm water	Oatmeal
1 heaping teaspoon salt	1 teaspoon salt
1 tablespoon molasses	2 tablespoons caraway seeds
1 cup lukewarm water	

Dissolve the yeast in the ¼ cup lukewarm water.

Mix salt and molasses, add the 1 cup lukewarm water, the dissolved yeast mixture and the flours sifted together.

Place on a floured board and knead until smooth, about 10 minutes. Place the dough in a greased bowl, cover with a towel and let rise in a warm place until doubled in bulk, about 2 hours.

Punch down and let rise again for 1½ hours.

Place again on the floured board, cover and let rest for 10 minutes.

Divide into 16 parts and shape each part into a roll. Place each on a greased baking sheet sprinkled with oatmeal. Make a gash lengthwise on top of each roll with a sharp knife. Brush tops with cold water mixed with the 1 teaspoon of salt and caraway seeds. (Use 2 scant teaspoons of salt if you enjoy very salty rolls.)

Preheat the oven to 400 degrees. Put the rolls on the lower shelf and a pan of boiling water on the top shelf. Bake for 25 minutes.

WHOLE WHEAT BISCUITS

•

HELHVEDE TEBOLLER

2 cups whole wheat flour	½ teaspoon salt
1 cup white flour	¼ cup soft butter
3 teaspoons baking powder	1 cup milk
2 tablespoons sugar	

Mix flours, baking powder, sugar and salt, and sift 3 times.

With the tips of your fingers work in the butter, mixing to a dough with the liquid.

Knead very lightly on a floured board. Roll into a sheet about 1 inch thick and cut into rounds.

Bake 15 to 20 minutes on a greased sheet in a preheated 375° oven.

SHROVE TUESDAY CRUMPETS

•

TIRSDAGS FASTELAVNSKAGER

4 eggs, beaten	*2 cups flour, sifted*
1 cup milk	*½ teaspoon salt*
3 tablespoons sugar	

Mix ingredients in order given. Drop the batter by spoonfuls on a preheated greased griddle and brown on both sides over low heat.

WINE PUFFS

•

TEBOLLER MED VIN

2 cups butter	*½ teaspoon salt*
4 cups flour	*⅝ cup red wine*
3 eggs, beaten	*1 egg yolk*

Cut 2 tablespoons cold butter into the flour. Add the beaten eggs, salt and the wine to form a firm dough. Knead it until you can feel and see dough blisters. Place in the refrigerator to chill for at least ½ hour.

Place on a floured board and roll thin. Dot generously with butter, fold edges together, then fold top and bottom to center, envelope fashion. Roll thin again. Chill for an additional ½ hour.

Place on floured board again and repeat the above procedure until all of the butter has been used, about 4 times in all.

Brush dough with beaten egg yolk, shape into small balls. Place on lightly greased and floured cookie sheets.

Bake in a very hot oven (preheated to 500 degrees) 15 to 18 minutes. Puffs should rise quickly and must be carefully watched during baking because they burn easily.

SHROVETIDE BUNS

•

FASTELAVNSBOLLER

1 cup unsalted mashed potatoes	2 tablespoons soft butter
(½ pound raw potatoes)	1 egg, beaten
1 cup potato water	¾ cup sugar
1 cake compressed yeast or	½ cup lukewarm water
1 package dry yeast	1 teaspoon salt
½ cup water	5 cups flour
2 cups flour, sifted	

Cook potatoes. Drain and reserve potato water. Mash potatoes. Mix mashed potatoes, potato water, yeast cake soaked in the ½ cup water, and the 2 cups flour. Let stand overnight.

In the morning add the butter, the egg and the sugar, and cream well. Add the lukewarm water, salt and the 5 cups flour. Beat well. Let rise in a warm place until doubled in size.

Punch down and roll ½ inch thick. Cut into rounds with a cookie cutter and drop each round into hot fat, browning on both sides. Remove and drain on paper towels. Roll in sugar while still warm.

NUT-FILLED MUFFINS

•

NØDDEFYLDTE TEBOLLER

2 cups flour	1 cup chopped almonds
½ teaspoon salt	2 tablespoons sugar
2 teaspoons baking powder	¾ cup milk
2 tablespoons soft butter	Chopped nuts

Sift together the flour, salt and baking powder. Mix the butter in well. Add the chopped almonds and sugar. Mix to a soft dough with the milk.

Mold into small balls and place well apart on greased cookie sheets. Brush each ball of dough with additional chopped nuts. Bake in an oven preheated to 450 degrees until lightly browned, 12 to 15 minutes.

WHOLE WHEAT MUFFINS

•

FULDKORNS TEBOLLER

1 cup whole wheat flour	*¾ teaspoon baking soda*
1 cup white flour	*1 egg*
2 tablespoons sugar	*1½ cups sour cream*
½ teaspoon salt	*2 tablespoons melted butter*

Sift the dry ingredients.

Beat the egg and beat into it the sour cream and melted butter. Add to the sifted dry ingredients in a few quick strokes (prolonged beating or stirring makes muffins tough).

Spoon the batter (which should be lumpy) into well-greased muffin tins. Fill the tins ⅔ full.

Bake in a preheated 400° oven 20 to 25 minutes.

Makes about 20 two-inch muffins.

RUSKS

•

SKORPOR

½ cake compressed yeast or	*2 tablespoons butter*
½ package dry yeast	*½ teaspoon salt*
2 tablespoons sugar	*1 egg, beaten*
1 tablespoon lukewarm water	*3 cups flour, sifted*
1 cup milk	

Mix yeast, sugar and water.

Scald milk, add butter and salt. When cool, add yeast mix, egg and flour.

Knead briefly. Let rise until doubled in bulk in a warm place and knead again.

Shape in an oblong loaf. Let rise again in a draft-free warm spot until doubled in bulk.

Bake in a greased loaf pan (9 x 5 x 3) in a preheated 450° oven for 10 minutes. Lower heat to 350° and bake 40 minutes more.

Cool, slice in thick slices, and return to the warm oven to dry.

QUICK RUSKS

•

SKORPOR

2 cups flour	*⅓ cup soft butter*
½ teaspoon salt	*1 egg, beaten*
2 teaspoons baking powder	*5 tablespoons sour cream*

Sift together the dry ingredients. Cut in butter until mixture is like dry meal.

Combine the beaten egg with the sour cream and stir into first mixture a little at a time.

Turn the moist soft dough onto a lightly floured board. Shape into a roll about ¾ inch thick and cut crosswise into about 10 pieces.

Place on a greased baking sheet and bake in a preheated 450° oven about 20 minutes. When well risen and light brown, remove and cut each piece into 2 pieces. Return rusks to warm oven to dry out.

ALMOND RUSKS

•

MANDELSKORPOR

2 eggs	*3 cups flour*
1 cup brown sugar	*1 teaspoon baking powder*
7 tablespoons soft butter, creamed	*Salt to taste*
3 tablespoons unblanched	
almonds, slivered	

Beat eggs and sugar together until light. Add the creamed butter and the almonds.

Sift dry ingredients and add a little at a time to first mixture, beating well after each addition.

Spread the dough 1½ inches thick on a lightly buttered baking sheet. Bake in a preheated 375° oven 15 minutes.

Remove from baking sheet and cut rusk diagonally into pieces ¾ inch thick. Cool.

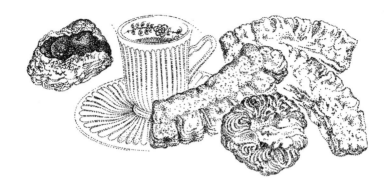

· 2 ·

SWEET BREADS,

COFFEE CAKES,

FAMOUS "DANISH PASTRY"

BASIC SWEET DOUGH

·

SØDBAGNING

½ cup milk
½ cup sugar
1 teaspoon salt
6 tablespoons butter
½ cup warm water

2 cakes compressed yeast or
    2 packages dry yeast
2 eggs
5 cups flour, sifted

Heat the milk until a fine film appears over the surface. Remove from flame and add the sugar, salt and butter. Let cool to lukewarm. Into the warm water (about 110 degrees) crumble the yeast (or sprinkle the dry yeast) and stir until dissolved. Blend in the milk mixture.

Beat the eggs and add to above mixture with 1½ cups of flour. Mix in all but ½ cup of the remaining flour.

43

Knead the dough on a floured board until it is smooth and shiny and air bubbles begin to break on the surface, adding more flour if necessary.

Put ball of dough in a buttered bowl, turning once so the top will be greased also. Put in a warm place until doubled in bulk. Punch down.

Turn dough on a floured board and knead lightly about 10 or 12 times. Shape the dough as you wish — into loaves, coffee cakes, rolls, braids — and fill, glaze or frost with any of the recipes to be found elsewhere in this book. Bake in accordance with directions given for size and shape of sweet bread you select.

APRICOT BUTTERMILK BREAD

•

ABRIKOS-KÆRNEMÆLKSBRØD

3 tablespoons soft butter
½ cup sugar
1 egg, beaten
1½ cups bran flakes, rolled lightly
1 cup dried apricots, chopped and
   soaked in
1½ cups buttermilk

2 cups white flour
2 teaspoons baking powder
½ teaspoon baking soda
¾ cup nut meats, coarsely
   chopped
½ teaspoon salt
1 teaspoon cinnamon
½ teaspoon nutmeg

Cream butter and sugar. Add egg and mix well. Add the bran and the apricot-buttermilk mixture.

When buttermilk has been almost absorbed, add the nut meats and the sifted dry ingredients. Mix well and put in a lightly buttered and floured pan (9 x 5 x 3).

Bake in a preheated 350° oven for 1¼ hours.

SWEET BREAD

•

SUKKERBRØD

2½ cups milk, scalded
1 cake compressed yeast or
   1 package dry yeast
6½ cups flour
½ cup butter, melted

⅔ cup sugar
1 heaping teaspoon cinnamon
1 teaspoon salt
1 egg, beaten to a froth

Cool milk to lukewarm. Set aside 1½ cups and soften yeast in the remaining 1 cup. Beat in 1 cup of flour and let this sponge rise until light.

Add the rest of the milk with 4 cups of flour. Beat again and let rise until doubled in bulk, about 1 hour.

Add the butter, sugar, cinnamon, salt and the egg. Stir well. Add the rest of the flour and mix thoroughly.

Put the dough on a floured board and knead for several minutes. Cover and let rise in a warm place until again doubled in size.

Roll the dough and cut into 3 strips. Braid them and pinch the ends together. Place the braided dough on a greased shallow baking pan and let rise in a warm place until doubled in bulk.

Bake in a preheated moderate oven (350°) 40 to 45 minutes. Remove from oven and brush with powdered-sugar glaze. (Sift ½ cup powdered sugar. Add 2 teaspoons hot milk and ¼ teaspoon vanilla.)

BRAN BREAD

•

KLIDBRØD

2 cakes compressed yeast or	*7 cups white flour*
2 packages dry yeast	*1 tablespoon salt*
½ cup lukewarm water	*1 teaspoon baking soda*
1 cup milk, scalded	*1 cup brown sugar*
½ cup butter	*1 cup filberts, ground or chopped*
1 cup cold water	*1 cup raisins*
¼ cup molasses	*1 cup dates, chopped*
3 cups bran flour	

Dissolve yeast in lukewarm water.

Add butter to scalded milk, stir until melted. Add cold water and molasses.

Set aside 1 cup of white flour. Combine all the remaining ingredients in a large mixing bowl. Blend thoroughly. In the center make a well. Into this pour the cooled liquids and dissolved yeast. Blend well. Work in the rest of the flour and turn the dough onto a floured board, kneading until smooth and elastic. Put into a greased bowl, cover, and let rise until doubled in bulk, about 2 hours.

Shape into loaves and place in 2 greased pans (9 x 5 x 3). Let rise again until twice their size.

Bake 1 hour in a preheated 375° oven.

OLD-FASHIONED STEAMED BROWN BREAD

•

BRUNBRØD

1 cup yellow corn meal	¾ teaspoon baking soda
1 cup rye meal	1 cup sour cream
1 cup whole wheat flour	¾ cup molasses
1 teaspoon salt	⅔ cup water or milk
2 teaspoons baking powder	

Sift the meals, flour, salt and baking powder together 3 times.

Add the soda to the molasses and sour cream, blending well. Add the water or milk.

Stir in the dry ingredients.

Fill generously buttered cans ¾ full. Butter inside of lids and tie securely. Place on trivet or rack in a heavy kettle to which boiling water to a depth of 1 inch has been added. Cover kettle and steam for 3 hours. Add additional boiling water occasionally if necessary.

CHERRY BREAD

•

KIRSEBÆRBRØD

12 to 18 large maraschino cherries, halved	¾ cup sugar
¼ cup blanched almonds, chopped	½ teaspoon salt
2 tablespoons butter	1 egg, beaten
¼ cup brown sugar	1 cup milk
2½ cups flour	¼ cup maraschino cherry juice
3 teaspoons baking powder	2 tablespoons melted butter
	1 cup bran flakes, crushed fine

Divide cherries into two equal portions. Do the same with chopped almonds. In a rectangular pan about 9 x 5 x 3, or a little larger, melt the first 2 tablespoons of butter, brushing the sides of the pan well. Sprinkle the brown sugar over the bottom of the pan, then a ½ portion of almonds. Now place ½ the maraschino cherries over these.

Sift together the flour, baking powder, sugar and salt.

Combine egg, milk, cherry juice and the last 2 tablespoons of melted butter and mix well. Add to the flour mixture and blend well. Add the bran flakes and mix only enough to moisten. Add the other portions of cherries and almonds and stir mixture well. Pour this batter into the pan lined with almonds and cherries.

Bake in a preheated 350° oven 60 to 65 minutes. When cool, slice thin.

Wonderful served with hot, spiced wine!

OLD-FASHIONED BROWN BREAD

•

BRUNBRØD

⅔ cup white flour
⅓ cup sugar
1 teaspoon baking soda
½ teaspoon salt
1 cup whole wheat flour

1 egg
⅔ cup molasses
1 cup milk
2 teaspoons vinegar

Sift flour, sugar, baking soda, and salt. Add whole wheat flour.

Add all other ingredients in the order given and blend well.

Pour the batter into a greased loaf pan (9 x 5 x 3) and bake in a preheated 350° oven for 45 minutes.

STEAMED BROWN BREAD WITH RAISINS

•

DAMPET BRUNBRØD

2 teaspoons baking soda
2 cups sour cream
1 teaspoon salt
1½ cups molasses

1 cup white flour
1 cup raisins
2 cups graham flour
1 cup corn meal

Dissolve soda in the sour cream. Add the salt and molasses. Add the white flour and the raisins. Add the graham flour and corn meal, and mix well.

Fill about half full 2 one-quart pudding pans or 3 one-pound tin cans which have been well buttered. Put on the lids and steam for 1 hour.

Remove the lids and bake the bread in a preheated 350° oven for about 10 minutes.

CURRANT SPICE BREAD

•

KRYDRET ROSINBRØD

1 cup dried currants
1⅓ cups red wine
2 cups flour
2 teaspoons baking powder
½ teaspoon salt
¾ teaspoon cinnamon
¼ teaspoon cloves

¼ teaspoon nutmeg
½ cup soft butter
1 cup sugar
3 eggs, unbeaten
1½ teaspoons vanilla
½ cup milk

Wash the currants and dry them on a towel. Soak them in the wine until they have expanded to roughly 3 times their size. Add more wine if necessary to keep the currants covered.

Sift flour, baking powder, salt and spices together.

Work the butter until soft and creamy, then add the sugar gradually. Beat eggs into the mixture until light and fluffy. Add vanilla and beat hard.

Stir in flour mixture and milk alternately, a little at a time. Beat well. Carefully stir in the currants.

Pour into a well-greased loaf pan (9 x 5 x 3) and bake in a preheated oven at 350° for 1 hour. Cool and slice very thin.

CARAMEL LOAF

•

BRYSTSUKKERBRØD

1 cake compressed yeast or
   1 package dry yeast
¼ cup lukewarm water
½ cup milk, scalded
¼ cup sugar

1 teaspoon salt
2 tablespoons butter
3 cups flour
1 egg
½ teaspoon grated lemon rind

Soften the yeast in the water.

Add the sugar, salt and butter to the scalded milk. Let cool to lukewarm. Add 1 cup of flour to make a thick batter. Beat well. Add the softened yeast, egg and grated lemon rind and beat well. Add the rest of the flour to make a soft dough.

Turn the dough onto a lightly floured board and knead until smooth.

Place in a greased bowl and let rise in a warm place until doubled in bulk, about 1½ hours. When dough is light, punch down and let rest for 10 minutes.

Divide the dough into chunks about the size of a plum. Place a layer on the bottom of a greased loaf pan (9 x 5 x 3) about 1 inch apart. Put a second layer on top so the spaces between the chunks in the first layer are covered. Continue procedure until all pieces are used. Cover with a caramel glaze as follows:

GLAZE

¼ cup dark syrup, corn or maple   1 teaspoon lemon extract
1 tablespoon melted butter

Combine the ingredients and mix well.
Pour the glaze over the layered balls of dough in the pan.
Let rise in a warm place until doubled in bulk, about 45 minutes.
Bake in a preheated 350° oven from 35 to 45 minutes. Let rest in pan for 5 minutes before turning out.

CHRISTMAS BREAD

•

JULEKAGE

1 cup sugar
½ cup butter
1 teaspoon salt
2 cups milk, scalded
2 cakes compressed yeast or
   2 packages dry yeast
¼ cup warm milk
2 eggs, unbeaten

7½ cups flour, sifted
2½ cups candied fruits
1 cup raisins
1½ teaspoons cardamom seeds,
   crushed, or 1 teaspoon ground
   cardamom
Melted butter

Put sugar, butter, salt and scalded milk in a large bowl. Stir until butter is melted. Let stand to cool.

Add yeast to warm milk, stir until dissolved and then add to the butter and milk mixture. Beat in the eggs, one at a time. Mix well. Add 5 cups of flour a little at a time, beating after each addition.

Coat 2 cups fruits and cardamom seeds with ½ cup of flour. Stir into basic mixture.

Place remaining flour on a board and knead the dough into it until smooth. Put dough in a greased bowl and brush with melted butter. Cover and let rise in a warm place until doubled in bulk.

Put back on the board and punch down. Divide into 3 portions and shape into loaves. Place in greased pans (9 x 5 x 3) and let rise until doubled in bulk.

Bake in a preheated 450° oven for 10 minutes, then lower heat to 350° and bake 45 minutes or until lightly browned on top. Remove from oven and cool. Top as follows:

FROSTING

1½ cups powdered sugar   ¼ teaspoon vanilla
2 tablespoons hot cream

Mix all ingredients together. Spread over the tops of the cooled bread, letting a little run over the sides.

Decorate with candied fruits of your choice.

EASTER BREAD

•

PÅSKEFESTBRØD

1½ cakes compressed yeast or   1 tablespoon melted butter
  1½ packages dry yeast   ½ teaspoon salt
1½ teaspoons sugar   4 tablespoons chopped citron
¾ cup lukewarm milk   ½ cup currants
1 egg, beaten   ½ cup raisins
3¾ cups flour

Dissolve yeast and sugar in lukewarm milk.

Add beaten egg and ½ of the flour a little at a time, beating after each addition. Add the melted butter and salt. Beat a few strokes. Add the rest of the flour with the citron, currants and raisins, blending well.

Knead on a floured board until smooth. Let rise in a greased bowl until doubled in bulk, about 2 hours. Return to floured board and form into 2 loaves. Place in greased 9 x 5 x 3 pans and let rise again until doubled in size.

Bake in a preheated 425° oven for 10 minutes, then lower oven temperature to 325° and bake 30 minutes more, or until the loaves shrink away from the sides of the pans.

SOUR-CREAM FRUIT BREAD

•

SURMÆLKSFRUGTBRØD

1 cup sugar	*1 teaspoon salt*
2 cups white flour	*1 egg, beaten*
2 cups whole wheat flour	*2 cups sour cream*
2 teaspoons baking soda	*2 tablespoons melted butter*
1 teaspoon baking powder	*1 cup chopped almonds*
¾ cup dried apricots, chopped	*2 tablespoons grated lemon rind*
½ cup dried prunes, chopped	*1 teaspoon vanilla*

Mix ingredients in order given and put in 2 greased and lightly floured loaf pans (9 x 5 x 3).

Bake in a preheated 325° oven for 1 hour.

Frost thinly with powdered sugar and decorate with candied fruits.

FRUIT AND BEER BREAD

•

FRUGTBRØD MED ØL

2 cups flour	*½ cup dried figs*
¼ teaspoon baking soda	*½ cup candied orange peel*
1 teaspoon cream of tartar	*½ cup candied lemon peel*
¼ teaspoon salt	*Grated rind of ½ lemon*
½ teaspoon cloves	*½ cup soft butter*
½ teaspoon allspice	*1½ cups brown sugar*
½ teaspoon nutmeg	*1 egg*
1 teaspoon cinnamon	*1 egg yolk*
½ cup currants	*½ cup beer*
½ cup raisins	

Sift dry ingredients into a bowl.

Chop the dried fruits and candied peels and add, with the grated lemon rind, to the dry ingredients. Mix well.

Cream the butter and sugar until smooth. Add the 1 egg and beat. Add the egg yolk and beat until light and smooth. Add the beer and beat again. Pour in the fruit mixture, blending well.

Spoon into a well-greased and floured baking pan (9 x 5 x 3, or a little larger). Level the dough in the pan with the back of a spoon.

Bake in a preheated 350° oven 1 hour, or until browned on top. Remove from oven and let the loaf stay in the pan for 5 minutes. Turn out on a rack. Spread top with a thin glaze, letting some drip over the sides.

HONEY BREAD

·

HONNINGBRØD

2 cups flour, sifted
¾ cup brown sugar
1 tablespoon baking powder
2 teaspoons cinnamon
¼ teaspoon ground cloves

¼ teaspoon ground nutmeg
1 teaspoon salt
1 cup sour cream
¼ cup honey
1 egg, beaten

Mix the dry ingredients. Add to them the liquids and beat well.
Bake in one large greased loaf pan in a preheated 325° oven about 60 minutes.

PRUNE BREAD

·

SVESKEBRØD

1 pound dry prunes
2 cakes compressed yeast or
  2 packages dry yeast
1 cup lukewarm water
5 cups flour

2 tablespoons sugar
1 teaspoon salt
½ cup milk, scalded and cooled
2 eggs

Cook the prunes in water to cover until soft. Drain, pit and chop them.

Soften or dissolve yeast in water.

Sift 4 cups of the flour with the sugar and salt.

Add yeast mixture, scalded milk and eggs to the sifted dry ingredients and beat well. Cover and let rise in a warm place until doubled in bulk. Add the chopped prunes.

Put the remaining cup of flour on a bread board. Turn the dough out on top of the flour and knead it until it has absorbed all the flour and is smooth.

Shape the dough into a loaf to fit a 9 x 13 pan. Grease pan, put in loaf and let rise until doubled in bulk.

Bake in a preheated 400° oven for 40 minutes. Frost with a powdered-sugar glaze.

SOUR-CREAM PRUNE BREAD

•

SURFLØDE-SVESKEBRØD

1½ cups white flour
1 cup graham flour
1 teaspoon baking powder
1 teaspoon salt
1 cup sugar
1 teaspoon cinnamon
1 teaspoon nutmeg
½ teaspoon ground cloves

1 cup nuts, ground
½ teaspoon baking soda
1 cup sour cream
1 cup cooked prunes, pitted
½ cup prune juice
2 tablespoons olive oil
1 egg, beaten

Sift together the dry ingredients. Add nuts.

Blend soda and sour cream thoroughly.

Combine all ingredients, mixing quickly and lightly.

Pour into buttered loaf pan (9 x 5 x 3) and bake in a preheated 350° oven for 1½ hours.

ALMOND PRUNE BREAD

•

MANDEL-SVESKEBRØD

2 cups flour
2 teaspoons baking powder
½ teaspoon baking soda
½ teaspoon salt
⅔ cup sugar
1 tablespoon grated orange rind
⅔ cup almonds, chopped

1 cup dried prunes, cooked, pitted
  and chopped
¼ cup prune juice
⅓ cup orange juice
1 egg
¼ cup melted butter

Sift together the dry ingredients. Add orange rind, chopped almonds and chopped prunes and mix well.

Beat the egg to a froth and add with the prune and orange juices to the dry mixture. Beat until well blended. Add the butter and mix well.

Spoon the batter into a greased, lightly floured baking pan (9 x 5 x 3). Thump the pan a little on a flat surface to expel any air bubbles which may have formed within. (This is a very old Danish custom; almost all Danish grandmothers gave their filled bread pans a careful thump before the pans went into the oven.)

Bake 1 hour in a preheated 350° oven. Remove and let cool. A thin glaze with ground almonds sprinkled on top may be used to decorate this bread.

RAISIN BREAD

•

ROSINBRØD

1 cake compressed yeast or	1 teaspoon salt
1 package dry yeast	4 cups flour, sifted
½ cup lukewarm water	2 eggs
1¼ cups scalded milk	¾ cup blanched almonds, halved
¾ cup butter	¾ cup white seeded raisins
½ cup sugar	Powdered sugar

Soften yeast in the lukewarm water.

To the scalded milk add the butter, sugar and salt, stirring until the butter is melted. Cool to lukewarm. Add 1 cup of flour. Add the eggs, one at a time, beating after each addition. Stir in the yeast. Add the remaining sifted flour to the mixture and beat hard from 3 to 7 minutes (an essential step because this dough is not kneaded).

Cover and let rise in a warm place until doubled in bulk, about 1½ hours.

Place almonds in the bottom of a well-greased mold or tube pan. Stir batter down and blend in the raisins. Spoon the batter into pan or mold. Cover and let rise until doubled in size, about 1 hour.

Bake in a preheated 350° oven for about 50 minutes, or until the top is browned. Let cool about 5 minutes, then turn out of pan upside down. Sprinkle with powdered sugar. The powdered sugar will make an attractive design on the almond-covered top if you sift it first, then lay a paper doily over the top of the bread, shake the sugar through the small holes in the doily, and carefully remove the doily.

SWEET SAFFRON BREAD

•

SØDE SAFRANBRØD

3 teaspoons sugar
1 package dry yeast or
    1 cake compressed yeast
1/4 cup lukewarm water
1/4 cup soft butter
3/4 cup sugar
1 teaspoon salt

1 cup milk
3/4 teaspoon saffron
3/4 cup hot water
6 cups flour
1/2 cup seeded raisins
1/4 cup currants
1/4 cup chopped almonds

Blend 3 teaspoons sugar and yeast in a small bowl. Add the luke-warm water and let the yeast dissolve.

Cream butter and sugar and salt in a large mixing bowl. Pour the milk over this mixture, stirring well until smooth.

Add saffron to hot water and let stand 10 minutes. Strain the saffron mixture through a fine sieve. Stir the saffron-flavored water well into the milk-butter-sugar blend. Add the yeast mixture. Stir.

When smooth, sift in 3 cups of flour, mixing well.

Blend 1 cup of flour with the raisins, currants and almonds in a bowl, until all fruits and the nuts are coated with flour. Add to the dough and mix well. Add the rest of the flour and knead with your finger tips on a board until very smooth.

Place the dough in a large bowl, cover with a towel and let rise in a warm place for 2 hours or until doubled in bulk. Cut dough in half and knead each half on a lightly floured board. Form into loaves and place each in a buttered, lightly floured loaf pan (9 x 5 x 3). Let rise again in a warm place 1 hour or until doubled in size.

Bake in a preheated 300° oven 45 minutes. Remove from oven and allow to cool gradually at room temperature.

SAFFRON BREAD

•

SAFRANBRØD

2 cups flour, sifted
2 cups lukewarm milk
2 cakes compressed yeast or
    2 packages dry yeast

2 tablespoons sugar
1/8 teaspoon saffron
1 cup soft butter, creamed
7/8 cup sugar

Salt to taste
2 eggs
1½ tablespoons blanched
   almonds, ground

½ cup seedless raisins
15 sliced almonds
Sugar
2 tablespoons butter

Add a little of the flour to 1½ cups of the milk and stir until smooth.

Mix the yeast with the 2 tablespoons of sugar in ¼ cup of milk. Add to the milk and flour base. Add enough more flour to make a smooth and elastic dough. Cover with a towel and put in a warm place until doubled in bulk.

Stir the saffron into the remaining ¼ cup of warm milk. Mix with the creamed butter, sugar and salt. Beat into the dough, then add 1 beaten egg, the ground almonds and the raisins, and mix well.

Turn the dough onto a lightly floured board and shape into two long, narrow loaves. Place side by side in a single greased loaf pan (9 x 5 x 3). Cover with a clean towel and let rise in a warm place for an hour or two. Brush the tops with the remaining egg, beaten. Sprinkle with sliced almonds and sugar.

Bake in a preheated 400° oven 15 minutes; lower heat to 350° and bake 30 minutes *without at any time opening the oven door*. If, at the end of the specified time, the loaves are golden brown, turn off oven heat. If they are not, continue baking until bread shrinks away from sides of pans and is golden brown.

Remove from oven and cool on racks. Rub tops of loaves with melted butter. Do not slice bread for about 4 hours. Slice thin.

DOUGHNUTS

·

HJORTETAKKER

1¼ cups scalded milk
1 cake compressed yeast or
   1 package dry yeast
5½ cups flour
2 eggs, beaten

1 teaspoon salt
⅔ cup sugar
½ teaspoon cinnamon
½ teaspoon nutmeg
2 tablespoons melted butter

Let scalded milk cool to lukewarm. Add the yeast to ¼ cup of the milk, stir until dissolved, and then add the rest of the milk.

Add half of the flour, mixing well. Add the rest of the ingredients in the order given, then the remainder of the flour.

Knead on a lightly floured board. Let rise in a warm place until doubled in bulk; punch down.

Roll to ¼-inch thickness. Cut in rounds with a doughnut cutter. You may want to try varying the traditional doughnut shape in one of the following ways: 1) Make a rectangle of the dough and cut into pieces about 2 inches x 4 inches. Make a slit 2 inches long through the center of each piece. Turn one end through the slit as if starting to tie a knot. 2) Roll dough to rectangular shape. Cut into long strips. Cut each strip into 4-inch lengths. Twist two strips together.

Let rise on the floured board until doubled in size. Drop carefully in deep fat heated to 375 degrees, and fry 1½ minutes on each side, or until golden brown.

Drain on paper towels. While still warm, shake in a bag containing a mixture of sugar and cinnamon.

Makes 3 dozen doughnuts.

ALMOND BUNS

•

FYLDTE MANDELKAGER

1 cake compressed yeast or	60 blanched almonds, chopped
1 package dry yeast	20 cardamom seeds, ground
2 cups lukewarm milk	4 teaspoons cinnamon
6 cups flour, sifted	¾ cup soft butter
2 eggs	1 egg, beaten (optional)
12 tablespoons sugar	

Mash the yeast in the milk, or dissolve dry yeast. Stir in enough sifted flour to make a light dough. Stir until it leaves the sides of the bowl.

Knead and fold a few times in the bowl, then cover with a cloth and set in a warm place to rise until doubled in bulk.

Beat eggs and beat in the sugar. Add chopped almonds, cardamom seeds, cinnamon and butter. Mix into the dough. Knead until smooth and until it leaves the sides of the bowl. Add remaining sifted flour and knead. Let rise again until doubled in bulk.

Knead on floured board until smooth and firm but not hard.

Shape into small round buns or rolls. Place on a greased baking sheet or pan, cover with a towel and let rise 1 hour. Brush with beaten egg.

Bake in a preheated 400° oven 15 or 20 minutes or until golden brown. Remove and fill.

FILLING

8 tablespoons almonds, ground	*2 egg whites, beaten stiff*
1½ cups powdered sugar	*1½ cups whipping cream*

Mix the ground almonds with the powdered sugar and the 2 beaten egg whites until smooth. Thin with a little cream if necessary.

Whip the rest of the cream.

Cut off the tops of the buns or rolls, spread each with the almond filling. Add a tablespoon of whipped cream. Replace tops. Sprinkle each with a little powdered sugar.

HOT CROSS BUNS

•

FASTELAVNSBOLLER

1 cup milk	*¼ cup currants*
¼ cup sugar	*2 tablespoons citron, chopped*
3 tablespoons butter	*½ teaspoon nutmeg*
1 package dry yeast or	*½ teaspoon allspice*
1 cake compressed yeast	*½ teaspoon ground cardamom*
¼ cup lukewarm water	*1 lemon rind, grated*
3 to 4 cups flour	*1 egg yolk, beaten*
½ teaspoon salt	*Sugar*
1 egg, beaten	

Scald the milk. Add the sugar and butter. Cool a little.

Soften the compressed yeast (or dissolve the dry) in the warm water and set aside for 5 minutes. Add to the first mixture.

Add the rest of the ingredients in the order given and mix well.

Let rise in a warm place until doubled in bulk. Shape into round, flat buns and place on a greased baking sheet, ½ inch apart. Let rise again until doubled in bulk. Brush with beaten egg yolk mixed with a little water. Sprinkle with sugar. With a sharp knife cut a cross in the center of each bun.

Bake in an oven preheated to 400 degrees for 20 to 30 minutes, or until golden brown. Remove from oven and frost the cross with a thick powdered-sugar frosting.

Makes 2 dozen buns.

RUM BUNS

·

ROMBOLLER

1 cake compressed yeast or	½ teaspoon salt
1 package dry yeast	½ teaspoon lemon extract
1 cup scalded milk, cooled	1 egg, beaten
¼ cup soft butter	3½ cups flour, sifted
¼ cup sugar	¼ cup currants

Soften the yeast in milk. Cream butter, sugar, salt and extract. Add beaten egg and ½ of sifted flour, mixing well.

Knead on a floured board until light. Put in a greased bowl, cover and let rise in a warm place until double in bulk.

Sift part of the remaining flour over the currants. Add them and the rest of the flour to the dough. Knead until smooth.

Shape into buns and let rise on greased pans until doubled in size.

Bake 30 minutes in a preheated 375° oven. Remove from oven and brush with rum syrup made as follows:

RUM SYRUP

¾ teaspoon cornstarch	3 tablespoons sugar
½ cup water	½ cup rum

Mix cornstarch and water until smooth. Add sugar and rum. Heat thoroughly.

ALMOND CINNAMON ROLLS

·

BLØDE MANDEL-KANELBOLLER

1 cake compressed yeast or	¼ teaspoon nutmeg
1 package dry yeast	¼ teaspoon lemon extract
½ cup lukewarm water	¼ teaspoon almond extract
¾ cup milk, scalded	3½ cups flour, sifted
¼ teaspoon salt	½ cup butter
3 tablespoons sugar	2 tablespoons sugar
2 tablespoons butter	1 teaspoon cinnamon
2 eggs	¼ cup almonds, ground fine

Dissolve yeast in the lukewarm water and set aside. Combine milk, salt, sugar and butter. Cool to lukewarm and add to the yeast mixture.

Beat eggs, add nutmeg and flavorings and stir into the milk and yeast mixture. Gradually work in 1 cup of flour, beating until smooth. Add more flour to make a very soft dough.

Turn dough onto a floured board and knead until smooth. Round up the dough and place in a greased bowl and let it rise until light, about 1 hour. Punch down and roll out on the board into a rectangle 8 x 10 inches.

Cut ⅓ of the ½ cup butter into small chunks over one long side of the dough. Press edges together. Chill for 1 hour.

Roll again. Butter the center ⅓ of the rectangle this time. Fold over one side of the dough, then the other side, and pinch the edges firmly. This time there will be 3 thicknesses of dough. Chill for 1 hour.

Divide dough into 5 pieces. Roll each into a small rectangle. Combine the 2 tablespoons of sugar, the cinnamon and ground almonds and sprinkle the mixture over each piece of dough. Roll each as for jelly roll. Cut into 1-inch pieces. Place on lightly greased baking sheets.

Bake 30 to 35 minutes in a preheated 375° oven. Brush with a glaze of syrup or thin powdered-sugar frosting.

CINNAMON ROLL-UPS

·

KANELBOLLER

1 cup scalded milk	*½ cup soft butter*
1 cup warm potato water	*½ cup sugar*
1 cup warm mashed potatoes,	*1 teaspoon salt*
unseasoned	*2 eggs, beaten*
1 cake compressed yeast or	*6 to 7 cups flour, sifted*
1 package dry yeast	

Mix scalded milk, potato water and mashed potatoes. Cool.

Add crumbled yeast. (If you're using dry yeast, dissolve in ¼ cup of the warm potato water first.)

Cream butter with sugar and add the salt and the eggs. Add to first mixture alternately with the flour to make a stiff dough, using additional flour if necessary.

Knead the dough 1 minute. Let rise overnight in a warm place.

In the morning roll out 1 inch thick, using more flour on the board if necessary to make the dough of good consistency. Sprinkle generously with brown sugar and cinnamon. Roll as for jelly roll. Cut into 1-inch pieces and place, edges just touching, on a greased baking pan at least 2 inches deep. Let rise until doubled in size.

Bake in a preheated 350° oven about ½ hour. Glaze with a thin water and powdered-sugar frosting.

Makes approximately 4 dozen medium-sized rolls.

CINNAMON BREAD

•

KANEL-SUKKERBRØD

1½ cups milk	*½ cup lukewarm water*
1 cup uncooked oatmeal	*1 egg*
1 cup raisins	*4½ cups flour, sifted*
¼ cup sugar	*2 tablespoons cinnamon*
¼ cup butter	*½ cup sugar*
1½ teaspoons salt	*Butter*
2 cakes compressed yeast or *2 packages dry yeast*	

Scald the milk and pour over the oatmeal, raisins, sugar, ¼ cup butter and salt. Stir until dissolved. Let cool.

Soften the yeast in the lukewarm water and add to the above mixture. Beat the egg separately until light and add, mixing well.

Add the flour gradually, mixing to a soft dough.

Knead the dough on a lightly floured board, about 10 minutes, until it is smooth. Shape the dough into a ball and place it in a greased bowl. Cover with a towel and let rise in a warm place (70 to 82 degrees, free from drafts) until doubled in bulk.

Punch down on a lightly floured board. Divide into 2 balls. Cover and let rest on the board for 10 minutes.

Form each ball into a rectangle ½ to ¾ inches thick. Mix the cinnamon with the ½ cup of sugar and sprinkle over both halves. Roll, starting with one of the 2 longer sides.

Place in greased loaf pans (9 x 5 x 3) with ends of rolls on bottom. Brush the tops with melted butter and set aside, covered with a towel, until doubled in size, about 1 hour.

Bake in a preheated moderate oven, 350°, from 40 to 50 minutes, until brown on top.

CINNAMON ROLLS

•

BLØDE KANELBOLLER

1 cup scalded milk	⅓ cup soft butter
2 cakes compressed yeast or	1 teaspoon salt
2 packages dry yeast	½ teaspoon grated lemon rind
1 cup lukewarm water	1 egg, beaten
¼ cup sugar	1 teaspoon cinnamon
4 cups flour, sifted	

Cool milk to lukewarm. Add yeast, dissolved in the lukewarm water, and 1 tablespoon sugar.

Sift flour and add 1½ cups to yeast mix. Beat until smooth. Cover and let rise in a warm place about 30 to 45 minutes until light and spongy. Add remaining sugar, butter, salt, lemon rind and the beaten egg, mixing well. (You may add the cinnamon now or mix with a small amount of sugar to sprinkle on top of the rolls just before baking.)

Add remaining flour to make a soft dough.

Turn out on a floured board and knead until smooth. Place in a greased bowl, turning the dough to grease it uniformly. Cover and let rise in a warm place until doubled in bulk. When dough is light, punch down a little. Shape into rolls and put on greased baking pans or in muffin tins. Cover and let rise until again doubled in bulk.

Bake about 45 minutes in a preheated 325° oven. Frost with a light powdered-sugar glaze.

ALMOND PASTRY RING

•

MANDELKRANS

PASTRY RING

4 cups flour, sifted	1 cake compressed yeast or
2 eggs, beaten	1 package dry yeast
4 tablespoons sour cream	½ cup lukewarm water
2 tablespoons white wine	2 cups butter
½ teaspoon salt	

Mix flour, eggs, sour cream, wine and salt, blending well.

Soften the yeast in the water. Add to above mixture and blend well.

Knead until bubbles appear on the dough.

Roll out to ¼-inch thickness. Place the butter on the dough, fold over completely, sprinkle with flour, roll and beat gently with the hands until very flat.

Fold the 4 corners envelope style to the center of the dough and roll very thin. Repeat this procedure 4 times. The dough will be very flaky and rich. To make the ring for which the Danes are famous, fill as follows:

FILLING

1 cup raisins, coarsely ground	6 eggs, beaten
6 tablespoons sugar	2 egg yolks (optional)
6 tablespoons unblanched	2 tablespoons almonds, ground
almonds, chopped fine	(optional)
Grated rind of 1 lemon	

Blend first five ingredients together well. Line a baking ring pan with half of the pastry dough. Place filling over this evenly. Cover with rest of pastry dough.

Brush with the beaten egg yolks and ground almonds to make the ring more decorative if you wish.

Let rise until doubled in bulk in a warm place.

Bake 40 minutes in a preheated 325° oven.

Makes 1 large or 2 small ones.

ALMOND SLICES

Make basic pastry as for Pastry Ring. Roll the dough to ¾-inch thickness. Divide dough in quarters. Line 2 rectangular baking sheets with two of the quarters. Reserve the other two quarters for covers.

FILLING FOR ALMOND SLICES

8 egg whites, beaten stiff	¼ teaspoon nutmeg
1 cup sugar	1 cup almonds, ground
¼ teaspoon cinnamon	

Mix the beaten egg whites with the sugar and spices. Cover the dough on the baking sheets evenly with filling. Cover with remaining dough. Sprinkle the top with ground almonds.

Bake 40 minutes in a preheated 350° oven, or until tops are dry and firm.

TWISTS

Make basic pastry as for Pastry Ring. Cut dough into narrow strips. Form into "S" shapes. Brush each one with a dab of egg white which you have beaten until frothy. Sprinkle with sugar.

Let rise until doubled in bulk.

Bake 15 to 20 minutes in a preheated 350° oven.

COPENHAGEN KRINGLES

•

KØBENHAVN-KRINGLER

1½ cups cream	*3⅓ cups flour, sifted*
½ cup soft butter	*¼ teaspoon cardamom seed,*
2 tablespoons sugar	*ground*
1 cake compressed yeast or	*Melted butter*
1 package dry yeast	

Scald the cream, add the butter and sugar, and stir until creamy.

When mixture has cooled to lukewarm, crumble in the yeast and stir until it is dissolved. Add half of the flour and the ground cardamom seeds, mixing thoroughly. Work in the remaining flour, blending well.

Knead until smooth on a lightly floured board. Place the dough in a greased bowl, cover and let rise until doubled in bulk in a warm place free from drafts.

Punch the dough down. Divide into 30 or 40 pieces. Roll each piece with the hands until it is about 10 inches long. Tie in a loose knot by pulling one end through the center and the other end up over the side.

Brush with melted butter and dip each kringle in

TOPPING

¼ cup sugar	*½ cup chopped almonds*
½ teaspoon cinnamon	

Place the kringles on a greased baking sheet about 2 inches apart and bake about 15 minutes in a preheated 400° oven.

DANISH KRINGLE

•

DANSK KRINGLE

4 cups flour	*1 cup milk*
1 teaspoon salt	*3 eggs, beaten*
1 cup butter	*1 teaspoon cardamom*
3 tablespoons sugar	*1 egg white*
2 cakes compressed yeast or	*Sugar*
2 packages dry yeast	*Cinnamon*
¼ cup lukewarm water	*Slivered almonds*

Blend flour, salt, butter and sugar, as for any crust.

Dissolve the yeast in ¼ cup lukewarm water.

Scald the milk, cool slightly and add to the beaten eggs. Stir. Add dissolved yeast, cardamom and flour-and-shortening mixture. Mix until smooth. Cover and let rise in a warm place until doubled in bulk.

Place the dough on a floured board, pat with the hands as though beating the dough.

Divide dough in half and place on 2 well-greased baking sheets. Spread out thinly. Spread through the middle with one of the fillings for which recipes are given in this chapter or in Chapter 5. Bring up edges to the center and press together to seal. Sprinkle with sugar and cinnamon and slivered almonds.

Bake 20 minutes in a preheated 350° oven, or until brown.

OLD DANISH KRINGLE

•

DANSK SMØREKRINGLE

This old Danish pastry is legendary. It symbolizes the Danish *hygge* (which means "comfortable and good") life.

Any fruit or nut filling is excellent, but almond is the most popular with the Danes.

It is always served at Christmas and Easter and on special anniversaries.

There is a secret to kringle baking: The dough is made with the butter *rolled* in — not mixed or blended with a fork or pastry blender.

DOUGH FOR KRINGLE

1 teaspoon salt
½ cup sugar
1 cup milk
2 eggs, lightly beaten
2 cakes compressed yeast or
   2 packages dry yeast
½ cup soft butter
2 cups flour

½ teaspoon grated lemon rind
Few cardamom seeds
Butter
Filling
Ground nuts
Powdered sugar
1 egg
Milk

Mix salt and sugar. Add ¾ cup milk and eggs.

Add yeast soaked in ¼ cup milk heated to lukewarm. Add butter, and cream all ingredients together with fingers. Add enough flour to make a medium-stiff dough; add grated lemon rind and cardamom seed.

On a lightly floured board spread the dough to an 8 x 12 rectangle. Dab the butter on half of this rectangle (4 x 6 inches). Fold the un-buttered half of the dough over the buttered half. Roll out to 8 x 12 inches again. Fold in half again. Roll again to an 8 x 12 rectangle. Fold in half. Chill dough 2 hours in refrigerator.

Cut in 4 strips lengthwise. For 4 kringles, roll strips out to 18 x 2½ inches. Spread filling (see 2 recipes which follow) in the middle and fold ends over. Sprinkle with ground nuts and powdered sugar.

Form in pretzel shapes and let rest in a warm place 45 minutes to rise.

Brush with a mixture of equal parts of egg and milk, sprinkle with sugar and ground slivered almonds.

Bake in a preheated 375° oven 12 to 15 minutes, or until a delicate brown.

RAISIN-NUT FILLING

1½ cups water
1½ cups golden raisins
½ cup soft butter
½ teaspoon cardamom seeds

2 cups powdered sugar
2 tablespoons cream
½ cup chopped almonds

Bring to a boil water and raisins. Drain off the liquid. Let cool.

Cream butter until very soft, add cardamom and blend well. Add powdered sugar and enough cream to enable you to spread mixture easily. Mix in raisins and chopped nuts and blend well.

Prune Filling

2 pounds prunes   ½ cup claret wine
1½ cups sugar

Cook prunes until tender, pit and mash. Add remaining ingredients
and cook until thick.

RAISIN RUM ROLLS

•

BLØDE ROMBOLLER

½ cup milk, scalded   1 cake compressed yeast or
¼ cup sugar   1 package dry yeast
1 teaspoon salt   1 egg, lightly beaten
3 tablespoons butter   2½ cups flour, sifted
                                         2 tablespoons melted butter

Add the sugar, salt and butter to the scalded milk. Stir until the
butter is melted and the sugar is dissolved. Cool to lukewarm. Crumble
fresh yeast into mixture (or sprinkle dry yeast over it) and stir well.
Add the egg and blend in the flour.

Turn out on a floured board and knead until the dough is smooth.
Put into a greased bowl and brush with 1 tablespoon of melted butter.
Cover and let stand in a warm place about 2 hours until doubled in
bulk.

Turn out again on the floured board, pat into a rectangle and roll out
about 15 inches long and 8 inches wide. Spread with remainder of
butter. Cover with raisin filling:

Filling

2 cups white raisins   1 egg, beaten
½ cup brown sugar   ½ cup rum
⅔ cup dry bread crumbs

Rinse and drain the raisins and put through a food chopper or
grinder. Add brown sugar, bread crumbs, egg and rum. Mix well.

Roll up as for a jelly roll and cut into pieces about 1½ inches thick.
Brush the tops with a little sugar and milk mixed together.

Place sugared side up in greased shallow pans and let stand in a warm place until doubled in size, 30 to 45 minutes.

Bake in a preheated 350° oven 30 to 40 minutes, or until browned. Makes 16 rolls.

You may frost these, if you wish, when they come out of the oven. The recipe given below adds a piquant and unusual flavor.

FROSTING

2 egg whites   ¾ cup apple jelly
Pinch of salt

Mix the egg whites with the salt and beat until they begin to hold their shape. Beat in the jelly a little at a time.

Place in the top of a double boiler over hot water and continue to beat for 2 or 3 minutes longer.

SNAILS
·
SNEGLER

½ cup milk	½ teaspoon salt
½ cup butter	5 cups flour
2 eggs, beaten	Sugar
1 cup sour cream	Cinnamon
1 cake compressed yeast or	Raisins, chopped
1 package dry yeast	Nut meats, chopped
½ cup sugar	

Scald milk. If you are using dry yeast, reserve ¼ cup of milk and add butter to the balance. If you're using fresh yeast, add butter to the total quantity of milk. Let cool.

Add eggs and sour cream.

Crumble fresh yeast in the sugar and let stand until liquefied. (Dissolve dry yeast in the warm milk you've been saving. Stir in sugar.) Add yeast blend to first mixture.

Add the salt and 4 cups of flour and beat well. Place in the refrigerator overnight.

In the morning remove and let dough rise in a warm place until doubled in bulk. Punch down and add remaining 1 cup of flour.

Knead well on a lightly floured board. Roll out in thin sheets and cover with sugar, cinnamon, nuts and raisins in whatever quantity best suits your family's tastes. Roll up like a jelly roll. Cut into 1-inch slices and lay slices flat on a greased baking sheet or in muffin pans. Let rise in a warm place until doubled in size.

Bake in a preheated 350° oven about 30 minutes. Frost with a glaze of water and powdered sugar.

LITTLE DANISH PASTRIES

•

SMÅ SMØRKAGER

1 cup soft butter
4 cups flour, sifted
1 teaspoon salt
1 cup warm milk
4 egg yolks, beaten
¼ cup sugar
Grated rind of 1 lemon

1 cake compressed yeast or
  1 package dry yeast
1 tablespoon warm water
½ teaspoon sugar
Prunes, or
Marmalade

Mix butter, flour and salt. Add milk, egg yolks, sugar and lemon rind. Add the yeast which has been mixed well with the water and the ½ teaspoon of sugar. Let rise in a warm place until doubled in bulk.

Roll out about 1 inch thick on a well-floured board. Cut in rounds with a large cookie cutter and press on top of each one a pitted prune which has been soaked in a little water until soft. Or make a well on top of each and fill it with a thick marmalade. Brush the tops with lightly beaten egg white and sprinkle with additional sugar. Place 1 inch apart on greased cookie sheets (or in muffin tins) and let rise until doubled in size.

Bake in a preheated hot oven (450°) 20 to 25 minutes.

SMALL CREAM CAKES

•

SMÅ FLØDEKAGER

2 cups heavy cream
5 eggs
6 tablespoons sugar

¾ cup flour, sifted
½ teaspoon ground cardamom

Whip the cream until stiff.

Beat the eggs with the sugar. Add the sifted flour and ground cardamom and mix thoroughly. Combine with whipped cream.

Half fill buttered, lightly floured muffin tins and bake 10 minutes in a preheated 350° oven, or until golden brown. Frost as desired.

SOUR-CREAM COFFEE ROLLS

•

SURFLØDEBOLLER

2 cups milk	4 eggs, beaten
1 cup sour cream	2 cakes compressed yeast or
¾ cup butter	2 packages dry yeast
1 teaspoon salt	¼ cup lukewarm water
1 cup sugar	13 cups flour

Scald the milk and cream. Add the butter, salt and sugar. Let cool. Add the eggs and yeast which has been dissolved in the water.

Stir in the flour gradually, using just enough to make a stiff dough.

Let rise until doubled in bulk. Punch down. Cover bottoms of lightly greased large muffin tins with dough ½ inch thick. Cover with filling (see below).

FILLING

½ cup sugar	1 teaspoon cinnamon
1 cup prunes, cooked and chopped	½ cup raisins
½ cup blanched almonds, chopped	

Mix all ingredients together, spoon over dough in muffin tins, and top with ½-inch-thick layer of dough. Let rise again in a warm place until doubled in bulk.

Bake in a preheated 450° oven 25 minutes.

This recipe may also be baked as 3 coffee loaves. Divide the dough into 6 equal portions. Cover the bottom of each lightly greased 9 x 5 x 3 bread pan with one portion of the dough. Spread filling over each, and top each with remaining portions of dough. Let rise until doubled in bulk. Bake 10 minutes in a preheated 450° oven. Reduce heat to 350 degrees and bake 40 minutes more.

Makes 3 large loaves or 8 dozen rolls. If you don't want to bake so many rolls at one time, wrap and freeze any quantity you wish for future baking.

OLD DANISH YEAST COFFEE CAKE
•
GAMMEL KAFFEKAGE

2 cups milk	*½ cup sugar*
1 cake compressed yeast or	*Grated rind of ½ lemon*
1 package dry yeast	*3 eggs, lightly beaten*
4 cups flour, scant	*1 teaspoon cinnamon*
½ cup melted butter	*2 tablespoons chopped almonds*

Scald milk and cool to lukewarm. Pour ¼ cup milk over yeast and let stand while beating remaining milk with 2¼ cups flour to make a smooth dough. Add dissolved yeast and beat well. Put in a warm place (70 to 82 degrees) to rise.

When dough is well risen (feels light to the touch and a finger indentation springs back), add melted butter, sugar, lemon rind and eggs. Stir in the rest of the flour. Mix well.

Spread dough about 1 inch thick on 2 greased baking pans or cookie sheets. Place in warm spot to rise again. When well risen, sprinkle with sugar and cinnamon. Dot well with butter. Spread with chopped almonds.

Bake in a preheated 400° oven about 15 minutes. Lower heat to 375° and bake until brown.

APPLE COFFEE CAKE
•
ÆBLEKAGE

Prepare dough as in Old Danish Yeast Coffee Cake, spreading on baking pans or cookie sheets to a thickness of about ½ inch before second rising.

When well risen, peel apples, cut into ½-inch slices and arrange evenly on dough. Sprinkle well with a mixture of sugar, cinnamon, and a pinch of nutmeg, if you wish.

Bake 10 minutes in a preheated 400° oven. Lower heat to 375° and bake until a toothpick inserted in the center comes out clean.

For a sweeter cake, sprinkle powdered sugar over the cake after it comes out of the oven.

Cherries may be substituted for apples in the above recipe.

QUICK DATE COFFEE CAKE

•

GALOP DADEL-KAFFEBRØD

1 cup hot water	3 cups flour
1½ cups dates, pitted	2 teaspoons baking soda
2 eggs	2 teaspoons baking powder
2 cups sugar	¼ cup soft butter
¼ teaspoon salt	1¾ cups hot coffee
½ cup blanched almonds, halved	1 teaspoon vanilla

Pour the hot water over the dates and let stand until the rest of the batter is mixed.

Beat eggs until frothy. Add the sugar and salt a little at a time, and blend well.

Mix nuts with flour and add to egg mixture, stirring well.

Combine baking soda and baking powder with the softened butter and blend with previously mixed ingredients.

Add the hot coffee, vanilla and dates, including any liquid which may remain from the soaking.

Pour into a greased tube pan and bake 1 hour in a preheated 350° oven.

SWEET BREAKFAST ROLLS

•

GOD MORGENKAGER

2 cups milk	½ cup melted butter
1 cake compressed yeast or	½ cup sugar
1 package dry yeast	3 eggs, lightly beaten
5 cups flour, scant	Grated rind of ½ lemon

Scald milk and cool to lukewarm. Pour ¼ cup of the milk over the yeast and let stand while beating remaining milk with 2¼ cups of the flour to make a smooth dough. Add the dissolved yeast and beat well.

Stir in about 2½ cups more flour. Add melted butter.

Beat eggs and add to above mixture with grated lemon rind. Mix well.

Put in a warm place to rise until doubled in bulk. Roll out on a lightly floured board or cloth to 1-inch thickness. Sprinkle with a mixture of:

1 cup sugar	½ to ¾ cup ground almonds
1 cup raisins	1 teaspoon cinnamon

Roll up carefully, like a jelly roll, and cut into slices. Place rolls in greased pans (with a cut side down) and let rise ½ hour. Dot the tops plentifully with melted butter.

Bake 10 minutes in a preheated 425° oven. Lower temperature to 375° and bake until rolls are browned. Remove from oven, brush tops with melted butter, and sprinkle with sugar.

QUICK COFFEE CAKE WITH FRESH FRUIT

•

GALOP KAFFEKAGE

1 cup ripe red currants	½ teaspoon nutmeg
(or blueberries or other fruit)	½ cup soft butter
2 cups flour	1 cup sugar
2 teaspoons baking powder	3 eggs
½ teaspoon salt	⅓ cup milk
½ teaspoon cinnamon	1½ teaspoons vanilla
¼ teaspoon cloves	

Wash and drain the currants. Remove the stems.

Sift the flour, baking powder, salt and spices together.

Work the butter until soft and creamy. Add the sugar gradually, blending well. Beat the eggs into the mixture and continue to beat until light and fluffy.

Stir in the dry ingredients and the milk alternately, a little at a time, beating well after each addition. Add vanilla. Fold in fruit.

Pour batter into a greased loaf pan (9 x 5 x 3) and bake in a preheated 350° oven for 1 hour.

FILLED COFFEE CAKE

•

KAFFEKAGE

1 cup milk	½ cup sugar
½ cup butter	1 teaspoon cinnamon
½ cup sugar	1 tablespoon sour cream
1 teaspoon salt	Melted butter
1 cake compressed yeast or	1 cup powdered sugar
1 package dry yeast	Juice of 1 lemon
3 eggs, beaten	Pecans
4½ cups flour	

Scald the milk. Remove from fire. Add butter, ½ cup of sugar and salt, stirring until lukewarm. Add the yeast and stir until dissolved.

Add the eggs, then enough of the sifted flour to make a stiff dough. Mix until smooth.

Knead well on a floured board. Put into a greased bowl and let rise in a warm place until doubled in bulk. Divide dough in half, patting into oblong shapes.

Mix ½ cup sugar, cinnamon and sour cream until creamy. Spread over the 2 oblong shapes of dough. Roll up and pinch the edges firmly together. Make slits here and there in the center of the oblongs, but not all the way through the dough. (Cut the dough into 3-inch slices if you prefer.)

Coat with melted butter and let double in size. Bake in a preheated 375° oven for 25 minutes. Before the pastry has cooled completely, mix the powdered sugar and lemon juice into a paste and ice the cakes. Sprinkle with ground nut meats.

This recipe is sufficient to make two filled cakes. If you prefer rounds to oblongs, and like your pastry a little richer, try the following:

FILLING

1 cup pecans, ground or chopped	¼ teaspoon salt
fine	2 egg yolks, beaten
½ cup cream	2 teaspoons butter
⅔ cup sugar	

Combine all ingredients in order given. Cook over low heat, stirring constantly, until thick.

Spread over dough, fold up and pinch the edges firmly together. Shape into rings slit as above, let rise and bake as directed in preceding recipe.

RAISIN COFFEE CAKE

·

ROSINKAFFEKAGE

2 cups milk	3 eggs, lightly beaten
2 cakes compressed yeast or	1 cup sugar
2 packages dry yeast	1 cup raisins
2½ cups flour	1½ cups flour
1 cup melted butter	

Scald milk. Cool. Add yeast, stir until dissolved. Beat in the flour. Let rise till bubbly. Add rest of ingredients and beat.

Half fill 2 round, buttered 9-inch tube pans with the dough. Let rise until forms are full.

Bake in a preheated 400° oven for 15 minutes. Lower heat to 375° and bake 45 minutes more.

QUICK COFFEE RING

·

GALOPKRINGLE MED BAGEPULVER

¼ pound butter	½ cup raisins
½ cup sugar	½ cup mixed candied fruit,
¾ cup milk	chopped
3 cups sifted flour	1 egg yolk
2½ teaspoons baking powder	Sugar
Pinch of salt	⅔ cup almonds, chopped

Mix first 8 ingredients. Blend well.

Knead 5 or 6 times on a lightly floured board. Form into 2 round loaves. Place on greased cookie sheet. Brush tops with lightly beaten egg yolk combined with sugar to taste. Sprinkle with chopped almonds.

Bake in a preheated 350° oven for 15 to 20 minutes.

This can also be made as a traditional ring by working in enough more flour so that the dough can be handled and shaped into a ring. Roll with your hands into a rope, joining the 2 ends together to form a circle.

FILLED DANISH PASTRIES

•

WIENERBRØD

1½ cakes compressed yeast or
   1½ packages dry yeast
¼ cup lukewarm milk
1½ cups milk
6 tablespoons soft butter
1½ teaspoons salt
6 tablespoons sugar
2 eggs
½ teaspoon nutmeg

½ teaspoon lemon extract
¼ teaspoon almond extract
7 cups flour, sifted
¾ cup soft butter
Filling
1 egg
½ cup powdered sugar
Almonds

Mash the yeast (or dissolve) in the ¼ cup lukewarm milk and set aside.

Heat the 1½ cups milk and with a fork beat lightly together with the butter, salt and sugar until sugar is dissolved. Add to the yeast mixture.

Beat the eggs well, add the nutmeg and flavorings and stir into the above mixture. Gradually work in 2 cups sifted flour. Beat well for a few minutes. Add remaining flour, a little at a time, and when mixed well, place the dough on a floured board and knead with floured hands until dough is smooth.

Turn into a warm buttered bowl, cover with a cloth and set in a warm place. When doubled in bulk, return to the floured board and roll out ½ inch thick. Spread half the softened butter over half the dough, fold other half over it and roll again to a thickness of ½ inch. Spread again with remaining softened butter and repeat above procedure. Cut into rounds, squares or triangles. Fill as follows:

FILLING

Jam, or cooked apples, or both
Spices of your choice

Small amount of cream

Mix all ingredients until creamy. Place a teaspoon of filling on each of the cut pastries. Fold over, letting a little of the filling peek out. Press the edges together lightly.

Brush with beaten egg and bake 15 to 18 minutes in a preheated 450° oven.

When cool, frost with icing made of powdered sugar and 1 tablespoon water. Sprinkle with ground almonds.

FILLINGS AND TOPPINGS FOR
COFFEE CAKES AND ROLLS

•

RAISIN-ZWIEBACK FILLING

1 cup chopped almonds, blanched
1 tablespoon sugar
1 cup seeded raisins

¼ cup heavy cream
½ cup zwieback, crumbled

Mix all ingredients together and stir well.

CRUMB TOPPING

1 cup soft butter
2 cups brown sugar
3½ cups flour

2 teaspoons cinnamon
1 teaspoon cloves
1 teaspoon nutmeg

Cream butter and sugar until light.

Sift the flour with the spices and mix with the butter and sugar until crumbly. This (enough for several cakes) will keep well in a covered jar in the refrigerator.

POPPY-SEED FILLING

3 cups poppy seed, ground
1¼ cups sugar

¾ cup milk
½ cup butter

Mix ingredients in order given and cook over low heat until mixture is slightly thickened. Remove from fire and let cool.

If filling becomes too thick while cooling, stir and mix in a little milk.

· 3 ·

DESSERT CAKES
AND TORTEN

ALMOND CAKE
·
MANDELKAGE

½ cup butter
½ cup sugar
1½ cups sifted flour
1 egg

1 teaspoon baking powder
⅔ cup blanched almonds
⅔ cup powdered sugar
1 egg, beaten

Cut butter, sugar and sifted flour together with a pastry knife or blender.

Beat the egg and, with the baking powder, blend with above mix.

Grate the almonds in a nut grinder or a blender; mix with the powdered sugar which has been sifted fine. Blend in the other egg.

Divide the dough into 2 parts. Put 1 ball of dough into a lightly greased 9-inch round cake pan, working dough to cover bottom and sides. Spread the almond mix evenly over the dough. Cut off pieces from rest of dough and roll with the hands into rolls about ½ inch thick. Place these crisscross over bottom layer, forming lattice work.

There will be some dough left which will make a thin roll to form an edge to the cake. Press the ends together to seal.

If dough becomes too sticky, place in the refrigerator 5 or 10 minutes to chill. Bake in preheated 375° oven about 30 minutes or until lightly browned. Cool on rack. When cooled, cut into small wedges and remove carefully from pan.

APPLESAUCE CAKE

•

ÆBLESAUCEKAGE

½ cup soft butter
2 cups sugar
1 egg, beaten
1½ cups thick applesauce
2½ cups flour, sifted
1 cup raisins, chopped
1 cup almonds, chopped

½ teaspoon salt
1 teaspoon cinnamon
1 teaspoon allspice
½ teaspoon cloves
1 teaspoon baking powder
½ cup buttermilk
2 teaspoons baking soda

Cream butter and sugar. Blend in the beaten egg and the applesauce. Sift flour, measure and sift again.

Dredge the raisins and the nuts with a little of the flour.

Sift the flour again with the salt, spices and baking powder. Add to the buttermilk with the baking soda. Blend well. Fold in the floured raisins and the nuts.

Bake in a buttered, lightly floured baking pan about 12 x 10 inches for 1 hour in a preheated 350° oven. Frost with your favorite light, creamy powdered-sugar frosting.

ANNIVERSARY CAKE

•

JUBILÆUMSKAGE

6 egg yolks
¾ cup granulated sugar
6 egg whites
1¼ cups flour
2 teaspoons baking powder

3 squares cooking chocolate
¾ cup soft butter
1¼ cups powdered sugar
2 eggs
2 cups whipping cream

Beat egg yolks with granulated sugar until light.

Beat egg whites until stiff but still a little moist. Fold in the flour and baking powder which have been sifted together three times.

Combine the two mixtures with a gentle hand. Pour into three 9-inch-square layer pans which have been greased and floured well.

Bake about 15 minutes in a preheated 375° oven, or until browned, or until a toothpick inserted in the center comes out clean. Invert on racks and let cool. Store in refrigerator or freezer 2 or 3 days. (The Danish recipe says: "Store in the cold part of the cellar or *kjelderrum*.")

When ready to use, thaw the cakes at room temperature. Shred the 3 squares of chocolate, reserving about ¼ cup. Mix the ¾ cup butter and the powdered sugar until creamy. Beat in the 2 eggs. Mix well. Cover each layer of cake with the butter-sugar-egg mixture, spreading each with the curls of chocolate.

Whip the heavy cream and frost the cake, after you have centered one layer over the top of the other. Swirl the whipped cream in deep indentations to be filled with the reserved curls of chocolate. Refrigerate until ready to serve.

BLACKBERRY JAM CAKE

·

BROMBÆRKAGE

½ cup soft butter
1 cup brown sugar, packed down
   as much as possible in cup
3 egg yolks, beaten
1½ cups flour
1 teaspoon baking soda
1 teaspoon nutmeg

1 teaspoon cinnamon
3 tablespoons sour milk
1 cup blackberry jam
Flour
¾ cup raisins, chopped
3 egg whites

Cream butter and sugar. Add egg yolks and mix well.

Sift dry ingredients together. Combine sour milk and jam with dry ingredients and blend thoroughly with butter-sugar-yolk mixture. Flour raisins lightly and add.

Beat egg whites until stiff and fold in.

Bake in 2 buttered and lightly floured 8-inch layer-cake pans 25 to 30 minutes in a preheated 375° oven. Frost as follows:

FROSTING

½ cup brown sugar
½ cup white sugar
½ teaspoon cream of tartar
¼ cup water

2 tablespoons strong coffee
Pinch of salt
Vanilla
2 egg whites

Boil sugars, cream of tartar, water, coffee and salt together without stirring until the syrup spins a thread. Remove from flame. Stir in vanilla.

Beat the egg whites until stiff. Add syrup slowly to egg whites, beating until the frosting will hold its shape and spread easily around the sides and over the top of the cake.

BEER CAKE FROM KOLDING, DENMARK

•

ØLKAGE FRA KOLDING

1 cup sugar
½ cup soft butter
2 eggs
½ cup molasses
2½ cups flour
¼ teaspoon salt

¼ teaspoon cinnamon
¼ teaspoon allspice
¼ teaspoon cloves
2½ teaspoons baking powder
¾ cup beer

Cream sugar and butter. Add the eggs, one at a time, beating well after each addition. Stir in the molasses.

Sift dry ingredients together and add, along with the beer, to the mixture.

Bake in 2 lightly greased and floured 8-inch layer-cake pans about 35 minutes in a preheated 375° oven. Fill and frost as follows:

FROSTING

4 cups powdered sugar
4 teaspoons cocoa
¼ teaspoon salt

⅓ cup soft butter
⅓ cup strong coffee
½ teaspoon vanilla extract

Mix and cream the ingredients well. Spread between layers, over top and around sides of cake.

BRANDY CAKE
FROM A ONE-HUNDRED-YEAR-OLD RECIPE

•

COGNACKAGE

5 egg yolks
Grated rind and juice of 1 lemon
1 cup flour, sifted three times
¼ teaspoon salt

5 egg whites
1 cup powdered sugar
¾ cup brandy

Beat the egg yolks until thick and lemon-colored. Add the lemon rind and juice. Fold in the sifted flour and the salt.

Beat the egg whites until stiff and fold the sugar into them a little at a time. Fold this mixture into the batter and mix gently but thoroughly.

Pour the batter into an ungreased tube pan and bake in a preheated slow oven (300°) for 1 hour, or until the cake is light brown and springs back when you touch it.

Invert the pan on a rack for at least 1 hour before moving the cake. Split the cake into 2 layers with a wire knife or cake separator. Put one layer on a serving platter and pour over it ½ cup of the brandy. When cake has soaked up the brandy, cover with ½ of the recipe for filling which follows:

CUSTARD FILLING

4 egg yolks
¼ cup sugar
Salt

2 cups milk
1 teaspoon vanilla
1 cup almonds (optional)

Beat the egg yolks lightly and stir in the sugar and a pinch of salt.

Scald the milk and when slightly cooled add to the yolk mixture. Cook over hot water in the top of a double boiler, stirring constantly, until the mixture coats a spoon. Do not overcook.

Remove from heat and stir in vanilla. Let mixture cool.

Place ½ of the custard on top of the brandy-soaked cake layer. Place second layer on top of this. Cover with the ¼ cup of brandy remaining. Let rest for about 15 minutes. Pour the rest of the custard over the top.

To give the cake a *smageligge* or tasty garnish, spread with a cup of blanched, split and toasted almonds.

CHERRY CAKE

•

KIRSEBÆRKAGE

3 tablespoons soft butter
⅔ cup sugar
2 egg yolks
1¼ cups flour
¼ teaspoon salt
2½ teaspoons baking powder

½ cup milk
1 teaspoon vanilla
2 egg whites
1½ cups black cherries, cooked
    and pitted

Cream butter and sugar. Beat in the egg yolks.

Sift together 3 times the flour, salt and baking powder.

Add flour alternately with the milk to the creamed mixture, beating after each addition. Add the vanilla. Beat egg whites stiff and fold in.

Drain the cherries. Place them in a buttered spring-form cake pan. Pour the batter over them. Swish the batter with a fork to distribute cherries through the cake.

Bake 35 to 40 minutes in a preheated 375° oven.

OLD-FASHIONED
SOUR-CREAM CHOCOLATE CAKE

•

CHOKOLADEKIKSEKAGE

½ cup soft butter
1 cup sugar
1 egg yolk, beaten
½ cup sour cream
1 teaspoon baking soda
½ teaspoon salt
1½ cups flour

½ teaspoon baking powder
1 teaspoon vanilla
3 tablespoons cocoa
¼ cup boiling water
1 egg white, beaten stiff but
    not dry

Cream butter and sugar. Stir in egg yolk.

Stir the soda into the sour cream.

Sift the dry ingredients together twice.

Add all ingredients to the butter-sugar mixture in the order given.

Bake in 2 buttered and lightly floured layer-cake tins about 20 to 25 minutes in a preheated 350° oven. When cool, spread top of one layer with the following:

FILLING

1 tablespoon cocoa	1 tablespoon butter
1 tablespoon cornstarch	½ cup hot water
⅔ cup sugar	1 teaspoon vanilla
½ cup cold water	

Mix ingredients in order given and cook 20 minutes, stirring often so mixture will not scorch.

Center plain layer over filled layer and frost top and sides as follows:

FROSTING

½ cup granulated sugar	3 tablespoons hot water
⅓ cup brown sugar	2 egg whites, beaten until frothy

Boil sugars and water until they spin a thread. Pour slowly over the beaten egg whites. Frost the cake.

Melt 2 ounces (2 squares) of unsweetened chocolate over hot water. Pour over cake and let drip down the sides.

CHOCOLATE BEER CAKE

·

CHOKOLADEKAGE

⅓ cup soft butter	1 teaspoon baking powder
1 cup sugar	½ teaspoon baking soda
2 egg yolks	½ teaspoon salt
2 squares unsweetened chocolate	¾ cup cold beer
1¾ cups flour	2 egg whites

Cream butter, add sugar slowly and beat well. Add the egg yolks one at a time, beating well after each addition.

Add the chocolate which has been melted over low heat and cooled. Beat until smooth.

Sift together three times the flour, baking powder, soda and salt. Add to the butter alternately with the beer, a little at a time, and blend well.

Beat the egg whites until stiff but not dry and fold in.

Bake in a buttered loaf pan (9 x 5 x 3) about 30 minutes in a pre-heated 375° oven. Serve plain or frost with a light frosting.

CIDER SPICE CAKE

•

CIDERKRYDDERIKAGE

3 cups flour, sifted	¾ cup soft butter
3 teaspoons baking powder	1½ cups brown sugar
¾ teaspoon salt	3 eggs
1 teaspoon cinnamon	1 tablespoon lemon juice
1 teaspoon nutmeg	1 cup cider
¼ teaspoon cloves	

Measure and sift together the flour and baking powder, salt and spices.

Cream the butter and sugar. Add the eggs and beat until thoroughly blended.

Add the lemon juice to the cider and add alternately with the dry ingredients to creamed mixture, beating after each addition.

Pour the batter into 3 greased and lightly floured 8-inch round layer-cake tins. Bake in a moderate oven (preheated to 375°) for 25 to 30 minutes. Take from oven and let rest for 10 minutes. Turn onto a rack to cool for 10 minutes. Spread a filling between the layers as follows:

CIDER FILLING

½ cup sugar	1 cup cider
¼ teaspoon salt	2 tablespoons lemon juice
3 tablespoons cornstarch	2 tablespoons butter

Combine sugar, salt and cornstarch in a saucepan. Add the cider and blend well. Cook over a low flame, stirring often, until thick and clear.

Remove from fire and add the lemon juice and butter, blending well. Top the cake with:

ALMOND-CIDER FROSTING

½ cup butter	½ cup cider
3½ tablespoons flour	3 cups powdered sugar
¼ teaspoon salt	½ cup almonds, ground

Melt butter in a saucepan. Blend in the flour and the salt. Add the cider, a little at a time, stirring well after each addition. Bring to a boil and cook for 1 minute over low heat, stirring constantly.

Remove from flame and add powdered sugar, stirring continually until the mixture has cooled somewhat. Add the ground almonds and frost the sides and top of the cake.

DARK CHRISTMAS CAKE

•

BRUN JULEKAGE

1 pound soft butter	*4 ounces red wine*
2 cups sugar	*4 ounces brandy*
1 cup dark molasses	*1½ pounds white or dark raisins*
12 eggs, beaten	*1½ pounds currants*
4 cups flour	*½ pound candied orange peel*
2 teaspoons baking powder	*½ pound candied lemon peel*
1 cup cream	*½ pound candied pineapple*
2 teaspoons nutmeg	*½ pound candied cherries*
1½ teaspoons cinnamon	*2 pounds shelled almonds*
1 teaspoon allspice	*1 cup flour*

Cream butter and sugar. Add molasses, then the eggs. Add the flour. Dissolve the baking powder in the cream and add to the mix. Add spices, wine and brandy.

Chop the fruits and nuts and dredge with extra cup of flour. Fold into the batter. Line cake pans with brown paper, and fill ⅔ full. Put cake pans into shallow pans ¼ filled with water. Bake slowly 4 hours in a preheated 275° oven. Cool thoroughly. Remove brown paper. To store, wrap in wine- or brandy-soaked cloth. Keep the cake moist by adding liquor now and then.

CURRANT CAKE

•

KORENDEKAGE

1 cup dried currants	*3 teaspoons baking powder*
1 cup soft butter	*½ teaspoon salt*
2½ cups sugar	*¾ cup milk*
6 egg yolks	*6 egg whites*
3¾ cups flour	*Dry bread crumbs*

Cover currants with cold water and let soak 1 hour.

Cream butter and sugar until light. Beat egg yolks and add. Add the drained currants and mix well.

Sift flour, baking powder and salt together and add alternately with the milk, beating well after each addition.

Whip the egg whites until stiff and fold in. Pour into 2 buttered 9-inch layer-cake pans which have been lined with finely rolled bread crumbs.

Bake 1 hour in a preheated 350° oven.

WHITE FRUIT CAKE

•

LYS FRUGTKAGE

1 cup butter
1 cup sugar
6 eggs
1½ cups flour
1½ teaspoons baking powder
1 teaspoon salt
½ cup white wine
1 cup dried apricots, chopped
1 cup dried figs, chopped

1 cup white raisins
1 cup candied lemon peel, chopped
½ cup citron, chopped
2 cups moist shredded coconut
½ cup flour
2 teaspoons rum
2 cups almonds, blanched and
  chopped

Soften the butter, gradually add the sugar, creaming well. Add the eggs, one at a time, beating after each addition.

Sift the 1½ cups of flour, baking powder and salt and add to the above mixture alternately with the ½ cup of wine. Beat well.

Combine all of the fruits and nuts and dredge with the ½ cup of flour. With the rum add the fruits and nuts to the batter, blending well.

Line 2 loaf pans (9 x 5 x 3) or 2 tube pans with brown paper. Pour the batter into the pans, filling about ⅔ full. Decorate with candied fruits or nuts if you wish. Bake about 2½ hours in a slow oven, 275 degrees. (Placing the baking pans in shallow pans ¼ filled with water prevents the cakes from scorching on the bottom while they bake.)

Cool in pans on racks 20 to 30 minutes. Turn out. Remove brown paper. Return to racks and cool completely before storing.

GERANIUM CAKE

•

GERANIUMSKAGE

2 cups flour	1 cup sugar
½ teaspoon salt	⅔ cup water
1 teaspoon baking powder	4 egg whites, beaten until frothy
½ cup butter	Fresh geranium leaves

Sift flour, salt and baking powder together.

Cream butter and sugar well. Add the water and mix. Add the sifted flour, salt and baking powder. Fold in egg whites, then beat hard for 5 minutes with a hand beater.

Line a loaf pan (9 x 5 x 3) with buttered waxed paper. Cover with a layer of crumbled geranium leaves. Pour batter over the leaves.

Bake in a moderate oven, preheated to 375 degrees, about 50 minutes. When removing waxed paper, don't worry about the fact that the leaves will pull off the cake with the paper. They are for flavor in this case, not for decoration. Shake powdered sugar through a paper doily over the cake.

GINGERBREAD

•

INGEFÆRKAGE

1 cup soft butter	2½ cups flour
1 cup sugar	1 teaspoon ginger
1 cup molasses	1 teaspoon cinnamon
2 teaspoons baking soda	1 teaspoon allspice
1 cup sour milk	4 eggs, beaten

Cream butter and sugar well. Stir in molasses and mix well. Stir soda into the sour milk. (To turn sweet milk sour quickly, add 1½ tablespoons of lemon juice or 1⅓ tablespoons of vinegar to lukewarm sweet milk. Let stand a few minutes to sour before you use it.) Add milk alternately to the creamed mixture with the sifted dry ingredients and the eggs. Beat well after each addition of the beaten eggs.

Pour into 2 greased and floured baking pans (9 x 12). Bake 45 to 55 minutes in a preheated 325° oven.

Serve plain or warm with your favorite hard sauce.

GRANDMOTHER'S CAKE FROM KOLDING

•

BEDSTEMODERS KAGE FRA KOLDING

1 egg
2½ cups flour
1½ heaping teaspoons baking
    powder
1½ teaspoons cinnamon
½ teaspoon nutmeg
¼ teaspoon allspice
¼ teaspoon cloves

1 cup soft butter
¾ cup molasses
¾ cup applesauce
1½ cups white raisins
⅓ cup candied orange peel
¼ cup candied lemon peel
½ cup almonds, chopped
½ cup lingonberry preserves

Beat the egg well.

Sift the dry ingredients together several times.

Cream the butter and add with the molasses and applesauce to the egg. Mix well. Add the sifted dry ingredients. Combine the fruits and nuts and add alternately with the preserves, beating well after each addition.

Line a tube pan with waxed paper. Pour the batter into the pan and bake for 1½ hours in a preheated 275° oven.

NUN'S CAKE

•

SØSTERKAGE

1 cup soft butter
1½ cups sugar
5 egg yolks
1 teaspoon almond extract
2 egg whites
3 cups flour, sifted twice

2½ teaspoons baking powder
½ teaspoon salt
1 teaspoon cinnamon
¾ cup milk
1 tablespoon caraway seeds

Cream the butter and sugar until light. Beat the egg yolks one at a time into the mixture, beating well after each addition. Beat egg whites slightly and add with the flavoring. Beat well.

Sift dry ingredients together twice. Add alternately with the milk to the butter mixture. Beat after each addition. Blend in the caraway seeds.

Pour batter into a greased and lightly floured tube pan. Bake in a 250° oven for 40 minutes, then 35 minutes more at 325 degrees.

ONE, TWO, THREE, FOUR CAKE

·

EN, TO, TRE, FIREKAGE

3 cups flour
4½ teaspoons baking powder
½ teaspoon salt
½ cup soft butter
2 cups sugar

4 egg yolks
1 cup milk
1 teaspoon vanilla
4 egg whites

Sift flour, baking powder and salt together.

Cream butter and sugar until light and fluffy. Add the egg yolks and beat well. Add milk and dry ingredients alternately and beat. Add vanilla.

Beat egg whites until stiff but not dry and fold in gently.

Turn the batter into 3 greased and lightly floured 9-inch layer-cake pans. Bake 30 to 40 minutes in a preheated 375° oven, then remove from tins and let cool. (Cut the 3 layers in halves to make 6 if you prefer.)

Fill as follows:

FILLING (for 3-layer cake)

2 tablespoons cornstarch
¼ cup sugar

2½ cups crushed pineapple
Juice of 1 orange

Mix cornstarch and sugar. Add to the crushed pineapple.

Cook until smooth and thickened. Add the orange juice and blend. Spread between the layers and frost as follows:

WHITE FROSTING

2 egg whites
1¾ cups sugar

6 tablespoons water
1 teaspoon orange extract

Put all ingredients, except extract, in the top of a double boiler and cook over hot water, beating continually, from 7 to 8 minutes, or until thick. Add flavoring, and spread around the sides and over the top of the cake.

POPPY-SEED CAKE

·

VALMUEFRØKAGE

½ cup poppy seeds
1 cup milk
1 teaspoon vanilla extract
¾ cup soft butter
1½ cups sugar

2 cups flour, sifted
2 teaspoons baking powder
½ teaspoon salt
4 egg whites (set aside yolks to use
in Filling recipe below)

Soak poppy seeds in the milk and vanilla overnight.

Cream butter until soft. Add the sugar gradually and cream well. Sift the flour, baking powder and salt together. Blend the flour and poppy-seed mixtures alternately into the creamed butter mix. Blend well.

Whip the egg whites until stiff and fold into mixture.

Pour the batter into 2 buttered and lightly floured 8-inch layer-cake tins, and bake 30 minutes in a preheated 350° oven. Let cool a little in the pans before turning out onto racks. If you wish you can cut each layer in half and spread filling between the four layers. Whichever you choose to do, here's a suggestion for a mouth-watering between-the-layers spread:

FILLING

4 egg yolks
¾ cup sugar
2 tablespoons cornstarch
1½ cups milk

¼ teaspoon salt
½ cup hazelnuts (substitute other
nuts, if necessary)
1 teaspoon vanilla

Beat the egg yolks until frothy. Mix sugar, cornstarch, milk and salt with the beaten yolks and cook in the top of a double boiler over hot water about 5 minutes. Stir constantly to keep the mixture from scorching.

Grind nuts and add to cooked mixture with vanilla. Mix well, and spread between layers.

Top the cake as follows:

FROSTING

1 cup powdered sugar
3 tablespoons rum

1 tablespoon water
½ cup hazelnuts, ground

Stir the sugar with the rum until smooth. Add the water and beat well. Ice the sides and top of the cake. Sprinkle the ground nuts over the top.

PLUM CAKE

·

BLOMMEKAGE

½ cup soft butter
1½ cups sugar
½ teaspoon salt
3 eggs
2¼ cups flour
1½ teaspoons baking powder
1 teaspoon cinnamon
1 teaspoon baking soda, scant

1½ cups plum juice (If you use fresh plums, cook them and put them through a sieve to get juice of the right consistency. Buy red plums if possible.)
1 cup white raisins
¾ cup chopped almonds

Cream butter, sugar and salt until light and creamy. Beat the 3 eggs until fluffy and add. Sift the flour, baking powder, cinnamon and soda together and add alternately with the plum juice to the butter mixture. Beat. If the batter seems a little thin, add a little more flour. Fold in the raisins and almonds.

Pour into a 10-inch-square pan greased and floured lightly. Bake 1 hour in a preheated 350° oven. After the cake has cooled cut it into squares. Serve with the following sauce:

OLD-FASHIONED PLUM SAUCE

2 tablespoons sugar
1½ tablespoons cornstarch
Pinch of salt
1 cup sieved red plums with juice

½ cup light corn syrup
1 teaspoon butter
1 teaspoon almond extract

Mix sugar, cornstarch and salt in a saucepan. Gradually add plums and juice and blend well. Add syrup and cook over low heat, stirring continuously until it thickens, about 3 minutes. Remove from stove and beat in butter. Add the almond extract.

PORK CAKE

·

FLÆSKEKAGE

Try this if you're tired of your traditional Christmas fruit cake.

1 pound salt pork
2 cups boiling water
2 cups dark brown sugar
1 cup molasses
1 teaspoon baking soda
1 pound raisins
1 pound dates, chopped

¼ pound citron, chopped
4 cups flour
1 teaspoon cinnamon
1 teaspoon cloves
1 teaspoon molasses
1 teaspoon allspice
1 teaspoon nutmeg

Put the salt pork through a food chopper. Pour the boiling water over it. Add the sugar, molasses and baking soda and mix well. Blend in the fruits.

Sift flour and spices together and add. Mix well.

Pour the batter into a greased and lightly floured loaf pan (9 x 5 x 3) and bake 1 hour in a slow oven preheated to 275 degrees.

This cake will keep indefinitely in your refrigerator or freezer.

PRUNE CAKE

·

SVESKEKAGE

¾ cup soft butter
1 cup sugar
3 eggs
½ cup buttermilk
2 cups flour
1 teaspoon baking soda

½ teaspoon salt
1 teaspoon cinnamon
1 teaspoon allspice
½ teaspoon cloves
1 cup cooked and pitted prunes
¾ cup nut meats, chopped

Cream butter and sugar. Add eggs and buttermilk and beat until creamy.

Sift flour, soda, salt and spices together. Add to creamy mixture. Add prunes (don't cut these up any more than necessary to pit them) and chopped nuts. Mix well.

Bake in 2 greased and floured 9-inch layer-cake pans for 30 minutes in a preheated 375° oven.

Cool layers in the pans on a rack for a few minutes. Remove from pans, cool completely and frost with Almond-Cider Frosting (*page 85*), White Frosting (*page 90*), or Fruit Frosting (*page 132*) .

WEDDING CAKE

•

KRANSEKAGE

This cake consists of at least 20 rings called *kranse,* of graduating sizes, placed on top of each other to make a cone. It is decorated with four large candles and as many smaller ones as you wish. Favors, white birds, and candy flowers in gay colors of the bride's choice are stuck on the cake with melted sugar. The traditional miniature bride and groom decorate the top.

3 pounds almond paste (buy this from a thoroughly reliable merchant, or make your own according to the recipe given below)

1½ pounds granulated sugar
8 egg whites, unbeaten

Mix ingredients well in order given into a stiff paste.

Heat the mixture, but do not let it boil, in the top of a double boiler over hot water.

Make the layers of the cake as follows: Roll paste into rings about ½ inch thick, taking enough of the mix at one time to make the size ring you wish. Pinch off the end of the dough before you close the circle to make the ring just a fraction smaller than the previous one. One of the easiest ways to get exact circles is to lay a length of waxed paper over a cookie sheet. Use a compass to draw the circumference of the bottom ring — the largest one — and as many more of the progressively smaller rings as you can fit on the cookie sheet. Continue in this fashion until you have marked out as many rings as you plan to have.

Butter and dust the cookie sheets with flour. Lay the rings on the sheets after they have been shaped on the waxed-paper patterns. With your fingers, squeeze the tops of the rings enough to make them somewhat pointed in the center to build the foundation for the smaller ring which will top each.

Bake in a slow oven, preheated to 250 degrees, until edges are browned. Place on a rack to cool. Frost between layers as follows:

Royal Icing

4 egg whites   *1½ cups powdered sugar*

Beat ingredients by hand until stiff. Squeeze out through a pastry bag to decorate each ring before putting the cake together.

Almond Paste

1½ pounds shelled almonds   *9 tablespoons orange juice*
3 cups sugar   *6 drops rose water*
1½ cups water

Blanch the almonds. Grind the nuts at least 4 times through the finest blade of your meat grinder to get the nuts as oily as possible.

Cook the sugar and water in a pan to the soft-ball stage, 240 degrees. Add the nuts, orange juice and rose water. Stir all until well blended and creamy. Cover with a towel and let rest 10 to 12 hours.

Dip hands in powdered sugar to make kneading easier. Place the almond paste on a clean, hard surface (ideally, a marble slab) dusted with powdered sugar. Knead the paste until smooth. Place in a covered jar or tin to ripen from 6 to 8 days.

WHIPPED-CREAM CAKE
·
FLØDEKAGE

1 cup whipping cream   *1½ cups flour*
1 cup sugar   *1 heaping teaspoon baking powder*
2 eggs   *1 teaspoon vanilla*

Whip the cream until stiff but not too dry. Add sugar gradually and beat well until blended. Add the eggs, one at a time, beating after each addition.

Sift the flour, measure, and add the baking powder. Sift again. Fold into egg and cream mixture. Add flavoring.

Bake either in a 9 x 5 x 3 buttered loaf pan or in 2 buttered 8-inch layer-cake pans. Loaf should be baked at a temperature of 350 degrees in a preheated oven, layers at 375 degrees. Cake is done when it is golden brown on top and springs back when touched with your finger tip.

RUM CAKE

•

RUMKAGE

1 pound candied cherries
1 pound candied pineapple
1 pound seeded white raisins
½ pound citron
1 pound white currants
½ pound candied orange peel
1 pint rum
1 pound butter
2½ cups sugar
1 teaspoon cinnamon

1 teaspoon cloves
1 teaspoon nutmeg
1 dozen eggs
2 pounds almonds, halved or
   coarsely chopped
1½ pounds filberts, halved or
   chopped
5 cups flour, sifted
2 teaspoons baking powder

Halve or coarsely chop all of the fruits, combine them with the rum and let soak overnight.

Cream the butter, the sugar and the spices well together. Beat in the eggs, one at a time, beating well after each addition.

Add nuts to the fruit mixture and sprinkle with ½ cup of the flour. Add baking powder with the rest of the flour and (using your hands) blend well into the mixture. Combine with butter, sugar and egg mixture.

Fill greased and floured loaf pans (9 x 5 x 3) ¾ full of the batter. Bake in a preheated 275° oven about 3 hours (more or less if your pans are larger or smaller than standard loaf tins). To prevent scorching while baking, set loaf pans into shallow pans ¼ full of water.

Cool completely and wrap with brandy-soaked cloths. If you wish to store these cakes for some time, moisten them now and then with additional brandy or rum.

ALMOND TORTE

•

MANDELKAGE

1 pound unshelled almonds
12 egg yolks

2 cups sugar
12 egg whites

Shell almonds and put them, unblanched, through a food chopper, using the finest blade you have. Or use a nut grinder or an electric blender.

Beat the egg yolks well. Add the sugar and beat again. Add the chopped almonds and blend well.

Beat the egg whites until stiff but not dry and fold into the above mixture.

Bake 70 minutes in a preheated 350° oven in 1 large cake pan, lightly greased and floured.

LAYER CAKE

•

LAGKAGE

4 egg yolks	1½ teaspoons baking powder
3 tablespoons cold water	½ teaspoon salt
1 cup sugar	4 egg whites
1 scant cup flour	1 teaspoon vanilla
1½ tablespoons cornstarch	

Beat the egg yolks until thick and lemon-colored. Add the water and slowly add the sugar, beating 2 minutes with a hand beater.

Mix and sift the flour, cornstarch, baking powder and salt and add to the first mixture.

Beat the egg whites until stiff and carefully fold them into the mixture. Blend in the vanilla.

Bake in four 9-inch cake tins, ungreased, in a quick, hot oven (preheated to 450 degrees) for 15 minutes.

Put a custard filling between the first and second layers, raspberry jam between the second and third layers, custard filling between the third and fourth layers.

Custard Filling

2 eggs	1½ cups milk
½ cup sugar	¼ teaspoon salt
1 tablespoon cornstarch	

Mix all ingredients in order given and beat well. Cook over low heat until thick.

An alternate filling is as follows:

CREAM FILLING

⅓ cup flour
¾ cup brown sugar
1½ cups milk

1 teaspoon vanilla
⅓ cup soft butter

Blend flour and sugar and gradually add the milk. Cook over low heat until thick and smooth, about 5 minutes. Cool. Add vanilla and butter. Beat until very smooth and creamy.

HAZELNUT TORTE

•

HASSELNØDLAGKAGE

9 egg yolks
⅔ cup sugar
¾ cup almonds, blanched and
  ground
¾ cup hazelnuts, ground
9 egg whites

¼ cup cherry liqueur (Cherry
  Heering)
¼ cup raspberry jam
1 pint whipping cream
24 whole nuts for top of torte
Powdered sugar

Beat the egg yolks until thick. Add the sugar and beat. Add the ground nuts and mix well.

Beat the egg whites until stiff. Fold into the yolk mixture.

Bake in 2 well-buttered layer-cake tins in a preheated moderate oven (350°) until the top of the cake springs back quickly when you touch it. Remove from oven and let cool.

Cover the top of each layer with half of the liqueur, then with a thin layer of the raspberry jam. Place one cake on top of the other.

Whip the cream and spread over top. Place whole hazelnuts here and there on the torte. Dust the top with powdered sugar.

BERTINE'S ALMOND TORTE

•

BERTINES MANDELKAGE

10 egg whites
2 cups sugar
1 pound shelled almonds, ground

⅓ cup red wine
Thick applesauce

Beat egg whites until stiff. Fold in the sugar and ground almonds, a little at a time. Put into a butter-cake tin (round or square, large size) and let dry in a very slow oven (175 degrees if possible) for 2 hours.

Remove from oven and cut in half. Sprinkle one layer with the wine, and cover it with applesauce. Place other layer on top. Pour the following sauce over the torte and serve at once:

SAUCE

10 egg yolks	1½ pints light cream
1 cup sugar	Whipped cream
½ teaspoon vanilla	

Beat the 10 egg yolks with the 1 cup of sugar and vanilla in a saucepan over low flame. Beat until the mixture begins to thicken. Add the 1½ pints of cream, stirring while you cook the mixture 1 minute more. When slightly cooled, pour over cake. Decorate with whipped cream. Not for dieters! This is Danish cooking at its richest.

RUM TORTE

•

LAGKAGE MED ROMCREME

4 egg yolks	⅓ cup flour, sifted
⅔ cup sugar	⅓ cup potato flour
¼ cup water	¾ teaspoon baking powder
1 teaspoon vanilla	¼ teaspoon salt
¼ teaspoon almond extract	4 egg whites

Beat the egg yolks until thick and lemon-colored. Slowly beat in the sugar. Add the water and flavorings and beat the mixture well.

Sift the flours together 3 times. Sift them again with the salt and baking powder. Fold into the egg-yolk mixture with a wire whisk.

Beat the egg whites until stiff and fold into the above mixture with the whisk.

Bake in an ungreased spring-form loaf pan in a preheated 350° oven 50 to 60 minutes. Remove from oven, cool upside down. Remove from pan and slice into 3 layers. Fill between the layers as follows:

FILLING

1 tablespoon flour	2 tablespoons rum
2 tablespoons water	1 tablespoon vanilla extract
½ cup milk, scalded	½ teaspoon salt
2 egg yolks, beaten	½ cup whipping cream
⅓ cup sugar	1 egg white, beaten stiff

Mix the flour with the 2 tablespoons of water. Add scalded milk and beat.

Beat the egg yolks well with the ⅓ cup of sugar. Add the hot mixture, rum, vanilla and salt.

Chill until somewhat cooled and thick. Whip the cream and fold it and the beaten egg white into the chilled ingredients. Spread between the layers. Top as follows:

TOPPING

⅓ cup raspberry or apricot preserves	1 cup whipping cream
1 tablespoon sugar	¼ cup almonds, toasted and slivered

Spread the preserves over the top of the torte, almost to the edge. Whip the cream with the 1 tablespoon of sugar. Put the whipped cream in a pastry tube and pipe around the edge of the torte, decorating the preserves with a few rosettes. Sprinkle with slivered almonds.

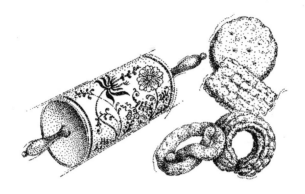

· 4 ·

COOKIES

AND SMALL CAKES

ANISE COOKIES

·

ANISKAGER

4½ cups flour, sifted
1 teaspoon baking powder
4 eggs
¼ teaspoon oil of anise*

3½ cups powdered sugar, sifted
4 teaspoons grated lemon peel
Anise seeds

Sift flour and baking powder together.

Beat the 4 eggs until thick and lemon-colored. Add the oil of anise. Add the powdered sugar a little at a time, beating until well mixed. Beat in the dry ingredients alternately with the lemon peel in small portions until thoroughly mixed. Chill the dough 2 hours, or until firm.

Grease cookie sheets lightly and sprinkle with a few anise seeds.

Roll dough ½ inch thick on a lightly floured board, with a springerle rolling pin. (This is a roller covered with intricate designs and figures

* This is sometimes, but not always, available at grocery stores. Try your favorite pharmacy.

which stamps the cookies as you roll. Each design is enclosed in a square or rectangle.) Press the roller heavily on the dough to get a good imprint, and then cut the cookies apart along the border lines stamped between the designs.

Lift the cookies carefully onto cookie sheets. Cover and let stand overnight in the refrigerator.

Bake in a preheated 350° oven for 30 minutes until lightly browned. Remove with a spatula at once onto a rack to cool. When thoroughly cooled, store in a tightly covered crock or jar for at least 10 days. Cookies will keep for months.

If you happen to have almonds on hand, put a sliver or half a blanched almond on each cookie.

ALMOND BUTTER BALLS

•

MANDELSMØRBOLLER

1 cup soft butter
3 tablespoons powdered sugar
1 teaspoon vanilla
¼ teaspoon almond extract

1 cup flour, sifted
1 cup almonds, chopped
Powdered sugar

Cream butter and sugar. Add flavoring and mix well. Stir in flour and fold in the chopped almonds.

Shape in small balls and place on ungreased cookie sheets.

Bake in a preheated 350° oven about 20 minutes. Roll in powdered sugar while warm.

ALMOND MACAROONS

•

MANDELMAKRONER

2⅔ cups shelled almonds
4 egg whites

2 cups powdered sugar

Pound the almonds to a paste.

Beat the egg whites and sugar to a stiff consistency and add them to the almond paste, mixing well with a wooden spoon.

Roll the dough in your hands into small balls the diameter of a nickel.

Place them on waxed paper on a cookie sheet about 1½ inches apart.

Bake until light brown in a preheated 325° oven. Makes 4 dozen macaroons.

AMMONIA COOKIES

•

AMMONIAKKAGER

2 level teaspoons baker's
  ammonia*
2 cups soft butter

2½ cups sugar
3 cups flour
1 teaspoon almond extract

Crush the ammonia cakes fine.

Cream the butter and sugar. Sift the flour and add. Measure ammonia and add. Beat well. Add the almond extract.

Form into small balls and bake in a slow oven preheated to 325 degrees for 10 to 12 minutes on greased and floured cookie sheets. Watch the cookies carefully because they burn easily.

* Baker's ammonia (ammonium carbonate) can be purchased by the ounce in drugstores.

BROWN COOKIES

•

BRUNEKAGER

6 cups brown sugar
2 cups buttermilk
2 teaspoons baking soda
1¼ cups soft butter

Pinch of powdered alum*
6 cups flour
Granulated sugar

Stir sugar into buttermilk. Dissolve the soda in the mixture.

Cream the butter and beat into the buttermilk mixture.

Add the alum to the flour and mix well. Combine with other ingredients. Let stand in a cool place overnight.

Roll out on a board, using very little flour. Cut with a cookie cutter. Brush a little sugar over each. Bake on a lightly floured cookie sheet 12 minutes in a preheated 425° oven.

* Obtainable in drugstores.

ALMOND WINE COOKIES

•

MANDELKAGER MED SHERRY

2 cups flour, sifted
4 egg yolks
1 cup soft butter
¼ teaspoon salt
⅔ cup sugar

½ teaspoon anise extract
1 teaspoon grated lemon rind
1 cup ground almonds
½ cup sherry
⅔ cup ground almonds

Mix ingredients in order given. Blend well after each addition. Drop by teaspoonfuls on greased cookie sheets.

Bake 15 minutes in a preheated 400° oven. Remove at once from baking sheets and allow to cool.

BRUNSWICK CAKES

•

BRUNSVIGERKAGER

⅝ cup soft butter
⅝ cup sugar
2 egg yolks
1 teaspoon lemon extract

½ cup almonds, chopped
1 cup flour, sifted
2 egg whites

Cream butter and sugar. Beat egg yolks and add with lemon extract and nuts. Gradually add the flour, beating well after each addition.

Beat egg whites until stiff and fold into mixture. Spread the dough about ¼ inch thick on a greased cookie sheet. Sprinkle with a topping as follows:

TOPPING

3 tablespoons powdered sugar
3 tablespoons chopped almonds

3 tablespoons dried currants, put
  through a meat grinder

Mix all ingredients thoroughly and sprinkle over the cookie dough.

Bake in a preheated 350° oven 8 to 12 minutes. Take from oven and cut into squares while still warm.

BUTTER FINGERS

•

SMØRFINGRE

2½ cups soft butter
1½ cups sugar
1 teaspoon salt
1 teaspoon vanilla

2 eggs
2½ tablespoons cream
5¼ cups flour
½ teaspoon baking powder

Cream butter and sugar until fluffy. Stir in the salt, vanilla, eggs and cream. Beat for 2 minutes.

Add flour, sifted together with baking powder. Blend well.

Press the dough through a pastry bag in 2-inch lengths about ½ inch apart on greased cookie sheets. With the pastry bag force a topping onto each strip or finger.

Bake 15 minutes in a preheated 350° oven.

TOPPING

1 cup butter
1 cup sugar
4 eggs

2 cups hazelnuts or filberts, ground
3 tablespoons cocoa
½ cup flour

Cream the butter and sugar well. Mix in the eggs. Add ground nuts, cocoa and flour, blending well after last addition.

CARDAMOM COOKIES

•

KARDEMOMMEKAGER

1 egg
1 cup sugar
½ cup melted butter
½ teaspoon baking soda

1 teaspoon crushed cardamom
    seeds or ground cardamom
1 teaspoon cinnamon
1 cup flour

Mix ingredients in order given. Roll into balls. Flatten down to the size of a fifty-cent piece.

Bake on a greased and floured cookie sheet in a preheated 350° oven until lightly browned on the edges.

CARAWAY COOKIES

•

KOMMENKAGER

1 cup soft butter
1 cup sugar
2 eggs
2 tablespoons buttermilk

¼ teaspoon baking soda
2 cups flour, sifted
1 tablespoon caraway seeds

Cream butter and sugar. Add unbeaten eggs, one at a time, beating after each addition. Add buttermilk with soda and flour. Add caraway seeds.

Chill for a few hours. Roll out to ½-inch thickness and cut with a cookie cutter. Sprinkle with sugar and bake 20 minutes in a preheated 350° oven.

COCONUT COOKIES

•

KOKOSNØDKAGER

6 egg whites
1 cup powdered sugar

1 pound shredded coconut

Beat the egg whites until stiff but not dry. Fold in the sugar and coconut.

Drop by spoonfuls onto lightly buttered and floured cookie sheets. Bake in a preheated 300° oven until lightly browned.

CHOCOLATE COOKIES

•

CHOKOLADEKAGER

1 cup soft butter
¾ cup granulated sugar
¾ cup brown sugar
2 eggs, beaten
1 teaspoon baking soda
1 teaspoon hot water

2¼ cups flour, sifted with
1 teaspoon salt
1 cup nut meats, chopped
1 pound chocolate bits, or grated
    chocolate
1 teaspoon vanilla

Cream the butter. Add the sugars and the eggs.

Dissolve the soda in the hot water and add to the creamed mixture alternately with the flour and salt. Add the chopped nut meats, chocolate and vanilla and beat well.

Drop by teaspoonfuls about 2 inches apart on a greased baking sheet. Flatten the small balls of dough a little with your finger tips.

Bake 10 to 13 minutes in a preheated 375° oven.

Dough may be refrigerated overnight if you wish.

CHRISTMAS STARS

•

JULESTJERNER

1 cup soft butter	1 teaspoon baking soda
2 cups molasses	2 teaspoons cinnamon
1 cup sour milk	½ teaspoon salt
8 cups flour	

Cream butter until very soft and beat in the molasses slowly. Add the sour milk and blend. Over this mixture sift 2 cups of the flour with the soda, cinnamon and salt. Blend well. Add the rest of the flour, mixing thoroughly. This will be a stiff dough.

Roll dough about ⅓ inch thick on floured board. If it seems a little soft, place more flour on the board and roll it until it becomes firm. Cut into stars with cookie cutter.

Bake 15 minutes on greased cookie sheets in a preheated 350° oven.

CINNAMON STARS

•

KANELSTJERNER

6 egg whites	Grated rind of 1 lemon
2 cups sugar	2⅔ cups shelled almonds, ground
1 tablespoon cinnamon	2 tablespoons flour

Beat egg whites until very stiff. Sift flour and add alternately, a little at a time, with cinnamon and lemon rind. Beat for 15 minutes.

Put aside enough of the batter to fill a small sauce dish (about 1 cup). To the dough which remains add the ground almonds, mixing well. Fold in the sifted flour gently.

Drop on buttered cookie sheets by teaspoonfuls in small mounds. Dot each mound with a pinch from the sauce dish.

Bake in a preheated 300° oven until light brown. Remove and let cool. Store in tightly covered containers. Makes 7½ dozen cookies.

COPENHAGEN COOKIES

•

KØBENHAVNERKAGER

1½ pounds soft butter
½ cup sugar
1 tablespoon water

4 cups flour, sifted
1 egg, beaten
1⅓ cups shelled almonds, ground

Cream butter and sugar, beating 10 minutes. Add water and flour a little at a time, beating after each addition.

Roll very thin on lightly floured board. Cut into desired shapes with a cookie cutter. Brush with beaten egg. Sprinkle with ground almonds. (For a Christmas touch, place a red or green maraschino cherry half on each cookie.)

Bake 10 to 12 minutes, or until the edges are light brown, in a preheated 400° oven on ungreased cookie sheets dusted with flour.

CRESCENT COOKIES

•

MÅNEKAGER

1 cup soft butter
⅓ cup sugar
2 teaspoons water

2 teaspoons vanilla extract
2 cups flour, sifted
½ cup almonds, ground

Cream butter and sugar. Mix in the water and vanilla. Add flour and the ground nuts. Chill 4 hours.

Form dough into long rolls about 1 inch in diameter. Cut into 3-inch lengths, shape into crescents.

Bake on ungreased cookie sheets 15 minutes in a preheated 325° oven. Watch carefully and do not allow crescents to brown. Remove from cookie sheets. Let cool slightly. Roll in powdered sugar.

CHERRY BALLS

•

KIRSEBÆRKUGLER

½ cup soft butter
¼ cup powdered sugar
1½ cups flour, sifted

Pinch of salt
1 teaspoon vanilla
Maraschino cherries

Mix butter and sugar to a creamy consistency. Add flour, salt and vanilla. Mix with the fingers.

Take a maraschino cherry and fold dough around it, making a small ball — the smaller the better. Put on ungreased cookie sheets and bake 12 to 15 minutes in a preheated 350° oven. Cool and dip in following icing:

ICING

1 cup sifted powdered sugar
2 tablespoons heavy cream

1 teaspoon vanilla

Blend well and roll cookies in the mixture.

TWO-DAY FILLED COOKIES

•

FYLDTE SMÅKAGER

1 cup honey
⅔ cup sugar
2 tablespoons water
2 tablespoons brandy
Grated rind of ½ lemon
2 teaspoons baking powder

4 cups flour, sifted
1 teaspoon anise seeds
¼ teaspoon cloves
¼ teaspoon ginger
¼ teaspoon cinnamon

Heat honey, sugar and water together until sugar is dissolved. Do not allow to boil. When cool, stir in the brandy and the grated lemon rind. (Reserve the other half of the lemon for the filling for the cookies.)

Sift the baking powder with the flour and the spices onto a kneading board.

Pour the honey mixture over the flour mixture, working into flour well. Place the dough in a greased bowl, cover and set aside for 2 days. Since the filling for the cookies can also rest for 2 days, you may make the following now if you wish:

FILLING

3 cups almonds, ground
1 cup sugar
⅓ cup honey

½ cup apricot jam
1½ teaspoons vanilla
Grated rind and juice of ½ lemon

Mix the nuts, sugar, honey, apricot jam, vanilla, lemon rind and juice. Blend well. Put aside in refrigerator for 2 days.

MAKING AND BAKING

Divide dough into 2 or 3 parts. Roll one at a time on lightly floured board to a rectangle about ¼ of an inch thick. Spread ½ of the dough with a layer of filling 1 inch thick. Leave a 1-inch edge all around the rectangle. Fold the unfilled half over the other and press the edges together with your fingers. The rolls should look like a miniature jelly roll.

Cut the filled rolls into 1-inch pieces. Place these on ungreased cookie sheets and bake about 30 minutes in a preheated 350° oven. Remove from sheets while warm, and glaze as follows:

GLAZE

1½ cups sugar

½ cup water

Boil sugar and water about 6 minutes or until the mixture reaches the syrup stage — 230° F. on a candy thermometer. Brush baked cookies with the glaze.

When glaze is dry, store the cookies in an airtight container to bring out their spicy flavor.

Yields 10 dozen cookies which will keep for weeks.

TOP-OF-THE-STOVE COOKIES

•

SMÅKAGER

1 cup soft butter
1 cup sugar
1 teaspoon vanilla

6 eggs
2 cups flour

Cream butter and sugar until smooth. Break one egg at a time into this mixture and beat well after each addition. Add enough of the flour to make the dough quite stiff.

Drop by teaspoonfuls into a preheated greased Danish cake pan. Cook over medium heat on top of the stove, 8 to 9 minutes on each side.

FILLED COOKIES

•

FYLDTE SMÅKAGER

Pastry Dough I

1 cup soft butter
2 cups brown sugar, packed
2 eggs
3½ cups flour, sifted
½ teaspoon salt
1 teaspoon baking soda

½ teaspoon baking powder
¼ teaspoon cinnamon
½ cup milk
1 teaspoon vanilla
Filling (see recipes below)

Cream butter and sugar, add eggs and beat well. Stir in the remaining ingredients, except filling. Set aside a small dish of batter. Drop the remainder by teaspoonfuls on a greased cookie sheet. Make a well with the bowl of a spoon in each mound of cookie dough. Place a teaspoonful of filling in each well and drop a small dab of the reserved batter on top of the filling.

Bake 12 to 15 minutes in a preheated 375° oven.

Pastry Dough II

1 cup soft butter
2 cups sugar
2 eggs
2 teaspoons lemon extract
6 cups flour, sifted

6 teaspoons baking powder
1 cup milk
Filling (see recipes below)
Powdered sugar

Cream butter and sugar. Add eggs and lemon extract in 3 or 4 additions, beating well after each. Sift in the flour and baking powder. Add milk gradually and beat after each addition. Divide dough into 4 parts and chill.

Roll out ⅛ inch thick and cut into rounds. Place half the rounds on greased and floured cookie sheets. Place filling generously on each. With a small cookie cutter take centers out of remaining rounds, leaving thin rings of dough. Place one ring over each filled whole round. Press edges of each cookie firmly together. Dust tops with powdered sugar. Bake 15 minutes in a preheated 375° oven.

POPPY-SEED FILLING

½ cup light corn syrup	½ cup raisins, chopped or ground
1 tablespoon butter	¼ teaspoon ginger
½ teaspoon cinnamon	2 tablespoons unsweetened
1 cup poppy seeds	chocolate, grated
½ teaspoon lemon rind, grated	

Cook all ingredients except chocolate over low heat, stirring until thick. Add chocolate and stir until it is melted.

DATE FILLING

1 pound dates, ground	½ cup orange juice
1 cup sugar	2 tablespoons orange rind, grated
1½ cups light corn syrup	½ teaspoon salt

Mix all ingredients and simmer over low heat until thick, stirring continually to prevent scorching.

NAPOLEON HATS

•

NAPOLEONSHATTE

7 tablespoons sugar	1 egg, beaten
¾ cup soft butter	1¾ cups flour, sifted

Beat sugar and butter until light. Add the egg, then the sifted flour, and mix well. Let dough rest 2 hours in a warm place in a bowl covered with a clean towel.

Roll as thin as possible on a floured board. Cut with a floured round cookie cutter. Put a small amount of almond filling (see following recipe) in the center of each cookie, and fold the dough over triangularly to make a hat shaped as much as possible like Napoleon's.

Place cookies on a buttered and lightly floured cookie sheet. Bake 18 to 20 minutes in a preheated 350° oven. Watch cookies carefully to make sure they are not getting burned.

ALMOND FILLING (MANDELFYLLING)

4 egg whites   ¾ cup almonds, ground very fine
1 cup powdered sugar

Beat egg whites until stiff and dry. Fold in the sugar and ground almonds to combine all ingredients lightly but thoroughly.

FILBERT COOKIES

•

HASSELNØDKAGER

3 eggs   1 tablespoon fine dry bread
½ cup sugar   crumbs
1 teaspoon vanilla   2 cups filberts, ground
2 tablespoons brandy   ½ cup filberts, halved

Beat the eggs and add the rest of the ingredients except the halved nuts in the order given. Mix well.

Shape into small balls. Put half a nut on each. Place the cookies about 3 inches apart on greased cookie sheets.

Bake in a preheated 300° oven for 20 minutes, or until lightly browned.

GROOM'S COOKIES

•

KAMMERJUNKERE

¾ pound soft butter   15 cups flour, sifted
¾ pound light brown sugar   2 teaspoons grated lemon peel
2 tablespoons cloves   8 ounces brandy
2 tablespoons cinnamon   2 tablespoons baking soda
4 cups molasses   4 tablespoons water or milk

Cream butter and sugar well. Mix spices in the molasses. Stir in the flour after the molasses has been added to the creamed mixture. (You'll find a large wooden spoon the best utensil for this.)

Add the lemon peel and brandy. Stir well. Soak the soda in the water or milk and add.

The dough should be *very* stiff. Add a little more flour at this point if necessary. Chill. Roll dough paper-thin and cut into whatever shapes you wish.

Bake on greased cookie sheets in a preheated 325° oven until brown. Ornament with icing, if desired.

In Denmark these were used as Christmas tree ornaments. They were made weeks before the great day and stored in tightly covered cans.

HAZELNUT SPHERES

•

HASSELNØDMARENGS

8 egg whites	¾ pound shelled hazelnuts or
2 cups sugar	filberts, ground
1 teaspoon vanilla extract	

Beat the egg whites until nearly stiff. Gradually add the sugar and beat 10 minutes after last addition. Add vanilla extract and the ground nuts.

Place a little flour and sugar on a board and roll the dough out to the thickness of your little finger. Cut into 1-inch-wide strips, and cut each strip into 1-inch lengths. Place on an ungreased cookie sheet.

Bake 20 minutes in a preheated 300° oven. These will puff up into spheres as they bake.

ALMOND ICEBOX COOKIES

•

MANDELSMÅKAGER

6 cups flour	1 cup brown sugar
2 teaspoons cinnamon	3 eggs
1 teaspoon baking powder	2⅔ cups shelled almonds,
1 pound soft butter	blanched and ground
1 cup white sugar	

Sift flour and measure. Add cinnamon and baking powder and sift 3 ꞈs.

Cream butter. Add sugars, a little at a time, and beat until light and fluffy. Add the eggs and beat thoroughly. Fold in the ground nuts.

Add flour gradually and mix well. Shape the dough in rolls about 1½ inches thick. Refrigerate them for at least 12 hours. Slice very thin. Bake 10 minutes on greased baking sheets in a preheated 400° oven.

LADYFINGERS I

•

FRUEKAGER

3 egg whites
⅓ cup powdered sugar, sifted
½ teaspoon vanilla
3 egg yolks, well beaten

½ cup flour
⅛ teaspoon salt
⅓ cup powdered sugar

Beat egg whites until stiff. Slowly beat in ⅓ cup powdered sugar. Fold in vanilla and egg yolks.

Sift together the flour, salt and the ⅓ cup powdered sugar which has first been sifted 4 times. Carefully fold in the beaten egg mixture, small quantities at a time, mixing well after each addition. Press through a cookie press onto an ungreased baking sheet, making finger-length strips or other shapes desired. Dust with sifted powdered sugar. Bake in a moderate oven, preheated to 350 degrees, about 10 minutes. Split or leave whole, depending on how you intend to use them.

LADYFINGERS II

•

FRUEKAGER

1 cup sugar
5 eggs
⅛ teaspoon salt

1 cup flour, sifted
Vanilla
Powdered sugar

Beat sugar, eggs and salt together until light and frothy. Sprinkle the sifted flour lightly over the egg mixture with your hands. Mix lightly. Add vanilla to taste.

The secret of making ladyfingers is to mix the batter lightly and quickly and get them into the oven as fast as possible. Drop the lady-fingers on a greased baking sheet by squeezing through a cookie press or pastry bag, shaping into little finger-sized cakes or cookies. Leave plenty of space between them.

Bake in a preheated 350° oven 7 minutes, or until a delicate brown. Let cool on the cookie sheet. Sprinkle with powdered sugar.

MACAROONS

•

MAKRONER

3¾ cups powdered sugar

2⅔ cups ground almonds

7 egg whites

1 teaspoon baking powder

Sift the sugar and mix with the ground almonds (½ pound of shelled almonds will produce a little more than 2 cups of ground almonds).

Whip the egg whites stiff with the baking powder. Fold in the almond mixture. Continue to fold gently until smooth. The mixture should be stiff enough to hold its shape.

Form into small round balls and place about 1 inch apart on a greased cookie sheet covered with waxed paper. Bake in a slow oven preheated to about 275 degrees 20 minutes, or until lightly browned. Remove from oven. Invert the cookie sheet on a clean flat surface and lift off. Wet the back of the waxed paper with a cloth wrung out in very cold water. Macaroons will slip off easily.

OLD-FASHIONED MACAROONS

•

GAMLE LINSEMAKRONER

3 egg whites

Pinch of salt

¼ teaspoon cream of tartar

1¼ cups light brown sugar

¼ cup granulated sugar

½ teaspoon vanilla

3 large tablespoons flour

¼ teaspoon baking powder

1⅓ cups shelled almonds, ground fine

Beat egg whites and salt until frothy and just beginning to get dry. Add cream of tartar and beat a little more. Fold the sugars into the mixture with a rubber scraper, a tablespoon at a time. Add vanilla.

Sift the flour and baking powder together and fold with the ground almonds gently into the mixture. Drop by teaspoonfuls on greased cookie sheets.

Bake in a slow oven, preheated to 325 degrees, about 35 minutes, or until a mellow brown. While warm remove carefully from sheets with a knife. Makes 4 dozen cookies.

LEMON WAFERS

•

CITRONSMÅKAGER

½ cup butter
1 cup sugar
4 eggs, well beaten

2 cups flour plus 4 tablespoons,
    sifted
2 teaspoons lemon extract

Cream butter and sugar until light and fluffy. Add eggs and beat until well mixed. Add the flour and beat until smooth. Add the flavoring. Drop by teaspoonfuls about 2 inches apart on greased cookie sheets.

Bake about 6 minutes in a preheated 350° oven, or until browned lightly around the edges. Makes about 10 dozen cookies.

MEDALLIONS

•

MEDALJER

2 cups soft butter
1 cup powdered sugar

1 egg
4½ cups flour, sifted

Cream butter. Add powdered sugar, beating until creamy. Blend the egg in well, then blend in the flour gradually. Set aside for 30 minutes. Do not chill.

Divide dough into 2 or 3 parts, depending on the size of your breadboard. Place one at a time on the lightly floured board. Roll out to about ¼ inch in thickness. Cut with a floured round cookie cutter and place the cookies on very, very lightly floured cookie sheets.

Bake 10 minutes in a preheated 375° oven, or until cookies are browned very slightly on the edges.

Remove from cookie sheets and place about ¾ teaspoon of the filling (see below) on each of ½ the total number of cookies. Top each filled cookie with a plain one.

FILLING

1 cup milk
2 tablespoons flour
⅓ cup sugar
Pinch of salt

2 egg yolks, beaten
1 tablespoon butter
1 teaspoon vanilla

Scald ¾ cup of milk in top of a double boiler until a thin film appears.

Sift flour, sugar and salt into a saucepan. Add to this the remaining ¼ cup of milk. Then add the scalded milk gradually, stirring constantly. Wash the rim of the double boiler to remove any scum of milk there may be left. Bring mixture rapidly to a boil, stirring constantly, and let boil for 3 minutes.

Transfer mixture back to the top of the double boiler and let cook over boiling water 5 minutes more.

Stir 3 tablespoons of this hot mixture into the beaten egg yolks. When the milk and flour combination has cooled somewhat, blend the egg yolks all at once into it and cook over low heat 3 to 5 minutes until smooth, stirring constantly.

Remove from flame and stir in the butter and the vanilla. Cover and set aside to cool, stirring now and then.

If you wish, you may frost the filled cookies as follows:

FROSTING

1 cup sifted powdered sugar   1 tablespoon heavy cream
1 teaspoon vanilla

Blend the sugar, vanilla and cream well so the mixture holds its shape. Spread on top of the cookies.

NUPTIAL COOKIES

•

BRYLLUPSKAGER

1 cup soft butter   ½ teaspoon salt
1 cup sugar   1½ cups flour
2 egg whites   Jam or preserves

Cream butter and sugar.

Whip egg whites with the salt until stiff. Fold into butter mixture. Sift flour and add slowly to the butter mixture.

Roll dough very thin on a lightly floured board and cut into rounds with a cookie cutter. Place on lightly greased cookie sheets and chill anywhere from 1 hour to overnight in the refrigerator.

Bake in a preheated 375° oven 10 to 12 minutes, or until a golden brown.

Remove from oven. Spread half of the cookies with a dab of jam or preserves. Cover with the other half. Make sure the oven is turned off and return the cookies to the warm oven to dry. Makes 6 dozen cookies.

NUTMEG BUTTER BALLS

•

MUSKATNØDKAGER

½ cup soft butter
½ cup sugar
1 teaspoon vanilla
1½ cups shelled almonds, ground

2 cups flour, sifted
½ cup powdered sugar
2 teaspoons nutmeg

Cream butter and sugar. Add vanilla and almonds. Work in the flour with your fingers to make a smooth dough.

Shape into small balls. Chill for several hours.

Place on greased cookie sheets and bake 15 minutes in a preheated 300° oven.

Remove from sheets and roll in a combination of the powdered sugar and nutmeg while still warm.

PEPPERNUTS

•

PEBERNØDDER

2 cups corn syrup
2 cups molasses
1 cup butter
1½ cups brown sugar
10 cups flour, sifted

1 teaspoon baking soda
2 teaspoons cinnamon
½ teaspoon cloves
Juice and grated rind of 1 lemon
2 egg whites

In a large saucepan over low heat beat syrup, molasses, butter and sugar together, stirring until sugar has dissolved. Remove from heat and let cool slightly.

Add the flour, soda, spices, lemon juice and grated rind. Mix well to make a stiff dough. Chill for several hours.

Shape into long rolls about 1 inch in diameter. Cut into pieces 1 inch long with a sharp knife.

Dilute egg whites with 2 tablespoons of water, and beat until frothy.

Brush over cut sides of cookies after you have placed them on a greased cookie sheet.

Bake 15 minutes in a preheated 350° oven.

This recipe makes the very hard peppernuts (*Pfeffernüsse*) which are an international language. These will keep indefinitely if stored tightly covered.

WHITE PEPPERNUTS
•
HVIDE PEBERNØDDER

4 eggs
3 ounces citron, chopped
Rind of 1 lemon, grated
2 cups sugar
1 tablespoon cinnamon

1 teaspoon nutmeg
½ teaspoon cloves
2 tablespoons baking powder
4 cups flour

Beat eggs well. Stir in citron and grated lemon rind. Add sugar, spices and baking powder. Work in the flour.

Form into small balls and place about 2 inches apart on a well-greased cookie sheet. Bake in a slow oven preheated to 275 degrees 12 to 15 minutes.

Remove from sheet and roll in powdered sugar, or glaze as follows:

GLAZE

½ cup powdered sugar
2 tablespoons water

2 tablespoons rose water

Mix until smooth. Dip cookies into glaze and dry for 10 or 15 minutes in a very slow oven (200 degrees or less).

PRUNE-FILLED COOKIES
•
SMÅKAGER FYLDTE MED SVESKER

½ cup soft butter
¾ cup sugar
1 egg
1 teaspoon vanilla

¾ cup flour
½ teaspoon salt
1¼ cups oatmeal
¾ cup shredded coconut

Cream butter and sugar. Add the egg and vanilla and beat to a creamy consistency.

Sift flour with the salt and add to the butter mixture. Add the oatmeal, mixing well. Chill.

Shape into small balls and roll in the coconut. Make a good-sized dent on top of each ball.

Bake on ungreased cookie sheets in a preheated slow oven, 275 degrees, for 30 minutes. Remove and let cool. Fill the dented centers as follows:

PRUNE FILLING

¼ cup sugar   1 cup cooked and pitted prunes

Chop the prunes, add sugar and cook until thick. Cool, and fill the centers of the cookies.

Warm your oven, turn off heat, and put cookies in to dry out for a few minutes.

POOR MAN'S COOKIES

•

FATTIGMANDSKAGER

3 tablespoons light cream
¼ cup sugar
3 eggs, beaten until light
1½ tablespoons melted butter
1 tablespoon brandy

½ teaspoon salt
½ teaspoon ground cardamom
3 cups flour
Fat or oil for frying
Powdered sugar

Blend cream and sugar well. Add eggs, butter, brandy, salt, cardamom and 2 cups of the flour, mixing well. Add enough more flour to make a stiff dough. Chill one hour.

Heat oil to a depth of 3 inches in a deep pan to a temperature of 365 degrees.

On a lightly floured canvas or board roll half of the dough paper-thin. Cut into diamond shapes 3 inches long, making a slit in the center of each. Pull one corner through the slit. Cook in the hot fat until a delicate brown. Dust with powdered sugar. Roll out remaining dough and proceed as above.

PLUM COOKIES

•

KATRINEBLOMMEKAGER*

½ cup soft butter
1½ cups sugar
2 eggs, beaten
1 teaspoon baking soda
½ cup sour cream

2 squares unsweetened chocolate,
    melted in top of double boiler
    over hot water
2½ cups flour, sifted with
1 teaspoon cinnamon
1 cup cooked, pitted and pureed
    plums

Combine ingredients in order given and mix well.

Drop batter by small spoonfuls on greased and floured cookie sheets and bake 15 minutes in a preheated 350° oven.

* A *Katrineblomme* is a kind of French plum. You may, however, use any variety available to you in this recipe.

RAISIN DROP COOKIES

•

ROSINKAGER

2½ cups raisins
1 cup water
1 teaspoon baking soda
1 cup soft butter
2 cups sugar
3 eggs, beaten
1 teaspoon vanilla
1 teaspoon lemon extract

4 cups flour, sifted
1½ teaspoons baking powder
½ teaspoon salt
1 teaspoon cinnamon
¼ teaspoon nutmeg
¼ teaspoon allspice
1 cup chopped nut meats

Wash and drain the raisins. Put in a saucepan, add water and let boil for 5 minutes. Cool a little. Stir in the soda.

Cream butter and sugar. Add eggs and the flavorings and beat until light and creamy. Add the cooled raisins.

Sift the dry ingredients together and fold into the batter, stirring a little after the folding-in. Add the nut meats and mix well.

Drop by teaspoonfuls on a well-greased cookie sheet far enough apart to allow them to spread out. Bake in a preheated 425° oven until browned. Remove at once to cool on a rack.

These cookies will keep soft and moist if you store them in tightly covered containers. Makes about 6 dozen.

ROCKS

•

ROKKEKAGER

1 cup soft butter	2 teaspoons cinnamon
2 cups brown sugar	½ teaspoon cloves
2 eggs	½ teaspoon nutmeg
2⅔ cups flour	⅓ cup milk
½ teaspoon salt	⅔ cup raisins, chopped
2 teaspoons baking powder	⅔ cup nut meats, chopped
½ teaspoon baking soda	

Cream butter and sugar. Add eggs and beat well.

Sift flour, measure, and add salt, baking powder, soda, and the spices. Stir into creamed mixture.

Add milk gradually, beating after each addition. Add nut meats and raisins. Blend well.

Drop by teaspoonfuls about 2 inches apart onto greased cookie sheets. Bake 15 minutes in a preheated 350° oven.

RUM BALLS

•

ROMBOLLER

1 pound vanilla wafers	½ cup rum
1 tablespoon cocoa	½ cup shelled hazelnuts, ground
½ cup corn syrup	Powdered sugar

Crush the wafers. Mix all ingredients together in the order given. Form into small balls about an inch in diameter. Place in refrigerator for 36 hours.

Bake on greased and lightly floured cookie sheets in a slow oven (preheated to 325 degrees) until lightly browned. Roll in powdered sugar while warm.

"S" COOKIES

•

S-KAGER

1 cup soft butter	2 egg yolks
1 teaspoon vanilla	2½ cups flour
½ cup sugar	

Cream butter and vanilla until soft. Add sugar slowly. Beat in egg yolks one at a time. Add flour slowly, blending well after each addition.

Fill a cookie press about ⅔ full of dough and press out cookies in "S" shapes (or in any desired shapes) on greased and lightly floured baking sheets.

Bake in a preheated 350° oven 12 to 14 minutes, or until golden yellow on edges. Watch the cookies while they bake because they scorch easily.

Makes 6 dozen cookies.

SPICE COOKIES

•

KRYDDERIKAGER

1 cup soft butter	5 to 6 cups flour, sifted
1 cup sugar	1 teaspoon salt
1 egg	1 teaspoon cinnamon
¾ teaspoon baking soda	1 teaspoon ground cardamom
½ cup boiling water	1 teaspoon cloves
1 cup molasses	

Cream butter and sugar. Beat the egg and add to the butter and sugar. Stir baking soda into the boiling water, add molasses, then beat into the creamed mixture.

Sift 5 cups of the flour together with the spices. Add as much of the remaining flour as is necessary to make a good stiff dough, but not *too* stiff.

Roll out about ¼ inch thick on a lightly floured board and cut into fancy shapes. Place on greased cookie sheets and let chill at least 1 hour, or as long as overnight if you wish.

Bake about 15 minutes in a preheated 375° oven.

SHORTBREAD

•

SANDKAGER

1 cup soft butter
1 cup sugar
2 egg yolks

2 cups flour, sifted
½ teaspoon baking powder

Cream butter and sugar. Add unbeaten egg yolks.

Sift flour and baking powder together and add, a little at a time, to the first mixture, stirring after each addition.

Let dough rest overnight in the refrigerator. In the morning, roll it about ½ inch thick on a lightly floured board, or flatten it out with your hands.

Cut into squares and place on greased and floured cookie sheets. Bake in a preheated 350° oven 12 to 15 minutes.

THIMBLE COOKIES

•

FINGERBØLKAGER

1 pound soft butter
1 cup sugar
1⅓ cups shelled almonds, ground

1 teaspoon vanilla
4 cups flour, sifted

Cream butter and sugar together. Add ground almonds, vanilla and flour. Refrigerate 3 hours.

Roll out to ⅛ inch thick. Cut with floured rim of a thimble or a small cookie cutter.

Bake on a greased cookie sheet in a preheated 400° oven until light brown.

Make a sandwich of two cookies with thick currant jelly or jam as the filling. Roll in powdered sugar.

THREE-CORNERED COOKIES

•

TREKANTEDE KAGER

2 cups flour
1 teaspoon salt

1 cup ice water
2 cups butter

Place flour on pastry board and make a well in the center. Add salt and work quickly to a paste with the ice water. Roll out to about 20 x 20 inches if your board is large enough. Place the butter in the center of the dough. Fold it like an envelope and put it in the refrigerator for 20 minutes.

Remove and roll into a long strip. Fold in thirds with open ends out. Roll again. Fold again, envelope fashion, wrap in a small towel and return to the refrigerator for ½ hour. Repeat this process 3 times. The last time roll very thin and cut into 3 long strips about 3 inches wide. Place on cookie sheets which have been moistened with water. Put the sheets in the refrigerator for 15 minutes.

Bake 15 minutes in a preheated 400° oven. Let cool, then spread with cream filling (see below). While still warm, cut into triangles.

FILLING

2 whole eggs	1½ cups hot milk
2 egg yolks	4 egg whites
6 tablespoons flour	1½ cups heavy cream
6 tablespoons sugar	4 tablespoons rum
1 tablespoon cornstarch	Powdered sugar
2 teaspoons vanilla	

Put eggs, egg yolks, flour and sugar in a mixing bowl. Beat well. Blend in the cornstarch and vanilla, mixing well. Pour the hot milk over it.

Place over a moderate heat until it comes just to the boiling point. Remove from heat and place over a pan of ice. Stir until it begins to thicken.

Beat egg whites until stiff. Whip cream. Fold alternately into cooked mixture. Fold in rum. Spread filling over strips, and dust with powdered sugar.

SAND COOKIES

•

SANDBAKKELSER

1 cup sugar	2½ cups sifted flour
1 cup soft butter	Heavy cream
1 egg	Strawberry preserves
½ teaspoon almond extract	

Cream sugar and butter. Add egg, flavoring and flour.

Pinch off small pieces of dough about the size of a walnut. Put them in the center of a *sandbakkel* tin (tiny, individual fluted tart shell tins) and press thinly and evenly into sides and bottom. Place the tins on a cookie sheet and bake in a preheated 375° oven about 12 minutes.

When cool, tap gently on the bottoms of the tins and the tarts will drop out easily. They are very fragile, so remove them carefully. Fill with whipped cream and strawberry preserves just before serving.

SAND COOKIES WITH ALMONDS

•

SANDKAGER

½ pound butter
1 cup sugar
¼ pound shelled almonds,
    chopped

2 eggs, beaten
4¼ cups flour
Granulated sugar

Melt butter and stir until light in color. Add sugar. Add almonds with the beaten eggs. Add flour and mix well. Let the dough cool.

Place the dough in the middle of a cookie sheet, then work it toward the edges with your thumbs to cover the whole cookie sheet as thinly as possible. Sprinkle with granulated sugar.

Bake in a moderate oven (preheated to 375 degrees) until golden brown. Cut into squares.

BUTTER COOKIES

•

SMØRDEJGSKAGER

2 cups soft butter
4 cups sugar
6 egg yolks, well beaten
1 cup sour cream
2 teaspoons almond extract

2 teaspoons nutmeg
2 teaspoons baking soda
2 teaspoons cream of tartar
9 cups flour
6 egg whites, beaten stiff

Cream butter and sugar, then add the egg yolks and beat again. Stir in the sour cream and almond flavoring.

Sift nutmeg, soda and cream of tartar with the flour. Combine with creamed mixture to make a stiff dough. Fold in the egg whites.

Roll the dough about ⅛ inch thick and cut into desired shapes with cookie cutters. Sprinkle with sugar. Place on greased cookie sheets.

Bake 10 minutes in a preheated 375° oven. Will yield about 12 dozen cookies.

WALNUT RUM COOKIES

•

VALNØDROMKAGER

1 cup soft butter
½ cup sugar
¼ teaspoon salt

2 teaspoons rum
2 cups flour
1½ cup walnut meats, ground

Mix butter and sugar till creamy. Add salt, rum, flour and nuts. Mix well. Chill dough until easy to handle (anywhere from 1 hour to overnight).

Shape dough into 1-inch balls and place on ungreased cookie sheets.

Bake 12 to 15 minutes in a preheated 350° oven, or until golden brown. While cookies are still warm, roll in sugar. Makes 4 dozen. Will keep well if stored in airtight container.

WHITE BUTTER COOKIES

•

LYSE SMØRKAGER

4 cups flour
1 pound soft butter, creamed
16 tablespoons powdered sugar

3 cups hazelnuts or filberts,
  ground
2 teaspoons vanilla

Sift flour, add creamed butter and mix with the powdered sugar. Fold in the ground nuts and vanilla.

Roll small quantities of dough between the palms of your hands into crescent shapes.

Place on greased cookie sheets and bake 20 to 25 minutes in a preheated 350° oven. Remove from cookie sheets and roll in powdered sugar while still warm. Yields about 80 cookies, depending, of course, on the size of the crescents.

· 5 ·

FILLINGS, FROSTINGS

AND GLAZES

RUM FILLING

·

ROMCREME

1½ cups light cream
½ cup sugar
2½ tablespoons flour
¼ teaspoon salt

3 egg yolks
2 tablespoons rum
1 tablespoon butter

Scald 1 cup of the cream.

Sift together the sugar, flour and salt. Blend in the reserved ½ cup of cream. Bring to a boil quickly and let boil 2 or 3 minutes, stirring gently. Remove from flame.

Pour this mixture over the scalded cream and cook over hot water in the top of a double boiler 5 to 7 minutes, stirring steadily.

Beat the 3 egg yolks slightly. Blend the yolk mixture into the mix in the double-boiler top. Remove from flame and add the rum and the butter.

You can convert this recipe to a vanilla filling by substituting 2 teaspoons vanilla and a little almond extract for the rum.

ALMOND FILLING

·

MANDELCREME

2 tablespoons soft butter
¼ cup sugar
1 egg yolk

1½ tablespoons rum
½ cup ground almonds

Work butter to a cream. Add sugar slowly and beat until fluffy. Add the egg yolk and beat well. Blend in the rum and fold in the ground almonds.

Will make about ½ cup.

DATE FILLING

·

DADELCREME

½ cup sugar
1 pound dates, pitted and ground
  in a food chopper

1 cup water
½ teaspoon grated lemon rind
½ cup chopped almonds

Mix all ingredients and cook over low heat about 5 minutes, stirring to prevent sticking or scorching. If filling becomes too thick while cooking, add a little more water.

SYLLABUB
FROM A 300-YEAR-OLD RECIPE

1 pint whipping cream
¼ cup sugar
2 egg whites

¼ cup sugar
4 tablespoons white wine

Beat whipping cream until stiff but not dry. Fold in the ¼ cup sugar.

Beat egg whites stiff and beat in the other ¼ cup sugar. Add the whipped cream and blend well, folding instead of stirring. Slowly add the white wine. Serve over cakes, custards, meringues or cookies.

RAISIN FILLING

•

ROSINCREME

1 cup seedless raisins
¼ cup sugar
½ cup water

½ teaspoon grated lemon rind
¼ cup ground almonds

Put raisins through a food chopper. Add sugar, water and grated lemon rind. Cook 5 minutes, or until thick and smooth, stirring constantly. Cool. Fold in the almonds.

TART CREAM FILLING

•

FLØDECREME

1 cup light cream
2 egg yolks, beaten
Juice of 1 lemon

1 heaping tablespoon flour
2 tablespoons sugar
1 teaspoon vanilla

Mix cream and egg yolks. Add lemon juice, flour and sugar. Mix well. Add vanilla.

Cook over low heat until smooth and thickened, stirring in a figure "8" to prevent scorching.

CHOCOLATE FILLING

•

CHOKOLADECREME

2 cups milk
3 tablespoons flour
2 tablespoons cornstarch
1 cup sugar

Pinch of salt
3 ounces unsweetened chocolate
2 eggs, beaten
1 teaspoon vanilla

Scald the milk. Mix flour, cornstarch, sugar and salt well and stir very slowly into scalded milk. Cook until thick.

Melt chocolate in top of double boiler over hot water and add to cooked mixture. Add eggs. Boil 2 minutes. Stir in vanilla. If you wish a glossy filling, stir in 2 tablespoons butter after the filling has been removed from the heat.

BUTTER CREAM FILLING

•

SMØRCREME

½ cup soft butter
1 cup powdered sugar
1 teaspoon sherry

1 teaspoon strong coffee
Chopped almonds

Cream butter. Beat in powdered sugar until smooth. Beat in the wine and coffee.

Use as a filling and/or frosting for any layer cake. Sprinkle chopped almonds on top, and spread around the sides of the frosted cake.

COCONUT-RAISIN FROSTING

•

FORSKELLIGE FRUGTCREMER

3 egg yolks
⅔ cup sugar
½ cup soft butter

½ cup white raisins
½ cup shredded coconut
½ cup chopped almonds

Combine the egg yolks and sugar. Beat until thick and lemon-colored. Add the soft butter and white raisins. Bring to a boil and cook over medium heat, stirring, until thick, 5 to 7 minutes. Add the coconut and the almonds. Spread over cake or cookies.

FRUIT FROSTING WITH CHOCOLATE

•

CHOKOLADEGLASUR

1 cup raisins
1 cup dates, pitted and chopped
¾ cup water
¼ cup brandy
1 cup sugar

1 tablespoon flour
½ cup chopped almonds
2 ounces unsweetened chocolate
2 teaspoons butter

Combine the raisins and dates and mix with the water, brandy, sugar and flour and let come to a boil. Boil slowly until thick.

Add the chopped almonds and mix well. Pour over the sides and top of a warm cake.

Melt the butter and chocolate together over low heat and drizzle over the cake.

CREAM FROSTING

•

FLØDEGLASUR

¾ cup whipping cream
3 tablespoons sugar

½ teaspoon vanilla
¼ teaspoon cinnamon

Whip the cream until very stiff. Fold in the sugar, vanilla and cinnamon.

You may vary this recipe by folding in a blend of very thick applesauce and 1 teaspoon lemon juice.

MARSHMALLOW FROSTING

•

LAEGE ALTHEE

20 marshmallows
1½ cups sugar
½ cup water

2 egg whites, beaten until stiff
1 teaspoon vanilla

Cut the marshmallows into small cubes.

Boil sugar and water until the syrup spins a thread. Pour over egg whites and beat well. Add marshmallows and vanilla to the hot mixture and beat until cool.

RUM CREAM FROSTING

•

FLØDEGLASUR MED ROM

1½ cups heavy cream
2 eggs, beaten
⅓ cup sugar

1 teaspoon rum
¼ cup melted butter

Whip cream until stiff, add the eggs, sugar and rum. Continue beating until thick.

Allow melted butter to cool somewhat, then stir into other ingredients and mix well.

EGG-WHITE CREAM FROSTING

•

ÆGGEHVIDEGLASUR

2 egg whites   *1½ cups light corn syrup*
Pinch of salt

Place all ingredients in the top of a double boiler over hot water. Cook 7 to 8 minutes, beating constantly, until the mixture stands in peaks.

If the frosting separates in the bottom of the pan, beat with a fork until it is well integrated again.

Danish cooks rely on glazes instead of thick frostings for tarts, breads, pastries of all kinds and cookies. Remember that these spread more easily when they're hot.

WHITE GLAZE

•

HVID GLASUR

2 cups sugar   *⅛ teaspoon cream of tartar*
¾ cup hot water   *3 cups powdered sugar*

Boil sugar, water and cream of tartar in a heavy saucepan until the syrup threads. Cool to a temperature just above lukewarm. Add sifted powdered sugar and beat until the right consistency for spreading thinly.

APRICOT GLAZE

•

ABRIKOSGLASUR

1 cup apricot jam

Place jam in a small, heavy saucepan and bring it to a boil. Cook slowly 10 minutes, or until very thick. Press through a sieve and spread while hot in a very thin film over breads, pastries and cakes.

ICE GLAZE

•

GLASUR

1 egg yolk   *Powdered sugar*
1 dessertspoon melted butter

Beat egg yolk and butter together well. Brush lightly over tarts or fruit cake. Sift powdered sugar over pastry.

Preheat oven to 450 degrees. Place glazed cake in oven for 3 or 4 minutes.

VANILLA GLAZE

•

VANILLA GLASUR

1½ cups powdered sugar   *3 tablespoons light cream*
2 tablespoons soft butter   *⅛ teaspoon salt*
1 teaspoon vanilla

Sift sugar. Add all ingredients and beat until smooth and creamy. Spread very thin on cakes or pastries while they are still hot.

· 6 ·

SMORREBROD:

THE OPEN-FACED SANDWICH

THE DANISH WORD *smørrebrød* can be traced back to the days
when a round of baked bread served as a plate for both hot and
cold food. The rich refrained from eating the plate, but the plate,
soaked by gravy or sauce, eventually found its way to the mouths of the
servants. Between the two classes, doubtless, was a group which served
delicious tidbits on the plate and ate both bread and topping. Eventually the open-faced sandwich was born, years before the Earl of
Sandwich discovered what could be done with two pieces of bread.

The fabulous "open-face" is Denmark's national dish. *Smørrebrød*
translates as "butter bread," but it is much more than that — now it
means an appetizing assortment of artfully constructed combinations
of food and garnish piled high on slices of well-buttered breads. At
least once a day, all over Denmark, housewives and renowned chefs
prepare, serve, eat and enjoy them. Restaurants take pride in the great
variety they offer, and the menus may be a yard or more long. One
restaurant in Copenhagen boasts hundreds of varieties.

The base of these little surprises is a single slice of bread (one of five
or more different kinds, depending on what is to go on top). Savory
and rich fillings, butters and dressings are heaped on succulent, sweet-

136

buttered bread cut in different shapes. The mere sight of the finished product stirs languishing appetites. Virtually anything goes — shrimps, lobster, spiced or kippered herring, onion rings, ham, cold meat or fowl, liver paste, parboiled eggs, smoked salmon, cheeses. Out of this variety the Danes turn four or five pieces of *smørrebrød* into a complete lunch, supper, or a late-evening dinner meal, served and eaten with knife and fork, in the same fashion as the courses of any meal. Each course is served on a fresh plate with fresh utensils, accompanied by ice-cold akvavit and Danish beer. Recent years have brought the "open-face" into popularity in America. It is a delightful way of entertaining informally at lunch or for an evening snack. The bite-size party *smørrebrød* is especially suitable for cocktail parties or afternoon teas or "coffees."

An open-faced sandwich must never be skimpy; the contents must completely cover the bread and be made with great care to appeal to the eye as well as the taste buds. The sandwich is most appealing when given height, as when shrimps are piled high, or meats are rolled into rounds and cheeses garnished with build-ups.

Today one may purchase so many delicious different kinds of bread it is no trick to have a wide gamut of bases for sandwiches. There are a number of suggestions for open-faced sandwiches in this chapter, but *smørrebrød* permutations and combinations are limited only by your own imagination. Be lavish and artistic; picture yourself living the good life in Denmark, and don't worry about calories until tomorrow.

SUGGESTIONS FOR
OPEN-FACED SANDWICHES

Fresh or canned salmon, mayonnaise, sweet pickle, seasonings
Fresh or canned salmon, grated onion, mayonnaise, seasonings to taste
1 cup fish, 2 hard-boiled eggs, lemon juice
1 cup fish, 1 teaspoon horseradish, mayonnaise
½ cup mashed sardines, lemon juice, chopped pimiento, olives and
    mayonnaise
Sardines, pickled beets
1 cup chopped cooked chicken, ¼ cup cubed pineapple, mayonnaise
Hard-boiled eggs, mustard, seasonings, catsup, chopped onion
Hard-boiled eggs, walnuts, sweet pickles, mayonnaise
Cream cheese, butter, onion juice, sage, celery salt, lemon juice

1 cup mashed cooked chicken livers, chopped cooked bacon, tomato
sauce, lemon juice

Flaked tuna, pickle relish, chopped stuffed olives, chopped parsley,
lemon juice, mayonnaise

Cooked ham, ground with pickle relish, celery, hard-boiled eggs, mixed
with mayonnaise

Tuna, crabmeat or lobster, celery chopped fine, mayonnaise

Chopped cooked chicken, walnut meats, pineapple and mayonnaise

Chopped cooked bacon, cream cheese, salad dressing of your choice

Chopped cucumbers, chopped chives, chopped shrimp, French dressing
or mayonnaise

Cream cheese, chopped almonds, chopped apples

Pineapple, almond slivers, cream cheese

Fried smelts with cucumbers

Fresh cooked, canned, or smoked salmon with scrambled eggs

Fried smelts in molasses and vinegar

Boiled tongue, chopped mushrooms, creamed butter with chopped
celery

Slices of goose breast, egg soufflé, chopped parsley

Cream cheese, water-cress leaves, onion juice

Liver paste with pickled-beet slices

Pressed meats or headcheese

Lamb or veal roast with sliced cucumbers

Pork roast, water-cress leaves, sliced tomatoes, slivered almonds

Coarsely chopped raw kale, sliced corned beef, water-cress leaves

Avocado with lemon juice, vinegar, salt, pepper, onion juice

Cream cheese, chopped turkey, chicken, chopped clams, dill pickles

Cream cheese, ground salami

Slices of a variety of cheeses on rye bread

Slices of fancy meats on slices of rye or white bread

Blue cheese, raw egg yolk, garnishes of chopped radishes

Blue cheese mixed with Cherry Heering

Salami, jellied consommé, on rye with a touch of seasoned lard

Pickled herring, sliced sweet onions, on rye or black bread

SUGGESTED GARNISHES
FOR OPEN-FACED SANDWICHES

Radishes, sliced very thin
Chopped parsley or chives

Hard-boiled eggs cut into small slices or wedges

Hard-boiled egg yolks, sieved, as a center for a flower whose petals may be made of any edible you choose

Paper-thin slices of cucumbers

Slivers of green or red peppers

Paper-thin slices of stuffed olives or pitted, diced black olives

Tiny balls of cream cheese

Mayonnaise squeezed through a pastry tube to form a decorative border or other design

Paprika

Natural red fruit juice tints; green or red artificial food coloring

Chopped fresh dill

Paper-thin slices of sweet onion

BREAD SHAPES FOR PARTY SMØRREBRØD

PINWHEELS (HJULBRØD)

1½-pound loaf unsliced bread   *Soft butter*
Parsley   *Lemon juice*

Trim crusts from bread. Cut very thin, lengthwise. Spread with parsley butter (in proportions of 1½ tablespoons very finely chopped parsley to 2 ounces soft butter; cream together with a few drops of lemon juice). Or use any other filling of your choice. Roll up.

Wrap each roll in waxed paper and twist the ends tightly. Store in refrigerator, seam side down. Remove and slice just before serving, placing seam side of paper down against board to slice. Remove paper.

FOLD-UPS (KONVOLUTTER)

Spread small bread squares with butter and filling of your choice. Toothpick two opposite corners together at the center.

CRESCENTS AND ROUNDS (HALVMÅNER OG CIRKLER)

One slice of bread will yield one crescent and one round. Use cookie cutters for best results.

TULIPS (TULIPANER)

Cut bread slices in petal shapes with cookie cutters and toast sufficiently to curl edges. Spread with egg salad, which may be tinted with food coloring if you wish.

CORNUCOPIAS (OVERFLØDIGHEDSHORN)

Trim thin slices of bread into squares, roll into cornucopias, one side overlapping the other. (Under the corner of the bread square place a little softened butter to hold it in place while chilling.)

Fill and wrap in waxed paper. Store them, seam side down, in the refrigerator until time to serve.

ANCHOVY PASTE

·

ANSJOSCREME

1½ cups soft butter   *4 hard-boiled eggs*
1½ ounces anchovy paste

Spread small rounds of bread with softened butter, then with anchovy paste. Cut narrow strips of the boiled egg whites to arrange in petal shapes. Fill center with sieved yolks.

SALMON SPREAD

·

LAKS-CREME

1½ cups freshly cooked or   *White pepper to taste*
  canned salmon   *⅓ cup soft butter*
¼ cup mayonnaise   *1 avocado*
1½ tablespoons lemon juice   *Pimiento*
Pinch of salt

Mix half the salmon and the mayonnaise, a little of the lemon juice, salt and white pepper. Spread small slices of dark bread with butter and cover with mixture.

Mix the other half of the salmon with mashed avocado and spread on small rounds of white bread. Garnish with strips of pimiento.

SHRIMP BUTTER

·

REJESMØR

1 cup soft butter
1 cup cooked shrimp, minced
1 tablespoon lemon juice

¼ teaspoon salt
Dash of paprika

Cream butter. Grind the shrimp to a very smooth paste and mix with the butter, lemon juice and seasonings. Rub through a sieve until smooth. Spread on trimmed bread, shaped as you wish.

CHIVE BUTTER

·

PURLØGSMØR

½ cup soft butter
¼ cup chives

4 drops Worcestershire sauce

Cream butter. Chop or grind the chives and mix with butter and sauce.

HORSERADISH BUTTER

·

PEBERRODSMØR

½ cup softened butter

¼ cup (or to taste) fresh grated horseradish

Mix horseradish well with butter.

DANISH BLUE CHEESE

·

DANABLU-CREME

Danish Blue Cheese
Sweet soft butter

Cold roast beef
Chopped chives

Spread white or whole-wheat bread with equal parts of Danish Blue Cheese and soft sweet butter, mixed together until smooth.

Top with slices of cold roast beef and sprinkle with chopped chives.

LIVERWURST SPREAD

•

LEVERPØLSE-CREME

Salt
Pepper
1 cup liverwurst
2 tablespoons mayonnaise
1 tablespoon lemon juice

1 cup broiled baby beef or
   chicken liver, chopped
1 tablespoon onion, chopped
½ teaspoon prepared mustard
2 tablespoons catsup

Mix all ingredients thoroughly. Cream until liver bits are completely integrated with other ingredients.

If not soft enough to spread, add 2 additional tablespoons mayonnaise.

EGG SANDWICH

•

ÆGGESMØRREBRØD

¼ cup soft butter
1 tablespoon chives, chopped fine
1 teaspoon lemon juice
Thin slices of your favorite cheese
4 hard-boiled eggs
2 ounces anchovies, drained and
   mashed

1 teaspoon minced onion
¼ teaspoon dry mustard
¼ cup salad dressing of your
   choice
Paprika

Cream the butter, add the chives and lemon juice and mix until very smooth. Spread on thin-sliced bread. Top with cheese slices. Cover with second slice of bread.

Mix the chopped eggs, anchovies, minced onion, dry mustard and mayonnaise until smooth. Spread on top part of double decker. Sprinkle with paprika.

MASHED ANCHOVIES

·

ANSJOS-SMØRECREME

1 cup mashed anchovies
2 hard-boiled eggs, chopped

1 teaspoon onion, minced
Strips of pimiento

Mix first 3 ingredients together well. Spread on dark bread and garnish with strips of pimiento.

CHICKEN SPREADS

·

SMØRECREME AF HAKKET KYLLINGEKØD

Mix the ingredients for each of these spreads well before spreading on open-faced sandwiches and garnishing.

¾ cup minced cooked chicken
⅓ cup crushed pineapple, drained

3 tablespoons mayonnaise

1 cup cooked chicken and giblets,
    chopped
1 cup chopped almonds, toasted

1 teaspoon grated onion
½ teaspoon curry powder
½ cup mayonnaise

1 cup cooked, ground chicken
    livers
2 teaspoons cooked, chopped
    bacon

1 tablespoon lemon juice
4 drops Tabasco sauce

CHICKEN LIVER SPREAD

·

SMØRECREME AF HØNSELEVER

1 pound chicken livers
1 onion
¾ cup melted butter
4 tablespoons onion, grated
⅓ cup chicken fat
2 scant teaspoons salt

½ teaspoon white pepper
¼ teaspoon mace
1½ teaspoons dry mustard
Pinch of anchovy paste
1 tablespoon brandy

Wash the livers carefully. Put in a saucepan with the onion, cover with water and bring to a boil. Let simmer 20 minutes. Drain, and discard the onion.

Put the livers through a food grinder 3 times until very smooth, or run in an electric blender 10 to 15 seconds. Add melted butter and mix well.

Render the chicken fat until smooth and liquid. Add with salt, pepper, mace, mustard and anchovy paste to ground livers. Mix until smooth. Add the brandy, mixing well.

Place the mixture in a mold, pressing it down until firm. Chill 3 hours. Turn out on a serving platter. Slice about ¼ inch thick and place on thin rounds of bread of your choice. Heap high with garnishes and serve with a knife and fork.

TONGUE SPREAD

•

TUNGESMØR

1 cup cooked tongue, chopped fine	*Yolk of 1 hard-boiled egg*
1 teaspoon prepared mustard	*Juice of 1 lemon*
1 tablespoon soft butter	*Dash of nutmeg*
¼ teaspoon paprika	

Chop the tongue *very* fine. Add balance of ingredients in order given and mix well.

CALVES' LIVER PASTE

•

KALVELEVERPOSTEJ

1½ pounds pork fat	*Salt*
10 tablespoons butter	*Pepper*
10 tablespoons flour	*Ground cloves*
Milk	*2 egg whites*
1 calves' liver	*1 teaspoon onion, grated*
2 egg yolks	*(optional)*

Put the fat through a food grinder or into an electric blender. Turn into a large, heavy skillet. Add the butter and the flour with enough milk to make a mixture of thick porridge-like consistency. Let cook until the fat has absorbed. Cook very slowly. Skim off any fat which does not absorb.

Wash and clean the liver thoroughly. Cut it in manageable pieces and feed through the finest blade of your meat grinder. Mix with the fat mixtures and put through a coarse sieve to make a smooth paste.

Add the egg yolks, salt, pepper and a good pinch of the ground cloves.

Beat the egg whites until stiff and add.

If you wish, add a little grated onion to the blend.

Fill bread tins about ¾ full of the mixture. Bake in a pan of hot water 1¼ hours, or until a knife inserted in the middle comes out clean. (Preheat oven to 325 degrees.) Do not remove any fat that may come to the surface; it will be absorbed.

Let cool in the pans and dip in boiling water to loosen after it has chilled overnight. Slice thin, serve on dark bread, imaginatively garnished.

With the permission of Denmark's famous Oskar Davidsen Restaurant, I am reproducing their 4-foot-long *smørrebrød* menu. You may get some ideas for your own combinations from this world-renowned sandwich maker. Patrons of the restaurant are free to choose rye, white, sour or crisp bread as the base for their sandwiches.

FISH, SHELLFISH

1. Superfine export caviar on toast
2. Shrimps
3. Shrimps, double portion (45–55)
4. "Rush Hour" (double layer of shrimps with 2 extra rows, 80–100 shrimps)
5. Shrimps, pyramid portion (180–200 shrimps)
6. Parboiled* egg in mayonnaise, garnished with shrimps
7. Smoked salmon
8. Smoked salmon with raw egg yolk
9. Smoked salmon with scrambled egg
10. Smoked salmon with stewed mushrooms
11. Purée of smoked salmon with raw egg yolk, horseradish and onion
12. Lobster, freshly boiled

* Hard-boiled, but just barely.

13. Lobster mayonnaise
14. Lobster with curry mayonnaise
15. Lobster with asparagus in mayonnaise
16. Lobster with lettuce, sliced egg and mayonnaise
17. ½ lobster, chopped heart of lettuce and raw egg yolk on toast
18. 6 split crawfish tails with dill mayonnaise
19. Eel, freshly smoked, and scrambled egg
20. Eel, with scrambled egg, spinach and fried mushrooms
21. Fried fillet of plaice and lemon
22. Fried fillet of plaice and remoulade
23. Dressed fried fillet of plaice
24. Fillet of plaice with de luxe garnish
25. Portuguese sardine in oil
26. Portuguese sardine and 2 boned anchovies in oyster sauce
27. Pickled herring "tit-bits" with raw onion
28. Potato salad with pickled herring "tit-bits" and seasoned beetroot
29. Pickled herring (Oskar Davidsen's special)
30. Fishcake and capers
31. Fishcake and remoulade
32. Freshly smoked herring
33. Freshly smoked herring with raw egg yolk
34. Freshly smoked herring, egg yolk and chopped radishes
35. Thinly sliced anchovies, beetroot, raw egg yolk, capers, onion and horseradish
36. 4 boned anchovies in oyster sauce
37. 4 boned anchovies with egg yolk and chives
38. 4 boned anchovies with chopped egg and capers
39. 4 boned anchovies with scrambled egg and chives
40. 4 boned anchovies in oyster sauce, fried egg on toast
41. Swedish anchovy bird's-nest
42. Hot fried eel
43. Hot fried eel and remoulade
44. Cod roe, fried
45. Cod roe fried with remoulade
46. Cod roe, fried with 2 boned anchovies in oyster sauce

FRESH MEATS, POULTRY, ETC.

47. "Clipper Sandwich" (raw, scraped beef, export caviar and smoked salmon)
48. Hans Andersen's Favourite (crisp bacon, tomato, liver paste with truffles, meat jelly and horseradish)

49. Rare, minced beef with capers and onions and fried egg
50. Boeuf Tartar (scraped raw beef)
51. Boeuf Tartar with pickles
52. "Strip Tease" (boeuf Tartar with raw egg yolk)
53. An Oskar Davidsen creation: scraped raw meat, shrimps, parboiled egg and fresh lettuce
54. "Union Jack" sandwich (raw, scraped fillet of beef with shrimps and raw egg yolk)
55. Boeuf Tartar with 2 boned anchovies in oyster sauce, egg yolk and chopped onions or chives
56. Raw, scraped meat, export caviar and 2 Limfjord oysters flanked by 2 rows of shrimps
57. Roast beef with tomato and cucumber salad
58. Roast beef with crisp bacon and onions
59. Roast beef with cold Béarnaise sauce
60. Roast beef with superfine export caviar
61. Roast beef and horseradish
62. Roast beef and remoulade
63. Roast beef with potato salad and chives
64. Fried calves' liver and onions
65. Fried calves' liver with fried egg
66. Fried calves' liver with cucumber salad
67. Fried calves' liver with bacon and mushrooms
68. Fried calves' liver with bacon and onions
69. Slices of juicy steak, parboiled egg, crisp onions, and sliced tomato on sour bread or toast
70. Steak and fried onions
71. Steak with fried egg
72. Roast duck with red cabbage and cucumber salad
73. Brisket of beef, freshly boiled, and horseradish
74. Brisket of beef and pickles
75. Brisket of beef and remoulade
76. Brisket of beef with tomato and 2 anchovies
77. Roast chicken with cucumber and tomato
78. Roast pork and beetroot
79. Roast pork with tomato and pickled cucumber
80. Roast pork with meat jelly and smoked ham
81. ½ young pigeon and stewed mushrooms
82. Liver paste with truffles, 2 anchovies in oyster sauce and fried egg
83. Liver paste with cucumber salad
84. Liver paste with thin slices of crisp bacon and stewed mushrooms
85. Liver paste with spiced lard, meat jelly and thinly sliced, juicy salt veal (The Vet's Supper)
86. Liver paste with 2 boned anchovies in oyster sauce and grated horseradish

87. Liver paste with Russian herring salad
88. Liver paste, sliced tomato and cucumber salad
89. Lamb's liver, fried tomato and mushrooms
90. Fried forcemeat cakes with red cabbage, meat jelly and beetroot
91. Fried forcemeat cakes and cucumber salad
92. Fried forcemeat cakes with meat jelly and thinly sliced, juicy salt veal

SALT AND SMOKED MEATS

93. Ham, sliced egg and meat jelly
94. Freshly boiled, mild-cured ham and meat jelly
95. Ham and scrambled egg
96. Ham with Camembert, raw egg yolk and chives
97. Ham with chicken salad
98. Ham with Bombay curry salad
99. Ham with vegetable salad
100. Ham with fried egg
101. Ham with fried calves' kidney and remoulade
102. Ham with bird's liver and fried egg
103. Ham with homemade goose-liver paste, Madeira jelly
104. Bayonne ham, roast beef and Madeira jelly
105. Crisp bacon and fried egg
106. Crisp bacon with tomato and Camembert cheese
107. Crisp bacon with fried onions
108. Crisp bacon with creamed mushrooms
109. Juicy, tender, salt veal and meat jelly
110. Freshly boiled tongue with meat jelly
111. Tongue with Italian salad
112. Tongue with fried egg
113. Tongue with homemade goose-liver paste
114. Tongue with sliced egg and meat jelly
115. Homemade collared pork
116. As above with spiced lard and meat jelly
117. Corned brisket of beef with horseradish
118. As above with spiced lard and meat jelly
119. As above with potato salad and chives
120. Salami sausage, liver paste and meat jelly (The Vet's Breakfast)
121. Salami with raw egg yolk, grated horseradish and chopped chives

EGGS, SALADS, ETC.

122. Salami sausage with meat jelly
123. Salami with scrambled egg and chives
124. Salami and fried egg on toast
125. Salami with spiced lard, sliced potato and chives
126. Luncheon sausage with meat jelly
127. Italian salad
128. Bombay toast (macaroni, chicken, giblets in curry mayonnaise with egg and smoked salmon)
129. Russian herring salad
130. Russian herring salad with egg
131. Vegetable salad
132. Curry salad
133. Hot scrambled egg with smoked salmon on toast
134. Hot scrambled egg, 4 boned anchovies in oyster sauce and chopped chives on toast
135. Hot scrambled egg and fried mushrooms on toast
136. Parboiled egg with shrimps
137. Parboiled egg with remoulade
138. Parboiled egg with export caviar
139. Parboiled egg with smoked eel
140. Parboiled egg with chives
141. Parboiled egg with smoked salmon
142. Parboiled egg and meat jelly
143. Parboiled egg with Russian herring salad
144. Parboiled egg and herring "tit-bits"
145. Parboiled egg and boned anchovies in oyster sauce
146. Parboiled egg and pickles
147. Parboiled egg with tomato and 2 boned anchovies in oyster sauce
148. Parboiled egg with tomato and fried onions
149. Parboiled egg with cheese mayonnaise and chopped radishes
150. Poached egg on toast with stewed mushrooms and fresh lobster
151. Parboiled egg, tomato and horseradish
152. Sliced tomato, scrambled egg, boned anchovies in oyster sauce and chives
153. Tomato and horseradish
154. Tomato with scrambled egg and chives
155. Tomato and 2 boned anchovies in oyster sauce
156. Tomato and fried onions
157. Tomato with cheese mayonnaise
158. Tomato, fried onions and fried egg
159. Tomato, scrambled egg, 2 boned anchovies in oyster sauce and chopped chives, on toast
160. Tomato, raw egg yolk, capers, horseradish and raw onion
161. Grated carrot with raw egg yolk and sliced lemon

CHEESE

162. Camembert with thin, juicy slices of salt veal and meat jelly
163. Swiss
164. Samsø (Danish Swiss)
165. Maribo (Dutch)
166. Old Holsteiner with butter or spiced lard
167. Old Holsteiner with red currant jelly
168. Smoked cheese with fresh cucumber and paprika
169. Christian IX
170. Danablu
171. Danablu with raw egg yolk
172. Smoked cheese with raw egg yolk and chives
173. Potkäse
174. Potkäse with raw egg yolk and chopped radishes
175. Camembert
176. Camembert with 2 boned anchovies in oyster sauce
177. Brie
178. 1 slice bread with butter or dripping

· 7 ·

DRINKS FROM DENMARK

A VARIED COLLECTION of unusual punches, toddies, eggnogs and lemonades — some alcoholic, some non-alcoholic, but all guaranteed to cool you on a hot day or warm you on a cold one, depending on the recipe you select.

BRANDIED COFFEE

·

COGNACKAFFE

6 eggs	*3 cups cooled coffee*
½ cup sugar	*1 cup brandy*

Beat the eggs until lemon-colored and fluffy. Add the sugar gradually and continue to beat until the mixture is thick and pale in color. Stir the cooled coffee in slowly. Add brandy, mixing well.

Chill and serve cold.

HOT CHRISTMAS "GLOGG"

•

JULEGLØGG

5 cardamom seeds	2 cups port wine
5 cloves	¼ pound blanched almonds
1 stick cinnamon	¼ pound seeded raisins
1 tablespoon chopped lemon peel	¼ pound loaf sugar
2 cups red wine	2 cups brandy

Put all spices and lemon peel in a double-thick cheesecloth bag. Tie it well.

Put the wine in a kettle and drop the bag into it. Let simmer for 20 minutes. Add the almonds and raisins. Let simmer 10 minutes more. Remove from heat. Remove the bag of spices. Pour the mixture through a sieve. Discard raisins and almonds.

Pour brandy over sugar cubes and ignite. Pour at once into wine mixture and serve hot in warmed mugs.

A CHRISTMAS TOAST FROM DENMARK

•

"SKOL" FRA DANMARK

2 bottles claret (4/5-quart size)	6 cinnamon sticks
2 bottles port (4/5-quart size)	1 pound shelled almonds,
2 tablespoons grated candied	blanched
orange peel	1 pound seedless raisins
20 cardamom seeds	1 pound lump sugar
25 whole cloves	2 cups cognac

Heat wine slowly in a large vessel. Put orange peel, cardamom seeds, cloves and cinnamon in a cheesecloth bag and place with the wine in the kettle. Boil slowly for 20 minutes, then add the almonds and raisins and boil slowly for another 20 minutes. Remove from flame and remove bag with spices and fruit peel.

Place a fine wire mesh over the kettle and put the lump sugar on it. Gradually pour the cognac over the sugar. Light a match and hold it near the sugar, letting it ignite the cognac. When all the sugar has melted and run over the mesh and through it, remove the mesh. Put the flame out by covering the kettle with a lid.

Serve hot in mugs with a few raisins and almonds in each mug. Will serve 40 generously.

HOT PORT TODDY

•

PORTVINSTODDY

1 teaspoon sugar
¼ cup boiling water
Pinch of allspice

Small piece of lemon
3 ounces port wine

Dissolve sugar in water. Add the allspice, lemon and wine. Serve in a warmed wineglass.

HOT RED WINE TODDY

•

RØDVINSTODDY

6 cups red wine
3 apples, peeled and sliced thin
2 teaspoons cinnamon

3 cloves
¼ cup sugar
1 teaspoon lemon juice

Combine the wine, apples, cinnamon, cloves, sugar and lemon juice in a saucepan. Bring to a boil and cook over low heat 20 minutes.

Strain through cheesecloth and return to saucepan. Reheat. Serve very hot in heated mugs during the winter holiday season as a change from eggnogs.

RED WINE TODDY WITH BRANDY

•

RØDVINSTODDY MED COGNAC

1 quart red wine
1½ cups sugar

2 teaspoons vanilla
2 cups brandy

Mix wine and sugar in a saucepan and bring to a boil. Cook over medium heat 10 minutes. Cool for 1 hour.

Add vanilla and brandy. Chill and serve cold.

The following two recipes taste better than aspirin and are equally effective for curing the common cold. It is, of course, not necessary to wait for wheezes and sneezes to try these. The merest hint of frost on the pumpkin is excuse enough.

HOT TODDY

·

VARM PUNCH

Boiling water	*4 cloves*
Small stick of cinnamon	*1 teaspoon sugar*
Slice of lemon	*3 tablespoons whisky*

Place a silver spoon in a glass. Fill ⅔ full with boiling water. Add the stick of cinnamon, slice of lemon, cloves and sugar. Add the whisky and stir well.

HOT MILK TODDY

·

VARM MÆLKEPUNCH

1 egg, separated	*2 tablespoons brandy*
1 tablespoon sugar	*Hot milk to fill a mug*
2 tablespoons rum	*Grated nutmeg*

Beat egg yolk until light. Add sugar and beat again.
Beat egg white until stiff and fold in. Add liquors.
Fill a mug half full with hot milk. Stir in other ingredients and sprinkle grated nutmeg on top.

SYLLABUB

·

1 cup sherry or port	*1 cup heavy cream, whipped until*
1 cup milk	*stiff*
	Sugar to taste

Beat together the wine, milk, cream and sugar. Beat well. Serve at once in champagne glasses.

If you prefer, whip the cream, then fold in the wine and sugar. Either version will keep your New Year's guests talking about your party for months to come.

WEDDING PUNCH

•

BRYLLUPSPUNCH

6 limes	1 bottle rum (4/5 quart)
1 medium-size fresh pineapple	1 quart sweet tea
Sugar	2 quarts club soda
1 bottle cognac (4/5 quart)	2 quarts champagne, chilled

Slice limes very thin. Peel the pineapple and slice it thin. Sprinkle sugar over fruits sparingly. Add cognac and rum. Mix well. Chill overnight.

When ready to serve pour into a punch bowl. Add the sweetened tea, soda, and champagne. Serve in glasses over cracked ice.

EGGNOG FOR AN INVALID

•

ÆGGEKOP

Almost all the recipes in this book are aimed at eaters in the most robust of health. Here's one for a single serving which can be made in a moment and is a refreshing drink any time for a convalescent. It's not only delicious but a rich source of nourishment.

1 egg yolk	1½ teaspoons vanilla
2 tablespoons sugar	1 egg white
1 cup milk	Nutmeg

Beat the egg yolk until lemon-colored and light. Add the sugar and beat well. Add milk and vanilla. Beat thoroughly.

Beat the egg white until stiff and fold it in gently. Pour into a tall glass and sprinkle with ground nutmeg.

To make it particularly tempting, add a dash of brandy or whisky.

COLD LEMON TODDY WITH WHISKY

•

KOLD CITRONTODDY MED WHISKY

1 dozen lemons

4 cups whisky (bourbon, rye, or
 Scotch)

4 cups water

1 cup sugar

Squeeze juice from lemons. Cut rinds into small pieces. Mix juice, rinds, whisky, water and sugar and let stand 24 hours. Stir often. Strain through cheesecloth. Serve cold.

EGG LEMONADE

•

LIMONADE MED ÆG

2 cups sugar

3 cups water

Grated rind of 1 lemon

Juice of 4 lemons

1 egg

1 quart club soda

Boil sugar and water 10 minutes. Add the grated lemon rind and juice. Let cool.

Beat the egg well until light yellow.

When you're ready to serve the drink, put cracked ice in glasses. Mix the egg and the lemon syrup in a large pitcher. Add the club soda. Stir. Pour into glasses from as much height as you dare to make mixture foam.

EGGNOG

•

ÆGGEKOP

6 eggs, separated

6 tablespoons sugar

9 ounces whisky

2 cups milk

3 ounces rum or brandy

1 pint whipping cream

Beat egg yolks and sugar together until light and fluffy. Slowly add the whisky and mix gently. Add the milk, then the rum (or brandy). Mix lightly. Do not beat or stir.

Whip the cream and fold into the mixture.

Beat the egg whites very stiff and fold in. Chill for at least 3 hours. Better still, refrigerate overnight.

SMØRGÅSBORD EGGNOG   !

·

SMØRGÅSBORD ÆGGEKOP

Don't expect your guests to be either able or willing to help with the dishes after sampling this.

12 eggs, separated	*¾ cup rum*
¾ cup sugar	*1½ pints heavy cream*
¾ cup whisky	*Vanilla ice cream (optional)*

Beat the egg yolks until lemon-colored and fluffy. Add the sugar a little at a time, beating well after each addition, until the mixture is light in texture. Add the whisky and rum in small quantities, beating as you add.

Beat the egg whites stiff and fold in.

Whip the cream and fold into the mixture a little at a time.

To make an extra-rich eggnog, add a scoop of vanilla ice cream to each cup.

Serves 10 to 12 generously without ice cream added. Eight more people can feast if you add scoops of ice cream to each cup.

QUEEN'S PUNCH

·

DRONNINGEPUNCH

2 cups water	*2 cups pineapple juice*
2 cups sugar	*2 quarts club soda*
Chopped rind of 1 lemon	*8 ounces small peppermints*
Small bottle maraschino cherries,	*Juice of 6 lemons*
plus juice	

Boil the water, sugar and lemon rind for 5 minutes. Strain, and while the liquid is hot, add the cherries and cherry and pineapple juices.

When ready to serve, put a cake of ice or several trays of ice cubes in a large punch bowl. Pour club soda over the ice and mix in the peppermints.

Mix the strained lemon juice with the fruit syrup. Pour into bowl. Stir lightly to mix well.

PART TWO

DANISH DINING

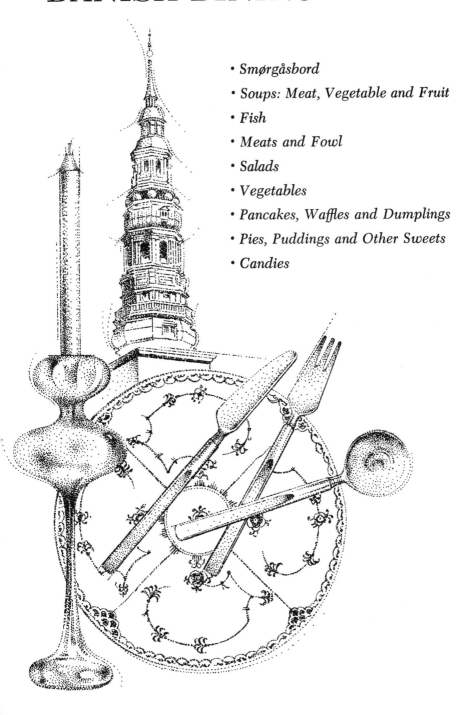

- *Smørgåsbord*
- *Soups: Meat, Vegetable and Fruit*
- *Fish*
- *Meats and Fowl*
- *Salads*
- *Vegetables*
- *Pancakes, Waffles and Dumplings*
- *Pies, Puddings and Other Sweets*
- *Candies*

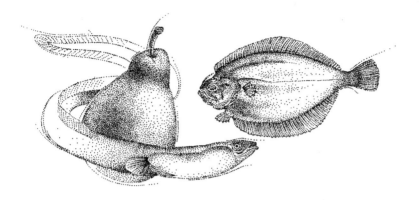

· 8 ·

SMORGASBORD

S MØRGÅSBORD is a lavish buffet consisting of separate dishes ranging from smoked fish to syllabub. A true smørgåsbord is expen-
sive and takes days to prepare. If you undertake it, you'll find it as easy
to do for forty as for four, so don't plan this for a small group of
intimate friends.

The great beauty of this method of entertaining is that you can prepare all of it in advance. This means that whether or not you have a
kitchen staff, you will have the leisure to enjoy the evening with your
guests.

A few simple suggestions will make a smørgåsbord dinner more
enjoyable for you and your guests. When you market for the party,
remember to select foods which have potential eye, as well as taste,
appeal.

There is an art to helping yourself at a smørgåsbord feast. The first
time around select only fish courses. Then start again with a clean
plate and choose salads and cold meats. With a third clean plate try
the hot dishes. Leave room, if you can, for luscious desserts and a
variety of cheeses.

The recipes in the pages which follow are intended only as teasers.

A distinctive smørgåsbord is the invention of the hostess, but the chapters in this book dealing with Fish, Salads, Meats and Fowl and the two sections on Desserts will provide ideas on a day when you're not feeling inventive.

SHRIMP IN BEER

·

REJER I ØL

1½ pounds shrimp
8 ounces beer
2 tablespoons minced onion
1 teaspoon salt
2 lemon slices
1 bay leaf

1 sprig parsley
2 tablespoons butter
2 tablespoons flour
½ teaspoon sugar
8 ounces tomato sauce

Shell and, if necessary, devein the shrimp. Cook 5 minutes in the beer with the onion, salt, lemon slices, bay leaf and parsley. Let cool in cooking liquid, then drain.

Melt the butter over low heat and blend in the flour and sugar. Cook and stir until smooth. Add the shrimp and the tomato sauce. Cook until thick, stirring continuously.

Place on a serving platter. Garnish with decorative raw vegetables of your choice. Serves 4 to 5.

FISH IN ASPIC

·

FISK I ASPIC

2½-pound whole fish (cod, haddock, bass, or any firm-fleshed fish)
2½ quarts boiling water
2 cloves
1 bay leaf
1 teaspoon salt
½ teaspoon white pepper
2 slices lemon

2 tablespoons white vinegar
4 tablespoons lemon juice
3 tablespoons egg whites, beaten until frothy
½ cup white wine
Parsley
Pickled beets
Spiced crab apples

Place fish in the boiling water with the spices, salt and pepper. Simmer 25 minutes, or until tender. Remove fish from the liquid. Let cool. Bone and skin and cut into large pieces.

Add the lemon slices, vinegar and lemon juice to the stock. Reduce over high heat until only 5 cups of liquid remain. Remove from heat and strain through a cheesecloth while the aspic is boiling hot. Add the beaten egg whites and mix well. Put the aspic back into the kettle and let come to the boiling point. Let stand 20 minutes without stirring.

Add the wine, fold in the fish pieces. Pour into a fish-shaped mold and chill until firm. Unmold and garnish with parsley, pickled beets and crab apples.

Serves 12 or more.

EEL IN ASPIC WITH CREAMED HORSERADISH

·

ÅLGELÉ MED FLØDEPEBERROD

1 3-pound eel	*1 tablespoon fresh grated*
Parsley	*horseradish*
1 envelope unflavored gelatin	*Pinch of salt*
¼ cup cold water	*1 teaspoon sugar*
1 cup heavy cream	*1 teaspoon vinegar*

Skin and clean the eel and cut into 1-inch pieces. (Get your favorite fish market to do this, if you can. These members of the fish clan have a habit, disconcerting to most housewives, of wriggling and leaping long after their heads have been cut off.) Remove all bones and replace with chopped parsley. Tie each piece with thread. Cook in salted water until tender. When done, take each piece from the liquid and let cool. Remove thread. Strain the hot fish liquid and add 2 cups of it to the gelatin which has been soaked in the ¼ cup of cold water. Stir until gelatin is dissolved.

Cover the bottom of a ring mold with about half of the aspic and let cool. When it has jellied, place small pieces of eel over the entire surface of the aspic. Cover with the rest of the jelly and allow to set.

Whip the cream until stiff. Add the grated horseradish, salt, sugar and the vinegar. Place a dish of the creamed-horseradish mixture in the center of the serving platter on which the eel salad has been unmolded on lettuce.

As a main course, a 3-pound eel will serve 6 people. It will serve many more as one of a number of smørgåsbord dishes.

SMØRGÅSBORD FISH PUDDING

·

SMØRGÅSBORD FISKE-BUDDING

4 pounds white fish	⅛ teaspoon ground nutmeg
2 tablespoons salt	2 cups milk
3 tablespoons cornstarch	2 cups cream

Clean the fish, remove all bones and cut into fillets. Cut the fillets into small pieces and sprinkle with salt. Put through the finest blade of your food chopper.

Mix the ground fish with the cornstarch and the nutmeg. Now put this mixture through the food grinder 4 times.

Slowly add the milk and the cream. Shape part of the mixture into small balls (will make approximately 18). Reserve balance for later use.

Cook the balls 20 minutes in boiling salted water. Drain and keep warm.

Pour the rest of the fish mixture into a buttered baking mold and place it in a shallow pan half filled with hot water. Bake in a moderate oven preheated to 350 degrees 40 to 60 minutes.

Turn out on a heated serving platter and garnish with the boiled small fish balls. Serve with Shrimp Sauce (*page 203*).

SMØRGÅSBORD PICKLED HERRING

·

SMØRGÅSBORD NEDLAGTE SILD

8 large salt herrings	2 tablespoons mustard seeds
3 medium onions, sliced	6 small pieces ginger root
1 large piece fresh horseradish, grated	10 bay leaves
	1½ cups vinegar
1 carrot, grated	1½ cups sugar
3 tablespoons whole allspice	2 cups water

Wash the herrings well; clean, scrape, and cut off the heads, tails and fins. Rinse several times in cold water until water is clear. Cut the fish into 1-inch pieces. Place in layers in a crock with the onions, horseradish, carrot, spices and bay leaves between the layers.

Heat vinegar, sugar and water just to the boiling point. Let cool. Pour over the herring. Press down firmly with a plate, putting a weight on top, and let stand in refrigerator about 6 days. Serves 10 or more.

HEADCHEESE

•

SYLTE

5 pounds pork shoulder, divided into 3 pieces of roughly equal size	Pepper to taste
	1 teaspoon cinnamon
	½ teaspoon allspice
2½ pounds breast or shoulder of veal	½ teaspoon cloves
	¼ teaspoon nutmeg
2 tablespoons salt	

Originally headcheese was made from a pig's head, but this method is simpler and more appetizing.

Put the pork and veal in a large kettle, cover with cold water and add salt. Simmer from 2 to 3 hours until the meat falls from the bones.

Line a pan or crock with a scalded white cloth roughly twice the size of the container. Cover with a layer of small pieces of meat. Press down with a wooden spoon.

Blend the remaining spices. Sprinkle about ⅓ of the quantity over the meat. Repeat in layers until all the meat is used.

Fold the cloth over the top of the container and tie securely so it is tightly covered. Press down hard on the pan or crock with the heel of your hand, then put a heavy weight on top of it.

Chill well before slicing.

VEAL IN ASPIC

•

KALV I ASPIC

3 pounds of veal shank	¼ teaspoon white pepper
1 pound of veal shoulder	1 tablespoon salt
2 quarts water	1 bay leaf
¾ teaspoon ginger	

Wash and wipe the veal shank and shoulder. Put in a large kettle of boiling water to cover. Boil 20 minutes. Skim now and then. Cover and reduce the heat and let simmer slowly 2 hours, or until meat is tender.

Remove the meat from bones and set meat aside. Discard bones. Strain the broth through a cheesecloth bag and return to the kettle. Bring to a boil and let boil uncovered until it is reduced to a quart.

Remove from heat and set aside.

Put meat through a medium blade of your food chopper and add it to the broth. Add the ginger, pepper, salt and bay leaf and boil for a minute or two. Let cool slightly.

Turn it into a loaf pan 10 x 6 x 4 inches. Chill in refrigerator until firm.

Unmold on a platter garnished with pickled beets and preserved lingonberries or other colorful garnishes of your choice.

MEAT ASPIC

·

KØDASPIC

Parsley	4 or 5 marrow bones
½ teaspoon white pepper	2 leeks
6 peppercorns	4 carrots
2 bay leaves	4 small onions
½ teaspoon celery seeds	1 stalk celery
1 stewing hen, cut into serving- sized pieces	1 large tomato
	2 tablespoons salt
1½ pounds boiling beef	6 egg whites, beaten until frothy
2 cracked veal knuckles	¾ cup Cherry Heering

Tie all the seasonings up securely in a small cheesecloth bag.

Put chicken, boiling beef, veal and marrow bones in a large kettle. Add 3½ quarts of water and let boil slowly, skimming occasionally.

Cut vegetables into medium-sized pieces. Add with salt to meat mixture. Simmer 3 hours. Let cool. Strain through a cheesecloth.

Discard the bag of seasonings, the vegetables and the bones. Reserve chicken and meat pieces for use at another time.

Put the strained stock in a crock and add the beaten egg whites. Mix well. Return the stock to the kettle, and while it is boiling slowly, beat it in a figure 8 until it comes to a full boil. Remove from heat and let stand 20 minutes without stirring.

Strain again through a double cheesecloth. Add the liqueur, which will make the aspic crystal-clear.

(If the aspic seems a little limp, add 2 or 3 tablespoons of plain gelatin softened in cold water and dissolved in some hot aspic.) Kept cold, this aspic will be usable for weeks.

GINGER SAUSAGES

•

INGEFÆRPØLSE

2 eggs, separated   ½ cup chopped dill pickles
1 pound bulk sausage meat   1 teaspoon ground ginger

Beat the egg yolks and mix with the sausage, pickles and ginger, blending well.

Beat the egg whites until stiff. Fold into the mixture.

Shape into very small sausages and fry in hot deep fat until browned. Serve at once.

Serves 4.

FISH BALLS

•

FISKEBOLLER

2 tablespoons butter   3 cups flaked, cooked fish
¼ cup sifted flour   1 egg yolk, lightly beaten
1 teaspoon salt   2 whole eggs, beaten
⅛ teaspoon white pepper   1 cup fine, dry bread crumbs
1 cup cream

Heat butter in a saucepan but do not let it brown. Blend in the flour, salt and pepper. Heat until the mixture bubbles. Add the cream slowly, stirring to keep the sauce from lumping. Cook as rapidly as possible until thickened. Remove from flame and let cool. Flake fish. When sauce has cooled, blend in fish and egg yolk.

Shape the mixture into small balls, about ¾ inch in diameter, and dip into the beaten eggs. Roll in fine bread crumbs.

Deep fry, uncovered, only as many of the balls as will float without crowding each other in your frying kettle. Turn often until lightly browned.

My favorite recipe for smørgåsbord. Yields 4 to 5 dozen fish balls.

HAM AND POTATO BALLS

·

SKINKE- OG KARTOFFELBOLLER

2 cups mashed potatoes	1 teaspoon minced parsley
1 cup cooked ham, chopped	1 cup soft bread crumbs
Salt	Oil for deep-fat frying
Pepper	

Mix mashed potatoes, ham, salt, pepper and parsley.

Shape into very small balls. Roll in the bread crumbs, then in the egg, and again in the bread crumbs.

Fry in deep-fat kettle in hot oil until well browned. Drain on paper towels. Serve hot with Mustard Sauce (*page 202*).

Serves 6. A true Danish smørgåsbord is not considered complete without these.

SCALLOPED POTATOES AND ANCHOVIES

·

KARTOFLER MED ANSJOS

2 ounces anchovy fillets	2 teaspoons onion, chopped
2 pounds raw potatoes, peeled and sliced	½ cup bread crumbs
	2 tablespoons butter
Salt	1 cup milk or cream
White pepper	

Cut fillets into small pieces.

Place half of the potatoes in a buttered baking dish and sprinkle with salt and pepper to taste, onion and bread crumbs. Dot with butter and anchovy bits. Layer the remaining potatoes over the top. Add the milk or cream, cover and bake 30 minutes in a preheated 350° oven. Uncover, reduce heat to 325 degrees and bake for another 30 minutes or until lightly browned.

COLD ROAST PORK

·

KOLD SVINESTEG

Cold roast pork
Anchovy fillets
Sweet pickled beets

Spiced crab apples
Parsley

Cut cold roast pork in small, thin slices.

Place on serving platter with rolled anchovy fillets on each slice. Surround with beets and crab apples, and garnish with sprigs of parsley.

CARAWAY CABBAGE

·

HVIDKÅL MED KOMMEN

1½ pounds shredded cabbage
2 eggs
2 tablespoons butter
½ cup milk

½ cup cream
½ teaspoon salt
White pepper to taste
1 teaspoon caraway seeds

Cover the cabbage with cold water. Chill 2 hours. Drain. Cover with boiling water and simmer 5 minutes. Drain well.

Combine the rest of the ingredients and mix lightly with the cabbage. Bake in a buttered baking dish 30 to 40 minutes in a preheated 350° oven, or until lightly browned on top.

PICKLED BEETS

·

NEDLAGTE RØDBEDER

2 pounds medium-sized beets
1 onion, sliced whole
1½ cups vinegar

1½ cups reserved beet juice
2 whole cloves

Leave 1- to 2-inch stems on the beets with the roots, if any. Scrub thoroughly and cook in water to cover for 30 to 45 minutes, or until tender. Drain, saving 1½ cups of the juice.

Plunge the beets at once into cold water. Peel. Discard the roots and the stems with the skins. Cut beets into ¼-inch slices.

Separate the onion into thin rings. Put a layer of beets in a shallow pan. Cover with some of the onion rings. Repeat the procedure until all beets and onion are used.

Warm the vinegar, beet juice and the cloves. Pour mixture over the beets. Chill overnight to blend the flavors.

PICKLED BEETS AND ONIONS

·

SYLTEDE RØDBEDER MED LØG

2 cups vinegar
1⅓ cups water
1 cup sugar
1 teaspoon whole cloves

½ teaspoon salt
6 cups cooked beets, sliced
    or diced
2 large onions, sliced

Boil the vinegar, water, sugar, cloves and salt in a kettle for 5 minutes. Add the beets and onions and let simmer for 8 minutes.

Remove from heat and put vegetables and syrup into sterilized jars. Seal at once.

PICKLED CUCUMBERS

·

SYLTEDE AGURKER

8 medium-sized cucumbers, peeled
1 quart vinegar
2 cups sugar
1 cup water
1 teaspoon mustard seed

1 teaspoon celery seed
5 drops oil of cinnamon* or ½
    teaspoon powdered cinnamon
5 drops oil of cloves* or ½
    teaspoon powdered cloves

Cut the cucumbers into 1½-inch chunks. Cover with boiling water and let stand overnight. In the morning drain well.

Boil the vinegar with the remaining ingredients for 10 minutes. Put the cucumber pieces into the hot liquid and heat through. Do not allow them to boil, or they will become mushy.

Put in sterilized jars with the syrup in which they were cooked, and seal at once.

* All well-stocked drugstores sell these essences.

PEARL ONIONS

•

PERLELØG

1 pound small white onions,   2½ cups white vinegar
   unpeeled   ¼ cup sugar

Wash onions, cover with boiling water and boil 5 minutes. Drain. Cover with cold water and drain again. Peel the onions. Cover with vinegar and sugar and boil again 5 minutes. Reserve liquid.

Remove onions to an earthenware crock or bowl. Pour over them the vinegar solution.

May also be served as a garnish for roasts. Serves 6 to 8.

PICKLED EGGS

•

EDDIKEÆG

3 dozen hard-boiled eggs   1 teaspoon ground ginger
1 pint vinegar   1 bay leaf
10 pieces whole allspice   1 pint vinegar

Remove the shells from the hard-boiled eggs and arrange them in large, wide-mouthed jars.

Boil 1 pint of vinegar, allspice, ginger and bay leaf. When vinegar has steeped long enough to extract the flavors of the spices, add the other 1 pint of vinegar, bring to the boiling point and pour over the eggs. When cold, seal the jars and let stand at least 48 hours before serving.

PICKLED RIPE CUCUMBERS

•

SYLTEDE KRYDREDE AGURKER

3 ripe cucumbers, 7 to 8 inches   1 pint vinegar
   long   1 lemon, sliced very thin
Salt   1 teaspoon cloves
1 pint water   1 teaspoon allspice
2 pounds sugar

Select large, firm, ripe cucumbers. Pare and remove the seeds and cut lengthwise into strips. Cut strips into pieces roughly 3 inches long. Soak overnight in salted water, using ¼ cup of salt to 1 quart of water. In the morning drain well and cook in water until tender.

Make a syrup of the sugar, vinegar and lemon slices.

Put the spices in a small cloth bag and drop into the syrup while it is heating. Drop the pieces of cucumber in the syrup for one minute. Remove and put in sterilized jars. Add the syrup to overflowing. Seal the jars at once.

SPICED GOOSEBERRIES

·

SYLTEDE KRYDREDE STIKKELSBÆR

Fresh gooseberries are a market rarity, but because they are occasionally available in some areas of North America, I am including this recipe which will make your smørgåsbord the talk of the town.

1 quart gooseberries	*¼ teaspoon cloves*
4 cups sugar	*¼ teaspoon cinnamon*
¼ cup cider vinegar	*¼ teaspoon nutmeg*

Wash and stem fruit.

Place in kettle, add remaining ingredients and cook slowly until syrup is thickened. Stir frequently to prevent burning.

Seal immediately in sterilized jars.

BRANDIED PEACHES

·

FERSKEN I COGNAC

5 pounds peaches	*2 cups water*
3 tablespoons lemon juice	*1 cup brandy*
3 cups sugar	

Pour boiling water over the peaches. Let stand a few minutes. Peel off the loosened skin. Put the peaches in a large bowl and cover with water to which the lemon juice has been added to keep the fruit from turning brown.

Cook sugar and water together until boiling. Drop the peaches in the syrup and cook slowly for 20 minutes. Add more water and sugar if necessary to make sure the syrup covers the fruit. Lift the peaches out of the syrup carefully with a slotted spoon.

Pack in sterilized jars. Pour 4 tablespoons of brandy into each jar, add syrup to overflowing and seal at once.

Store at least 2 weeks before using.

SPICED PEACHES

•

SYLTEDE FERSKEN

2 quarts peaches	4½ cups sugar
Whole cloves	Cinnamon sticks
2 cups vinegar	

Select firm, ripe peaches. Remove skins by scalding. Insert 3 whole cloves in each peach.

Put vinegar in a kettle, add the sugar and 2 sticks of cinnamon. Bring to the boiling point and let boil 5 minutes. Drop peaches into the boiling syrup, a few at a time. Let boil 5 minutes or until the peaches are tender and transparent. Discard cinnamon sticks.

Pack the peaches in sterilized jars, placing a small piece of a new cinnamon stick in each jar. Pour the hot syrup over them until jars overflow. Seal tightly.

GINGER PEARS

•

INGEFÆR PÆRER

4 pounds green pears	3 pounds sugar
Juice of 2 lemons	2 ounces ginger root

Select hard, unripe pears. Peel, core and slice them. Squeeze a little of the lemon juice over the slices.

Cover pears with the sugar and let them stand for several hours. Scrape and cut the ginger root into very small pieces, and add to the pears and the remaining lemon juice. Simmer over low heat until the mixture is clear and the syrup is thick.

Put the pears in sterilized jars and pour the syrup over them. Seal.

WINE-PICKLED PEARS

·

KRYDRET PÆRER I VIN

1 cup honey	*1 stick of cinnamon*
¾ cup wine vinegar	*¾ cup port wine*
10 whole cloves	*1½ quarts small, firm pears*

Combine honey, vinegar, cloves and cinnamon. Simmer 5 minutes. Add wine and whole, peeled pears and simmer 15 minutes, or until tender.

Place in sterilized jars and fill with the syrup. Seal at once.

RHUBARB CONSERVE

·

RABARBERKOMPOT

2½ pounds rhubarb	*1 tablespoon cinnamon*
1 cup vinegar	*1 tablespoon ground cloves*
2 cups sugar	

Wash and cut rhubarb into small pieces.

Mix all ingredients in a kettle and boil slowly, approximately 1½ hours, or until thick.

Seal at once in sterilized jars.

CHEESE SPONGE CREAM

·

OSTEFROMAGE

¾ pound soft butter	*Butter*
4 ounces Danish Blue cheese	*White bread*
¼ pint whipping cream	*Rye or pumpernickel bread*

Cream butter. Press cheese through a sieve twice and add to butter. Cream well.

Whip cream until stiff and fold into above mixture.

Butter a small mold and line with alternate very thin slices of white and dark bread. Fill with the butter and cheese mixture, and chill thoroughly. Unmold it onto a cold serving plate and garnish with any-thing you wish. This is supposed to be not only a taste treat but a delight to the eye of the beholder.

FROZEN FRUIT SALAD

·

FROSSEN FRUGTSALAT

1 cup tart red cherries	1 cup sliced oranges
2 cups pineapple chunks	3 cups heavy cream
1 cup candied, or maraschino, cherries	2 cups small marshmallows, cut
	Slivered almonds (optional)
2 cups seedless white grapes	Fresh strawberries

Pit the cherries. Drain all the fruits. Save the juice to make a dressing for other salads.

Whip the cream until stiff. Fold in the marshmallows and fruits, mixing well. (Now is the time to add slivered almonds.)

Place in the salad bowl you will use on the table and set under the coil of the freezing compartment of your refrigerator until frost ap-pears on top. Move the bowl to a warmer spot in the refrigerator so it will not freeze, and leave overnight.

Decorate with large fresh strawberries and place in the center of your smørgåsbord table.

SPICED PEARS

·

SYLTEDE PÆRER

8 pounds small, hard pears	1 pint water
12 sticks of cinnamon	1 quart vinegar
2 tablespoons whole cloves	4 pounds sugar
2 tablespoons whole allspice	

Select firm but ripe fruit. Wash and remove blossom ends only. Cover fruit with water and boil 10 minutes. Drain. Prick skins gently with a fork.

Put the spices loosely in a small bag (clean white cloth or double thickness of cheesecloth) and tie closed.

While pears are draining, put the water, vinegar, sugar and spice bag in a kettle. Bring syrup to a boil and keep it boiling for 5 minutes. Remove from heat, place pears in syrup, cover and set aside to cool overnight.

In the morning remove the spice bag and the pears and bring the syrup to a boil. Stir frequently to prevent scorching.

Pack pears in sterilized jars, pour the hot syrup over them, filling to overflowing. Seal at once with sterilized rubbers and lids.

· 9 ·

SOUPS: MEAT,
VEGETABLE AND FRUIT

I N THE United States soups are in general either appetizers or hearty,
meal-in-themselves dishes, like chowders and the fish stews we
have borrowed from France and Portugal and never returned.

The Danes, however, have soups not only of the kind with which all
of us are familiar but soups for dessert. Almost every fruit that grows
has been used as the basis for a dessert soup by an enterprising Dane
somewhere on planet Earth. You'll find these soups light, refreshing,
welcome windups, particularly for summer meals when appetites bog-
gle at pastries, pies and cakes.

I: FIRST-COURSE SOUPS

BARLEY SOUP

·

BYGVANDGRØD

6 tablespoons pearl barley	6 tablespoons chopped
3 pints stock or water	mushrooms
1 onion, chopped	4 tablespoons butter
3 carrots, diced	1 teaspoon salt
4 tablespoons celery, chopped	½ teaspoon white pepper
	4 tablespoons thick sour cream

Simmer barley in ½ of the stock or water for 1 hour. Boil the vegetables and mushrooms in the other half until tender. Add the cooked barley mixture, butter, salt and pepper while still over heat. Remove from burner and blend in the sour cream.

Serve hot or cold. Serves 6 or 7.

POTATO SOUP

·

KARTOFFELSUPPE

1 pound breast or shoulder	2 tablespoons butter
of veal	1 bay leaf
¼ pound boneless beef chuck	3 sprigs parsley
3 pints water	1 teaspoon salt
4 large potatoes, peeled and sliced	½ teaspoon white pepper
2 medium onions, chopped	1 cup white wine
2 leeks, sliced	12 tablespoons thick cream

Cook the veal and beef in the water until tender. Remove meats from stock and reserve for use as slices with Horseradish Sauce (*page 216*).

Brown the potatoes, onions and leeks in the butter over low heat for 10 minutes.

Add all the ingredients except the cream to the liquid in which the meat was cooked, and cook 1½ hours. Press through a sieve.

Reheat, and add the cream slowly. If the soup is thicker than you want it to be, add a little more cream.

Serves 4 to 6. Serve with croutons.

BEER SOUP

·

ØLSUPPE

1 quart beer	1 tablespoon butter
1 quart water	3 egg yolks
2 tablespoons sugar	1 cup cream

Combine the beer and water and bring to a slow boil. Add the sugar and butter. Cook 30 minutes over low heat.

Beat the egg yolks, add the cream and beat together until light. Gradually add to the beer mixture, beating to prevent curdling. Do not allow to boil.

Serves 12 generously.

BEET SOUP

·

RØDBEDESUPPE

12 large beets	1 onion, sliced
2 pounds short ribs of beef	Salt to taste
½ cup lemon juice	¼ teaspoon white pepper
½ cup sugar	Sour cream
1 teaspoon allspice	

Wash the beets and scrape but do not peel them. Cut beets into small chunks. Place in a kettle with the remaining ingredients, except the sour cream. Cover with water, put a lid on the kettle and simmer 2½ hours over low heat. Strain through a sieve or colander.

Serve cold with a topping of sour cream. Serves 6 to 8.

HAM AND PEA SOUP

·

SKINKE- OG GRØNÆRTESUPPE

4 cups dried green peas	4 tablespoons minced celery
1 ham end (smoked butt or shank)	1 small onion
	1 teaspoon salt
3 pints water	½ teaspoon white pepper

Soak the peas overnight in cold water. In the morning combine with ham, celery, onion, salt and pepper. Cover with water and cook slowly for 4 or 5 hours.

Remove ham from bone. Cut into small strips and serve separately as a main course, topped with Horseradish Sauce (*page 216*), and accompanied by boiled, buttered potatoes.

Soup serves 6.

CELERY SOUP

·

SELLERISUPPE

1 bunch celery	½ teaspoon salt
1 quart boiling water	¼ teaspoon white pepper
4 tablespoons butter	1 egg yolk
4 tablespoons flour	½ cup peas, cooked
6 cups stock or bouillon	½ cup sherry wine

Cook celery in the boiling water until soft. Drain and save liquid. Put celery through a sieve.

Melt the butter, stir in flour, add celery, 2 cups of the water in which it was cooked and stock, stirring until smooth. Add salt and pepper.

Beat egg yolk and add with the peas. Boil 3 minutes. Turn off heat. Add sherry and stir well to blend.

Serve hot. Serves 6.

MUSHROOM SOUP

·

CHAMPIGNONSUPPE

6 tablespoons butter	2 pints chicken stock
4 tablespoons flour	1 pound mushrooms, chopped fine
Salt to taste	8 tablespoons cream
½ teaspoon white pepper	Parsley

Heat the butter in a pan; add the flour and seasonings. Gradually stir in the stock, stirring until thick.

Add the chopped mushrooms and simmer 20 minutes. Add the cream slowly, and sprinkle with minced parsley.

Serve at once. Serves 4 or 5.

QUEEN'S SOUP

•

DRONNINGSUPPE

4 egg yolks	*4 tablespoons sherry wine*
⅜ cup cream	*2½ quarts boiling chicken broth*

Beat the egg yolks, add the cream and the wine and stir well in a warmed soup tureen.

Pour the chicken broth into the tureen, stirring while you pour in the broth. Add small dumplings (*see Index for suggested recipes*) an\ serve hot.

Serves 8.

TURTLE SOUP

•

TURTELSUPPE

You may have to look a long time to find the chief ingredient for this soup, but the results will be worth the search.

1½-pound turtle	*2 tablespoons flour*
¾ cup melted butter	*4 quarts stock*
1 medium onion, chopped	*8 stems of fresh parsley*
1 cup celery, chopped	*4 hard-cooked eggs, chopped*
6 tablespoons brandy	*1 cup white wine*
8 tablespoons dry red wine	*6 tablespoons brandy*
1 teaspoon paprika	*1 teaspoon white pepper*
1 bay leaf	*Salt to taste*
6 cloves	

Buy a cleaned and ready-to-use turtle from a reliable fish market, or pay such a market to prepare your own catch. Cut the turtle meat into small pieces.

Put the butter in a skillet; add the onion and celery to brown lightly. Add the turtle meat and fry 15 or 20 minutes. Transfer to kettle.

Add 6 tablespoons of brandy, flame it and let burn. Add the 8 tablespoons of red wine, spices and the flour. Mix well. Add the stock. Let the mixture boil slowly for 4 hours.

Add the parsley, eggs, white wine and brandy while still hot and blend well.

Serve at once. Serves 8.

WHITE WINE SOUP WITH BUTTER BALLS

·

SUPPE MED VIN OG SMØRBOLLER

4 pounds knuckle of beef	*3 sprigs parsley*
2 quarts or more cold water	*1 bay leaf*
3 carrots	*4 tablespoons white wine*
1 onion	*1 cup cream*
6 stalks celery	*1 tablespoon salt*

Wipe the knuckle of beef and cut meat from the bone into small pieces. Put bone and meat in a kettle, cover with water.

Dice the carrots and slice the onion. Add to kettle with the celery, parsley and bay leaf. Bring to a quick boil, reduce the heat and let simmer 5 hours.

Strain. Chill and remove fat. Reheat and add the butter balls (see recipe which follows). Remove the balls to soup bowls with a slotted spoon after they have boiled 10 minutes. Add the wine, cream and salt to the soup in the kettle and heat through. Do not allow to boil.

Serves 12.

BUTTER BALLS (SMØRBOLLER)

1 cup soft butter	*1 teaspoon salt*
2½ cups flour	

Cream the butter; add 2 cups of the flour sifted with salt. Moisten with ice water. Form into balls about the size of a walnut. Roll the balls in the remaining flour. Add to the soup, cover and keep at low boil for 10 minutes.

Makes approximately 24 balls.

II: DESSERT SOUPS

APPLE SOUP

•

ÆBLESUPPE

2 pounds tart apples
1 stick of cinnamon
Peel of 1 lemon
2 pints boiling water
5 tablespoons fine dry bread
   crumbs

Juice of 1 lemon
6 tablespoons sugar
2 cups dry red wine
4 tablespoons currant jelly

Wash, core and slice the apples. Put apples, cinnamon stick, lemon peel, boiling water and the crumbs in a kettle and boil until apples are tender.

Remove cinnamon stick and lemon peel. Put apples through a sieve. Add lemon juice, sugar, wine and jelly.

Stir well, reheat briefly, and serve at once. Serves 6.

BREAD AND BEER SOUP

•

ØLLEBRØD

1-pound loaf whole-wheat bread
1-pound loaf pumpernickel bread
8½ cups water
8½ cups dark beer or ale
½ teaspoon salt

12 tablespoons sugar
2 sticks of cinnamon
Rind of 1 lemon, grated
Heavy cream

Pour the water over the breads and let stand in a crock covered with a lid overnight.

In the morning transfer to a kettle which has a lid, and cook, covered, over low heat, stirring often, until the mixture thickens. Stir in the beer or ale, salt, sugar, cinnamon and lemon rind. Let soup come to a boil.

Serve it hot topped with plenty of whipped cream. Serves 12 generously.

RASPBERRY SOUP

•

HINDBÆRSUPPE

1½ quarts raspberries
3 quarts water

4 tablespoons cornstarch
½ cup sugar

Wash the raspberries and drain. Cover the berries with the 3 quarts of water and bring to the boiling point. Lower the heat and let the berries simmer until soft. Put through a coarse sieve and return to the kettle.

Mix the cornstarch with a little cold water and stir gently into the soup. Add the sugar and heat again to the boiling point, stirring to prevent scorching.

Serve at once. Serves 12 to 16.

BUTTERMILK SOUP

•

KÆRNEMÆLKSSUPPE

1½ quarts buttermilk
1 pint sweet milk
2½ tablespoons tapioca
1 stick of cinnamon

3 lemon slices
¾ cup sugar
Pinch of salt

Combine buttermilk, sweet milk, tapioca, cinnamon and lemon. Cook slowly 1 hour, stirring often to prevent scorching. Add sugar and salt.

Serve hot or cold. Serves 8.

COLD BUTTERMILK SOUP

•

KÆRNEMÆLKS KOLD SKÅL

4 cups buttermilk
3 eggs
4 tablespoons sugar

Juice of 1 lemon
1 teaspoon vanilla
Heavy cream

Beat the buttermilk.

Beat the eggs, sugar, lemon juice and vanilla together. Add egg mixture to the buttermilk, a little at a time.

Chill and serve in bowls topped with whipped cream. Serves 4.

COLD CHERRY SOUP

•

KIRSEBÆR KOLD SKÅL

2¾ pounds ripe cherries
2½ cups powdered sugar
2½ quarts water
1 stick of cinnamon

Peel of ½ lemon, cut into long,
  thin strips
1 pint sherry wine

Wash the cherries; remove the pits but reserve them. Combine the cherries, sugar and water. Heat to the boiling point, stirring often. Lift the cherries out into a deep bowl.

Crush the cherry pits with nut crackers or mortar and pestle or in a blender and add them to the hot juice with the stick of cinnamon and the lemon peel. Let boil 5 minutes, strain and pour over the cherries in the bowl. Chill.

Just before serving add the sherry wine and blend well. Serves 6.

CHOCOLATE SOUP

•

CHOKOLADESUPPE

3 pints milk
2 squares bitter chocolate
¼ cup sugar
¼ cup milk

6 eggs, separated
1 cup sugar
1 teaspoon vanilla
6 tablespoons sugar

Scald the 3 pints of milk in the top of a double boiler over hot water.

Melt the chocolate and ¼ cup sugar in the ¼ cup milk over low heat. To this mixture add the scalded milk, beating gently to blend well.

Beat the egg yolks, 1 cup sugar and vanilla together until frothy and lemon-colored. Add the chocolate mixture in small quantities, beating gently but thoroughly.

Return to the top of the double boiler and let stand over the hot water, heat turned off, until it thickens.

Whip the egg whites stiff with the 6 tablespoons of sugar.

To serve, place the mixture in bowls and top generously with the egg-white mixture. Serves 6.

WARM FRUIT SOUP

·

VARM FRUGTSUPPE

½ cup dried pears
½ cup dried peaches
½ cup dried apricots
½ cup dried, pitted prunes
½ cup dried apples
½ cup white raisins
½ cup dark raisins

¼ cup tapioca
½ cup sugar
2 cups water
1 stick of cinnamon
½ cup lemon juice
2 drops oil of cloves*
½ cup grape jelly

Soak dried fruits in separate bowls overnight, using 1½ cups of water for each variety of fruit.

Drain the fruit, saving all the juices. Cut soaked fruit into small pieces. Simmer the fruit in the fruit juices until soft.

Drain again and into the juice put the tapioca, sugar, the 2 cups of water and the stick of cinnamon. Let boil until the tapioca is clear, 30 to 35 minutes.

Stir in the lemon juice, oil of cloves and the jelly. Cook until the jelly dissolves. Add the fruits and heat through.

Serves 6 to 8.

* Try a well-stocked drugstore instead of a grocery store for this.

FRUIT SOUP FROM KOLDING, DENMARK

·

FRUGTSUPPE FRA KOLDING

½ pound mixed dried fruits
½ cup dried apples
¼ cup currants
¼ cup seeded white raisins
2 quarts cold water
2 cups red sago (or tapioca)

1 stick cinnamon
2 tablespoons sugar
1 tablespoon grated lemon rind
½ teaspoon salt
½ cup heavy cream
Slivered almonds

Wash the dried fruits and drain. Add enough of the 2 quarts of water to cover. Reserve the balance. Let stand overnight.

In the morning add the sago (or tapioca), cinnamon and the remainder of the water. Bring slowly to the boiling point, cover with a lid, reduce the heat and simmer very slowly for 2 hours.

Add sugar, lemon rind and salt. Simmer a few minutes more. Chill.

Serve cold, topped with dabs of whipped cream and slivers of almonds. Serves 6.

ORANGE SOUP

·

APPELSINSUPPE

6 oranges	1 small stick of cinnamon
8 tablespoons sugar	1 cup orange juice
1 pint water	1 cup white wine

Peel oranges and divide into sections. Remove any seeds and place the fruit in a soup tureen.

Cook the sugar, water and stick cinnamon to a syrup. Add the orange juice and wine, blending well. Chill briefly, then pour over the orange sections, after removing the cinnamon stick.

Serves 4.

RIPE PLUM SOUP

·

BLOMMESUPPE

3 pounds ripe plums	4 quarts water
¾ cup sugar	10 dessertspoons cornstarch
2 sticks of cinnamon	1 cup white wine

Wash the plums. Do not peel. Cut in half, remove pits and boil with the sugar, cinnamon and water until plums are soft.

Put through a coarse sieve and heat again.

Mix the cornstarch with a little cold water and stir into the soup. Stir and let boil 5 minutes. Add the wine and remove from stove at once.

Serve hot or cold. If you wish to serve it chilled, top with whipped cream. Serves 8 to 10.

PRUNE AND SAGO SOUP

·

SVESKESAGOSUPPE

18 large prunes
½ cup seedless raisins
6 tablespoons sago (or tapioca)
2 quarts water
1 stick of cinnamon

1 cup grapefruit juice,
   unsweetened
Sugar to taste
½ cup white wine (optional)
Heavy cream (optional)

Wash the prunes, cover with water and cook until tender. Remove pits. Wash the raisins and drain. Cover with hot water and let stand until soft and plump.

Simmer sago (or tapioca) slowly in the 2 quarts of water with the cinnamon stick until soft, about 1 hour.

Add the prunes, raisins and juice. Taste, and add whatever amount of sugar suits your palate. Simmer slowly for 1 hour more.

If you have white wine in the house, add ½ cup and blend while the soup is warm. Top with whipped cream if you wish.

Serve at once. Serves 6.

RHUBARB WINE SOUP

·

RABARBERSUPPE MED VIN

1 tablespoon cornstarch
¾ cup sugar
1 cup water
2 sticks of cinnamon
½ teaspoon ground cinnamon
½ teaspoon nutmeg

3 slices lemon
2 cups red wine
2 cups rhubarb, cut into small
   pieces
Heavy cream

Combine cornstarch, sugar and water and cook, stirring continually, until mixture reaches the boiling point.

Add the spices, lemon, wine and rhubarb and cook 5 minutes. Remove the cinnamon sticks and serve hot.

Served cold, this makes a wonderful summer dessert. Try it, topped with whipped cream and a sprinkling of cinnamon. Serves 4.

SAGO FRUIT SOUP

•

FRUGTSAGOSUPPE

1 pint white wine	*4 slices lemon*
1 pint water	*1 pound lingonberries or*
1 stick of cinnamon	*raspberries*
2 tablespoons sugar	*Heavy cream*
5 tablespoons sago (or tapioca)	

Put all ingredients in a kettle and boil 20 or 25 minutes. Remove cinnamon stick and what is left of the lemon slices. If soup is too thick, add a little more wine and blend well.

Chill and serve, topped with whipped cream. Serves 4 to 6.

SWEET SOUP

•

SØD FRUGTSUPPE

1 cup tapioca	*2 cups currant jelly*
6 cups warm water	*½ teaspoon cinnamon*
½ cup raisins	*3 cloves*
½ cup cooked, pitted prunes	*3 tablespoons white vinegar*

Boil the tapioca in the water until clear. Add raisins, prunes, currant jelly and the spices and mix well. Add vinegar and blend.

Boil as slowly as possible for 1½ hours, uncovered. If boiled slowly enough, no more water will need to be added.

Serves 10.

· 10 ·

FISH

UNLESS RECIPES in this chapter specifically call for salted fish, use the fresh variety. The surest guarantee that fish are fresh is to catch them yourself and cook them at once. If this isn't practical, go out of your way to find a good sea-food market which has fish which are firm-fleshed to the touch, bright-eyed and so newly arrived from their native waters they snap their jaws at you. Anything less is borderline. You won't be poisoned, but you'll waste a lot of good ingredients trying to make a tasty dish from a poor fish.

From the cook's standpoint, one of the best arguments for a good fishman is his willingness to scale, clean and bone fish to specifications. These are jobs for an expert, as anybody who has ever struggled over her proud husband's catch for the day can testify.

190

BOILED SALMON

·

KOGT LAKS

5- or 6-pound dressed salmon	*¼ cup lemon juice*
3 quarts boiling water	*2 tablespoons salt*

Wrap salmon in cheesecloth and tie ends loosely. Place salmon on a rack in a pan and cover with combination of boiling water, lemon juice and salt. Cover and let simmer for 35 to 40 minutes. Lift to a serving platter or baking plank. Chill.

Prepare a sauce, and when ready to serve fish, remove the cheesecloth carefully. Remove any small particles of skin clinging to the fish. Garnish with sprigs of parsley and serve with sauce. Serves 8 to 10.

If you are skillful and lucky, your salmon will be a thing of beauty which you will want to display proudly. In this case, have your sauce available in a separate sauce boat from which guests may help themselves. If the fish looks a little limp and despondent, pat him into shape and cover his deficiencies with a thin coating of sauce. Reserve the rest to be added to individual servings as your guests choose.

SAUCE

1 cup sour cream	*½ teaspoon salt, scant*
2 teaspoons horseradish	*½ teaspoon sugar*

Blend ingredients together and chill until the salmon is ready to be served. Makes 1 cup sauce.

HERRING BITS IN SOUR CREAM

·

SILD I SURFLØDE

1 pound herring fillets	*1 teaspoon salt*
1 cup thick sour cream	*Paprika*
3 tablespoons lemon juice	*Parsley*
1 large sliced onion	*Lemon slices*
1 tablespoon peppercorns	

Cut herring fillets into bite-sized pieces.

Mix together sour cream, lemon juice, onion slices, peppercorns and salt. Pour the mixture over the herring and toss with a fork to coat all pieces. Refrigerate 3 hours at least, or until very cold.

Serve on platter. Sprinkle with paprika. Garnish with sprigs of parsley and slices of lemon. Serves 4.

SOUR HERRING

·

SURSILD

3 large salt herrings	*Vinegar*
3 or 4 large onions	*Parsley*

Put herrings in cold water and let soak 12 hours. Dry fish well between paper towels. Skin, bone and cut into 1-inch lengths.

Place a layer of herring in a large mixing bowl. Cover with a layer of sliced onions. Repeat until all the fish is used.

Cover with a solution made of 2 parts vinegar to 1 part water. Chill for at least 12 hours.

Remove fish from vinegar solution when ready to serve. Garnish with sliced onions and sprigs of parsley. Will keep for several weeks refrigerated.

PICKLED HERRING

·

NEDLAGTE SILD

2 salt herrings	*1 cup water*
3 quarts cold water	*1 bay leaf*
1 large onion	*Parsley*
1 cup vinegar	

Prepare the salted herrings as follows: Cut off the heads and discard. Slit the fish from head to tail. Remove entrails and scrape the inside well. Cut off tail and fins. Rinse the fish thoroughly in cold water. Scrape and pull off the bluish skin. Be careful not to tear outside of fish. Remove backbone and as many bones as possible without breaking the flesh.

Let fillets soak in cold water in a large bowl for 2 hours. While fish is soaking, slice onion into thin rings. Mix together the vinegar, water and bay leaf.

Drain herring and cut into pieces about 2½ inches square. Put a layer of herring into a shallow baking pan and top with some of the onion rings. Repeat the layers until all the fish and onion rings are used. Pour the vinegar and water mixture over it. Chill overnight in refrigerator to blend the flavors thoroughly.

When ready to serve, drain off the liquid. Toss the herring and onion rings lightly to mix. Garnish with chopped parsley.

QUICK PICKLED HERRING

•

HURTIGE KRYDDERSILD

3 large salt herrings	3 bay leaves
1 cup vinegar	12 whole allspice
½ cup sugar	3 sprays fresh dill
½ cup chopped onion	White pepper

(This recipe takes less time to prepare than the preceding one, though it must chill just as long before it is ready to serve.)

Cover the herring with cold water and let stand overnight. Drain. Split, clean, skin, and remove all bones from the fish.

Mix the remaining ingredients and let stand while you cut the herrings in small chunks across the width of the fish. Place in a bowl. Pour the pickling solution over the herring bits.

Chill overnight or longer in refrigerator before serving. Serves 6 to 8.

MUSTARD HERRING

•

SENNEPSSILD

1 large smoked herring	3 tablespoons minced cucumber pickles
3 tablespoons mixed dry mustards	
2 tablespoons sugar	6 tablespoons minced pickled beets
¾ cup olive oil	

Clean and wash the herring. Cut off the head and tail, and remove bones. Cut into small chunks and cover with cold water. Let stand overnight.

When ready to serve, drain and arrange on a serving plate.

Combine mustards and sugar. Stir in olive oil a little at a time and stir until smooth. Add the pickles and beets. Mix well. Pour over the fish. Serves 6 to 8.

Decorate with small boiled new potatoes, lightly sautéed in butter and sprinkled with chopped parsley.

SHRIMP WITH SPICES IN BEER

•

REJER I ØL

36 ounces beer	1 teaspoon caraway seeds
6 pounds large shrimps	1 teaspoon toasted sesame seeds
1 tablespoon salt	1 teaspoon anise seeds
¼ cup chopped parsley	1 teaspoon cardamom seeds
1 onion, chopped	1 teaspoon thyme
1 small stalk celery, chopped	1 teaspoon marjoram
1 teaspoon mustard seeds	½ teaspoon cayenne pepper
1 teaspoon celery seeds	¼ teaspoon curry powder

Open canned or bottled beer an hour or so before you plan to start cooking to allow it to become flat at room temperature.

Wash the shrimps; do not peel. Place in a large kettle with the remaining ingredients except the beer. Cover with beer and bring to a boil. Cover the kettle and boil over high heat for 8 minutes, stirring occasionally.

Remove from stove. Drain, and reserve the broth. Shell and devein the shrimps. Serve in deep tureen with the boiled liquid, accompanied by individual serving bowls of any sauce you choose. Serves 6 to 8.

You can convert this to an hors d'oeuvre by chilling the drained shrimp (discard the broth) and serving them with the following dip:

DIP

1 cup butter	4 tablespoons prepared mustard

Melt butter together with mustard. Keep the sauce warm in a small chafing dish or over a warming candle. Have plenty of toothpicks handy and let each guest spear as many shrimps as he wants to dip into the hot sauce.

HERRING CROQUETTES

·

SILDEKROKETTER

2 salt herrings
1½ pounds cooked potatoes,
   cooled and finely diced
1½ cups cooked, finely chopped
   leftover meat

1 cup milk
½ teaspoon white pepper
1 cup brown bread crumbs
Butter for frying

Soak the herrings overnight in cold water. In the morning dry between paper towels. Skin and bone the fish. Chop very fine. Add the potatoes, meat and milk. Season with the pepper.

Shape into croquettes and roll them in the brown crumbs. Fry to a golden brown in butter. Serve with a currant sauce. Serves 6.

CURRANT SAUCE

3 tablespoons dried currants
2 cups water
1 tablespoon butter
2 tablespoons flour

½ tablespoon syrup
1 tablespoon vinegar
½ tablespoon sugar
¼ teaspoon salt

Wash the currants and boil until tender in the 2 cups of water. Drain. Mix with the remaining ingredients in the order given. Serve hot over the croquettes.

FISH FILLETS WITH ALMONDS

·

FISKEFILETER MED MANDLER

2 pounds fish fillets
Salt

Pepper
2 tablespoons melted butter

Arrange fish fillets in a single layer in a shallow greased baking dish. Sprinkle with salt and pepper and brush with the butter.

Broil in a preheated broiler about 5 minutes, or until fish begins to flake.

Drain liquids from baking dish carefully to avoid breaking fillets. While the fish is broiling, start to prepare the following:

TOPPING

½ cup mayonnaise
1 tablespoon lemon juice
1 teaspoon minced onion

2 egg whites
½ cup blanched, slivered and
    toasted almonds

Mix the mayonnaise, lemon juice and onion together.

Beat the egg whites until stiff and fold into the mayonnaise mixture very gently. Spread over the broiled fillets. Sprinkle with the slivered almonds. Return to broiler and broil until the top is lightly browned and a little puffy. Serves 4.

FISH COOKED IN BEER

•

FISK KOGT I ØL

1 whole fish
1 medium onion, sliced
2 or 3 carrots, sliced
Grated rind of 1 lemon
Juice of 1 lemon
2 tablespoons vinegar
1 tablespoon molasses
½ cup butter
2 bay leaves

½ teaspoon salt
Pepper to taste
1 teaspoon paprika
½ cup bread crumbs
Beer
Pickled onions
Mushrooms
Parsley

Wash, clean and if necessary scale a good-sized fresh fish. Place in a shallow baking pan large enough to give the fish plenty of head and tail room. Spread over the fish the onion, carrots and lemon rind. Add lemon juice, vinegar, molasses, butter, bay leaves, salt, pepper and paprika. Sprinkle the bread crumbs on top. Pour in your favorite beer three-quarters covering the fish.

Bake about 40 minutes in a preheated 350° oven, or until well browned.

Place on a warm platter surrounded by pickled onions and mushrooms browned in butter. Cover with a sauce, if you wish, and decorate with parsley.

A 3-pound fish should serve 4 to 6 people.

CURRIED EEL

•

ÅL I KARRYSAUCE

3-pound eel
1 tablespoon salt
2 quarts boiling water
4 tablespoons butter

4 tablespoons flour
3 cups eel stock
1 teaspoon curry powder

Clean, skin and bone the eel. Wash several times in cold water. Cut into pieces about 3 inches long. Cover with salted, boiling water and boil for ½ hour, or until tender. Place eel on a heatproof platter and keep warm in oven.

Strain the water in which the eel boiled.

Melt the butter and stir in the flour. Add the stock, stirring until thick. Mix the curry powder with 1 tablespoon of the sauce. Stir into balance of sauce and mix well. Remove from fire and pour over the warm boiled eel.

Serve with rice and hot rolls. Serves 5 to 6.

STUFFED EEL

•

FYLDTE ÅL

2 eels about 2 pounds each
3 tins sardines packed in oil
Salt
Pepper
3 tablespoons butter

Corn meal
Parsley
Pickled beets
Lemon slices

Remove fins from eels. Wash and clean well. Bone them to get long, flat pieces from both. Season with salt and pepper to taste, tapping the eels gently to distribute the seasoning.

Remove tails of the sardines and place them lengthwise between each pair of fillet strips. Close each eel with skewers, or tie together with string.

Lightly brown butter in a large skillet.

Roll the fish in fine corn meal and fry in the browned butter over low heat, turning only once to brown on both sides.

Remove to a warm platter and serve surrounded with sprigs of parsley, pickled beets and slices of lemon. Serves 4 to 6.

FRIED FISH WITH SAGE

•

STEGT FISK

3 fish, about 1 pound each	*Nutmeg*
Salt	*3 sage leaves or ¼ teaspoon*
Pepper	*ground sage*
⅓ cup flour	*Parsley*
6 tablespoons butter	*Lemon slices*

Bone fish (or have your fish market do this chore), wash, and dry well. Sprinkle with salt and pepper. Roll in flour.

Brown 4 tablespoons of the butter in a frying pan and cook fish about 5 minutes on one side over moderate heat. Turn and brown the other side. Place on a warm platter.

Melt the other 2 tablespoons of butter and add to it a little nutmeg and the sage. Heat until butter has absorbed flavors of spices, but do not allow butter to brown. Pour over fish.

Garnish with sprigs of parsley and slices of lemon. Serves 5 or 6.

FRIED MACKEREL

•

STEGTE MAKREL

Salt	*2 teaspoons baking powder*
2 pounds mackerel fillets	*¼ teaspoon salt*
⅔ cup milk	*Butter for frying*
2 eggs	*2 ripe tomatoes, sliced*
1½ cups sifted flour	*Parsley*

Salt the fillets. Beat milk and eggs together. Combine with flour, baking powder and salt. Dip fillets in batter, one at a time.

Sauté slowly in hot butter until browned (from 7 to 10 minutes on each side, depending on size of fillets).

Serve with sliced tomatoes and sprigs of parsley. Serves 4.

CODFISH BALLS

·

TORSKEBOLLER

1½ cups salt codfish	2 tablespoons soft butter
3 cups raw diced potatoes	¼ teaspoon pepper
1 egg	⅛ teaspoon dry mustard

Soak the codfish overnight in cold water. Drain in the morning and soak for 1 hour in cold water. Drain.

Put the fish and raw potatoes in a saucepan, cover with water, and cook until the potatoes are tender. Drain off the water.

Beat the egg and blend in butter. Add the pepper and dry mustard. Add fish and potato mixture, beat well.

Drop by tablespoonfuls into hot fat and fry, turning to brown all over, until a rich golden brown. Serves 4 or 5.

FISH PUDDING

·

FISKEBUDDING

2½ pounds fresh cod or halibut (delicious with trout, too, if you can spare any)	1 teaspoon salt
	1½ cups whipping cream
	3 egg whites

Clean, skin and bone the fish. Set skin and bones aside. Chop fish and grind fine. Add the salt.

Whip the cream until stiff and fold in, mixing well.

Beat the egg whites until stiff and fold into the mixture.

Butter a mold generously. Fill it ¾ full. Set it in a pan containing a little hot water. Cover and bake 1 hour in a preheated 325° oven. Unmold on a hot serving platter and serve with Mushroom Sauce (page 202).

FRIED FILLETS OF FLOUNDER

•

STEGTE RØDSPÆTTE FILETER

2 pounds flounder fillets	2 zwiebacks, ground fine
Salt	½ cup butter
Flour	1 lemon, sliced
1 egg, beaten	1 tablespoon minced parsley

Sprinkle the fillets well with salt and let stand in refrigerator 1 hour.

Dry each fillet between paper towels and dredge lightly in the flour, then in the egg. Coat with zwieback crumbs.

Melt the butter in a deep skillet, and when hot, lay the fillets in it and cook until brown and crisp. Lift them out carefully onto a warm platter or serving plate. Serve garnished with the lemon slices and parsley. Serves 4.

FILLET OF SOLE

•

SØTUNGE

1½ pounds fillet of sole	2 glasses dry white wine
Salt	Butter
Pepper	Parsley
2 tomatoes, peeled	

Put the fillets in a well-buttered baking dish and season with salt and pepper.

Dice the tomatoes over the fish. Pour the wine over all and bake in a preheated moderate oven (375°) 25 to 30 minutes. Remove from oven, and dot top with butter. Sprinkle with finely chopped parsley. Serves 3 generously.

ROLLED FISH FILLETS

•

FILETRULLER

1½ pounds halibut fillets	Green pepper
3 cups water	Parsley
1½ teaspoons salt	

Wipe the fish with a damp cloth and dry between paper towels. Cut the fillets into narrow strips about 8 to 10 inches long and about 2 inches wide. Roll up the strips, starting at the narrower end. Fasten with a toothpick.

In a saucepan, bring the water and salt to the boiling point. After the water boils, reduce the heat somewhat. Put the fish rolls into the pan and let simmer about 8 minutes. Remove, drain and chill. When ready to serve, cover the rolls with either of the following sauces and serve on a platter, garnished with chopped green pepper and sprigs of parsley. Serves 3 to 4.

MAYONNAISE SAUCE

1 tablespoon sugar
1 cup mayonnaise

¼ cup lemon juice

Mix ingredients and chill. Spread over rolled fish fillets.

WINE SAUCE

3 tablespoons butter
1½ tablespoons flour
½ cup cream
½ cup white wine

¼ teaspoon salt
⅛ teaspoon white pepper
1 teaspoon lemon juice

Melt the butter. Stir in the flour and blend. Add the cream and the wine a little at a time, stirring after each addition. Cook until smooth and creamy. Add the salt, pepper and lemon juice. Mix well. Serve warm over the chilled fillet rolls, or cold, if you prefer.

SAUCES FOR FISH

DRAWN BUTTER SAUCE

·

SMØRSAUCE

¼ cup butter
¼ cup flour
½ teaspoon paprika

½ teaspoon salt
2 cups cold water
¼ cup butter

Melt ¼ cup butter. Stir in the flour to make a smooth paste. Add paprika and salt. Mix well. Add the water and let come just to the boiling point.

Just before serving, while still warm, add the last ¼ cup butter, cut into small pieces. Beat the butter pieces gradually into the mixture until they disappear from the surface.

Serve over fish which has a very pronounced flavor of its own, not on bland fish which needs a distinctively flavored sauce.

MUSTARD SAUCE

·

SENNEPSSAUCE

1½ cups fish stock	1 teaspoon sugar
1 tablespoon dry mustard	1 teaspoon paprika
1 tablespoon vinegar	Pinch of salt

Mix all ingredients and bring to the boiling point, stirring continuously to prevent scorching. Remove from heat and serve at once. Serve over fish requiring a thin, clear sauce.

This may also be used as a sauce for meats. Substitute meat stock or bouillon for fish stock.

MUSHROOM SAUCE

·

CHAMPIGNONSSAUCE

Fish bones and skin	3 tablespoons butter
3 cups water	1 cup sliced mushrooms
1 bay leaf	3 tablespoons flour
3 tablespoons minced parsley	¾ cup cream
½ cup diced carrots	1 teaspoon salt
¼ cup diced onions	2 egg yolks, beaten
6 peppercorns	

Combine water and reserved fish skin and bones in a saucepan. Add bay leaf, parsley, carrots, onion and peppercorns. Cover and let mixture boil slowly for 45 minutes until the liquid has boiled down to about 1½ cups. Strain.

Melt the butter and sauté the mushrooms until tender and lightly browned. Stir in the flour. Add the strained fish stock, cream and salt. Cook 5 minutes. Add 2 tablespoons of this hot liquid to the beaten egg yolks a little at a time to prevent curdling. Stir into the hot sauce gradually and cook over a low flame until thickened.

Serves 4 to 6.

(While particularly good as an accompaniment for Fish Pudding (*page 199*), this sauce is an asset for many other fish and meat entrées.)

SHRIMP SAUCE

•

REJESAUCE

1 pound shrimps, shelled, cleaned and boiled	1 tablespoon sour cream
	½ teaspoon sugar
6 tablespoons butter	Salt
4 tablespoons flour	1½ tablespoons sherry
3 cups milk	

Cut large shrimps in half.

Melt half of the butter over low heat, stir flour into it and mix until smooth. Add the milk a little at a time, stirring well. Add the rest of the butter, sour cream, sugar, shrimps and salt to taste. Boil for about 2 minutes. Add sherry and remove from heat. Serve hot over fish fillets or steaks.

MUSHROOM-SHERRY SAUCE

•

CHAMPIGNONSSAUCE

¼ pound mushrooms	Salt to taste
4 tablespoons butter	1 egg yolk
4 tablespoons flour	3 tablespoons sherry
1½ cups milk	

Wash mushrooms and sauté whole (including stems) in 2 tablespoons of the butter. When browned, remove the mushrooms and mince. Stir the rest of the butter into the pan. Add the flour and stir until smooth. Add the milk a little at a time and mix well. Let cook until smooth and thickened, stirring constantly.

Just before removing from the heat, add the salt, beaten egg yolk, mushrooms and sherry. Stir thoroughly and heat for just 1 minute. Serve hot over fish, meats or fowl.

EGG SAUCE

•

ÆGGESAUCE

6 egg yolks
1 teaspoon flour
¼ teaspoon sugar
1½ cups water

Juice of 1 lemon
¾ cup butter
Salt
Pepper

Beat the egg yolks until frothy and lemon-colored. Add the rest of the ingredients. Heat to a low boil, stirring until thick.

Wonderful for fish and equally good as an unusual sauce for vegetables.

· 11 ·

MEATS AND FOWL

ROAST REINDEER (VENISON)

·

RENSDYRSSTEG

8 pounds reindeer
Salt
White pepper
1 teaspoon ground ginger
1 tablespoon sugar
1 teaspoon celery salt
1 cup olive oil
2 bay leaves

6 whole allspice
6 peppercorns
1 lemon, sliced thin
1 cup water
2 cups wine
1 cup cream
2 eggs, separated
1 tablespoon black currant jelly

Clean, wash and wipe meat with a cloth. Leave in a single piece or cut into serving-size pieces. Rub with salt, white pepper, ginger, sugar and celery salt in generous amounts.

Brown the meat in hot olive oil in a roasting pan on top of the stove or under the broiler. Turn to brown well on all sides. Add the remaining ingredients except the cream, eggs and jelly.

205

Cover and roast slowly in an oven preheated to 300 degrees for 3 hours. Turn every 15 or 20 minutes. Do not pierce the meat. When done, place on a hot platter and return to oven to keep warm.

Pour the cream into the roasting pan, mix well with juices. Boil about 10 minutes, stirring often. Stir in the beaten egg yolks and the jelly, stirring until mixture thickens. Do not boil.

Beat the egg whites until stiff and fold into the gravy.

Garnish with lingonberries if desired. Serves 12 or more.

ROASTED HARE

•

HARESTEG

6-pound hare	*½ cup butter*
4 slices salt pork	*3 cups milk*
¼ cup flour	*¾ cup cream*
Salt	*Hot water*

Clean hare well. Soak in cold water for several hours. Drain.

Lard the back and legs with strips of salt pork. Sprinkle with flour and salt.

Melt the butter and brown the hare in it on top of the stove.

Preheat oven to 350 degrees and roast hare 2 or 3 hours, or until joints move easily in sockets. Roast in covered or uncovered roaster, as you prefer.

Baste often with the mixture of milk and cream, adding a little water if necessary at the end of the roasting period.

Serves 8 to 10.

BREAST OF LAMB WITH DILL SAUCE

•

KALVEBRYST MED DILDSAUCE

3 pounds breast of lamb	*2 sprigs of dill, fresh*
1 quart boiling water	*1 teaspoon salt*
1 bay leaf	*3 peppercorns*

Rinse the meat quickly with hot water. Place in a roaster and cover with the boiling water. Let come to a boil. Skim. Add the bay leaf, dill, salt and pepper. Simmer covered on top of the stove for 1½ hours. Remove lamb and reserve 2 cups of the stock.

Cut the lamb into small serving pieces and place on a hot serving platter. Serve with the following sauce:

DILL SAUCE

2 tablespoons butter
2 tablespoons flour
2 cups stock reserved from cooking
    lamb
2 tablespoons crushed dill

1½ tablespoons vinegar
1 tablespoon sugar
1 egg yolk
½ teaspoon salt
Parsley

Melt the butter in a skillet, add the flour and stir continuously until smooth. Add the stock gradually, stirring after each addition. Add the rest of the ingredients alternately, beating a little after each addition.

When mixture is smooth, remove from the flame and serve over the lamb. Garnish the platter with sprigs of parsley. Serves 6.

APPLE- AND PRUNE-FILLED SPARERIBS

•

RIBBENSTYKKE MED ÆBLER OG SVESKER

8 pounds spareribs
1 teaspoon salt
1 teaspoon celery salt
2 tablespoons sugar
1 teaspoon cinnamon
1 pound apples, cored and peeled

1 pound prunes, cooked and pitted
2 tablespoons flour
1 cup milk
1 cup light cream
Salt
White pepper

Rub both sides of spareribs with the salts, sugar and cinnamon.
Cut apples into sixths.
Make sandwiches of the racks of ribs, a pair at a time, using apples and prunes, mixed, as the filling. Tie securely to retain the filling.

Brown in butter in a roasting pan, basting with enough warm water to cover the bottom of the pan. Cook slowly for 2½ hours in an oven preheated to 275–300 degrees. Add warm water from time to time if necessary to keep ribs from sticking and scorching.

Remove from oven and keep hot while you make the gravy. Add flour to the stock in the pan, stirring until smooth. Place pan over low heat on top of the stove. Slowly add the milk and cream. (If gravy becomes too thick, add more milk.) Stir until it comes just to the boiling point. Season with salt and pepper to taste.

Place spareribs on a serving platter. Remove string. Pour a small amount of gravy over the ribs, and serve the rest in a gravy boat to be savored over small boiled potatoes. Serves 8.

STUFFED TENDERLOINS

•

FYLDT MØRBRAD

2 pork tenderloins
2 large apples, peeled, cored and
   diced
8 dry prunes, cooked and pitted
3 tablespoons butter

1 cup sweet cream
1 cup sour cream
2 tablespoons white wine
Salt
White pepper

Slice the tenderloins lengthwise in half. Open and pound flat. Replace top half of each tenderloin.

Place apples over 1 tenderloin. Drain prunes and pull into chunks. Place prunes over the apples. Place the other tenderloin over the filling. Roll like a long sausage and tie securely.

Heat the butter in a deep, heavy skillet and brown the tenderloin slightly. Add the creams, wine and seasonings to taste and cook slowly, covered, for 1½ hours.

Serves 6 to 8.

BEER MEAT LOAF

•

KØDRULLE I ØL

2 pounds lean pork
1 pound raw smoked ham
1½ cups cracker crumbs
2 eggs, beaten

1 teaspoon salt
¼ teaspoon white pepper
Beer

Have your butcher grind the pork and ham together.

Mix well with the cracker crumbs, eggs, salt and pepper. Form into a loaf. Roll in cheesecloth and tie the ends securely.

Place in a kettle and add sufficient beer to cover the loaf. Simmer slowly for 2¾ hours.

Very good served on thin-sliced open-faced sandwiches. Or serve with cole slaw, your favorite sharp cheese, pickled beets and potato salad.

Serves 4 to 5.

ROAST LOIN OF PORK
·
SVINESTEG

5-pound loin of pork	*Prunes, pitted*
Salt	*Butter*
Pepper	*Cream*
Apples	*1 cup red or white wine*

Have your butcher slit the pork loin lengthwise. Salt and pepper it and fill the cavity with slices of pared tart apples and prunes. Tie or skewer the roast.

Brown on all sides in butter in a roasting pan. Add a little water at first, then baste with as much cream as you need to keep the bottom of the pan moist.

Let simmer 25 minutes on top of the stove, uncovered.

Roast 3½ hours in a preheated 350° oven. Reduce heat to 275 degrees. Add the wine and baste often for the next 40 minutes. Serves 6 to 8.

For a change of flavor, try the following instead of the apple-and-prune stuffing (pork does not have to be slit for this):

PORK DRESSING

1 egg	*1 small onion, minced*
⅓ cup soft butter	*1 teaspoon salt*
2 cups hot mashed potatoes	*¼ teaspoon white pepper*
1 cup dry bread crumbs	

Mix ingredients in order given. Place in mounds around the pork loin roast during the last ¾ hour of roasting. Dressing should be nicely browned.

PORK LOIN WITH PRUNES

•

MØRBRAD MED SVESKER

6-pound loin of pork
20 large cooked, pitted prunes
Salt

White pepper
1 teaspoon ground ginger
1 tablespoon light brown sugar

Have your butcher remove bone from loin. Fill cavity with the prunes. Make another incision if necessary to use all the prunes. Skewer the roast and rub it with the salt, pepper, ginger and brown sugar. Place in a shallow open roasting pan and cook in a preheated 450° oven until browned. Lower the temperature to 350 degrees and roast 3½ to 4 hours, or until very tender.

Serves 6 to 8.

PORK ROAST AND SAUERKRAUT IN BEER

•

SKINKE OG SURKÅL MED ØL

2 pounds fresh sauerkraut
1 teaspoon pepper
1 clove garlic

1 quart beer
3-pound pork loin or rib roast

Simmer the sauerkraut, pepper, garlic and beer on top of the stove for 2 hours.

Brown the pork roast on all sides. Place the kraut around the roast in a baking or roasting pan. Cook in a preheated 375° oven for 3½ hours or until very tender.

Serve with plain boiled potatoes, grated fresh horseradish and beet and apple salad. Serves 5 to 6.

SMOKED HAM IN MADEIRA

•

RØGET SKINKE I MADEIRA

10-pound smoked ham
4 bay leaves

6 whole cloves
1 quart Madeira wine

Wash ham well. Cover with cold water and let soak for 1 hour, or soak overnight if convenient.

Drain the ham, cover with boiling water. Add the spices and cook slowly just below the boiling point about 3 hours, or until tender. Drain. Reserve the liquid.

Cover with the wine and let simmer in the oven (preheated to 350 degrees) uncovered for 30 minutes. Slice, and pass around a bowl of the following sauce to be spooned over individual servings:

BROWN SAUCE

4 tablespoons butter	1 cup Madeira wine
4 tablespoons flour	Salt to taste
2 cups ham stock	

Melt the butter and stir in the flour to make a smooth paste. Add the ham stock and cook, stirring, until thick. Add the wine, a little at a time, and the salt, stirring to prevent lumps.

HAM BAKED IN WINE
•
SKINKE I VIN

10-pound ham*	2 tablespoons butter
2 small onions, chopped	½ cup water
1 leek, chopped fine	Salt
2 4/5-quart bottles domestic rosé	Pepper
or other light American red wine	2 tablespoons butter
½ pound mushrooms, sliced	2 tablespoons flour

Loosen the skin from the ham and simmer with the onions and the leek for 1 hour in a roasting pan with all but ½ cup of the wine.

Remove ham from roaster. Cut away and discard tough outer skin. Brown mushrooms in butter. Cut a slash in the top of the ham suf-

---

* There are hams and hams. This recipe is intended not for the canned or cellophane-wrapped hams available at your supermarket but for the so-called "country" or Smithfield ham which requires precooking preparation. A gourmet feast will repay you for the loving care these hams call for.

ficiently large to hold the mushroom mixture, water, salt and pepper. Skewer the opening to keep the filling in place.

Make a sauce of the 2 tablespoons of butter, 2 tablespoons of flour and the liquid from the roaster. Stir over a low heat. Add the reserved ½ cup wine a little at a time and mix well. Pour over the ham in the roasting pan and bake until tender (about 25 minutes to the pound) in a preheated 375° oven. Baste at least every ½ hour with juices from the pan.

HAM IN A BLANKET

·

SKINKE I SENGETÆPPE

18-pound ham	*6 teaspoons baking powder*
1½ cups domestic rosé or other	*2 teaspoons salt*
light American red wine	*1 teaspoon sage*
3 tablespoons honey	*1½ cups butter*
9 cups flour	*2 cups milk*

Score fat of ham and place, fat side up, in a shallow baking pan. Bake until tender (about 25 minutes to the pound) in a preheated 350° oven.

About 45 minutes before the ham is done remove from oven and drain off liquid from the pan. Mix the wine and honey and pour over the ham.

Increase oven temperature to 375 degrees and return ham to oven to bake for 45 minutes more, basting often.

Take ham from oven, and while it cools, make the crust. Sift the flour, baking powder and salt, and add the sage. Cut in the butter, mixing well. Add the milk and mix quickly.

Roll the dough out until it is large enough to completely envelop the ham. Place ham on dough, wrap around ham and pinch edges together.

Preheat oven to 450 degrees and bake the ham for 1 hour, or until the crust is golden brown and crunchy.

CHAMPAGNE HAM

•

CHAMPAGNESKINKE

15-pound ham
10 cloves
1 teaspoon thyme
1 26-ounce bottle champagne

1 cup sugar
2 medium onions, quartered
4 tablespoons flour

Place the ham in a roasting pan with water to cover. Bring to a boil on top of the stove over a high heat. Place the cloves in the ham, sprinkle the ham with thyme.

Roast 2½ hours covered in a preheated 350° oven. Drain ham of stock, reserving 2½ cups. Remove as much skin and fat as possible from the ham. Pour the reserved stock back over the ham and add the bottle of champagne. Return to oven and let cook for another hour, basting often.

Drain off the stock and reserve. Sprinkle ham with the sugar. Drop the onions in the pan.

Raise oven heat to 500 degrees, return ham to oven to brown and glaze. Remove ham to warm serving platter.

Mix flour with stock until smooth and cook over low flame, stirring constantly until it boils.

Carve ham and serve sauce individually over slices.

A ham this large, depending on how thinly it is sliced, serves a great many people — certainly a sufficiency for a large buffet supper.

HAM IN BEER

•

SKINKE MED ØL

1 tenderized ham
½ teaspoon dry mustard
4 tablespoons water
1 cup brown sugar
20 whole cloves

10 bay leaves
3 12-ounce cans beer
Candied cherries
Candied pineapple

Remove all but a thin layer of fat from the ham. Score the top. Place in a roasting pan. Mix mustard, water and sugar to the consistency of prepared mustard. Cover ham with this mixture. Stick cloves in the ham surface. Fasten the bay leaves to the ham with small skewers or toothpicks broken in half.

Pour the beer over the ham and bake, uncovered, 30 minutes to the pound in an oven preheated to 425 degrees. Just before serving, decorate with candied cherries and slices of pineapple fastened to the ham with toothpicks. Return to oven to brown for 20 minutes. Use the liquid in the pan as a sauce for the ham.

Allow ⅓ pound ham per person to be served, and keep in mind that leftover ham has a multitude of uses, as well as being a meat that retains its flavor well in a freezer.

COOKING ROASTS WITH BEER

•

KOGEKUNST MED ØL

Beer is wonderful for basting any roast — lamb, veal, beef and especially pork.

Rub any size or type of pork roast with a little flour mixed with ginger, ¼ teaspoon for each 4 pounds of roast. Put the roast in a preheated 475° oven for 10 minutes, then reduce the heat to 325 degrees. Pour a bottle of beer over the roast and baste every 20 minutes until done (35 minutes per pound).

Make a brown gravy with the juice in the pan by pouring off as much of the fat as possible and stirring in a paste made of 3 tablespoons of flour and 3 tablespoons of water.

Stews and meat balls also take kindly to the beer treatment. The following 2 recipes will have a piquant flavor your guests will find hard to identify.

ROUND STEAK WITH BEER

•

OKSEKØDSSKIVER MED ØL

3 pounds boneless sirloin or top round steak	1 small onion
Flour	10 ounces beer
Salt	2 cups thin beef stock
Pepper	2 teaspoons sugar
½ cup butter	2 teaspoons vinegar

Cut meat into small squares, about 2½ inches on a side, and dust with seasoned flour. In a large heavy skillet or casserole brown lightly on both sides in the butter. Slice the onion into the pan. Add the beer, stock, sugar and vinegar. Cook slowly on top of the stove or in an oven preheated to 250 degrees for 2 hours, or until tender. Remove meat from pan.

If juice is not thick enough for gravy, add a paste of 2 tablespoons of flour and 2 tablespoons cold water. Return meat to pan and let simmer for a few more minutes.

Serves 4 to 5.

MEAT BALLS IN BEER

•

FRIKADELLER MED ØL

1 onion, minced	4 slices dry bread
2 tablespoons butter	1 egg, beaten
1 teaspoon salt	Flour
¼ teaspoon pepper	3 tablespoons butter
¼ teaspoon grated nutmeg	12 ounces beer
1 pound ground pork	2 tablespoons lemon juice
1 pound ground beef chuck	

Brown onion in butter, salt, pepper and nutmeg. Mix pork, beef and dry bread rolled into crumbs. Combine with onions. Add the egg; mix well, and form into small balls. Roll them in a small amount of flour.

Brown the meat balls in the 3 tablespoons of butter. When well browned, add beer and lemon juice. Cover and let simmer 30 minutes.

Serve with buttered noodles sprinkled with toasted crumbs. Serves 4 to 6.

MEAT BALLS

•

FRIKADELLER

2 pounds boneless beef chuck	1 cup milk
6 tablespoons soft butter	1 teaspoon salt
4 tablespoons bread crumbs	¼ teaspoon pepper
6 teaspoons flour	

Put the beef through a meat grinder 3 times. Add the butter, bread crumbs, flour, milk, salt and pepper. Mix well with your hands until well blended.

Shape into small balls. Boil in salted water 15 minutes.

These meat balls may be used as dumplings to be dropped into beef broth or soups or served with small boiled potatoes with horseradish sauce, as follows:

Horseradish Sauce (Peberrodssauce)

½ pint whipping cream	*2 tablespoons grated fresh horseradish*

Whip cream until stiff. Beat in grated horseradish.

If you prefer a heated sauce for the meat balls, prepare your favorite cream sauce and stir in the grated horseradish.

Serves 4.

MEAT BALLS IN ONION SAUCE

•

FRIKADELLER I LØGSAUCE

2 pounds ground beef	*1 egg*
1 pound ground pork	*1 teaspoon salt*
1 cup bread crumbs	*2 small onions*
1 cup milk	*½ cup butter*

Mix beef, pork and bread crumbs which have been soaked in milk.

Add egg, salt and minced onions. Shape into small balls about the size of a large walnut. (You should have about 45 meat balls.)

Brown the meat balls in the butter. Cover and simmer 1 hour. Serve with either of the following sauces:

Onion Sauce (Løgsauce)

3 cups onions, minced	*1 teaspoon salt*
1 cup butter	*3 cups milk*
6 tablespoons flour	

Cook minced onions in butter until transparent. Blend in the flour and salt. Slowly add the milk and stir continually until thickened. Pour over the meat balls.

MUSHROOM SAUCE (CHAMPIGNONSSAUCE)

1 pound mushrooms, sliced
4 tablespoons butter
4 tablespoons flour
Salt
Pepper

4 cups milk
2 tablespoons Worcestershire
    sauce
½ teaspoon dry mustard

Brown mushrooms in the butter; dredge with flour to which salt and pepper have been added. Add milk slowly when the flour begins to brown. Season with Worcestershire sauce and mustard. Stir until thick and smooth.

MEAT BALLS WITH SALT PORK

•

FRIKADELLER

1 onion, minced
¾ pound salt pork
1 pound beef chuck
1 hard-crust roll
2 cups milk
5 eggs

1 cup cracker crumbs or dry bread
    crumbs
Salt
Pepper
1 cup butter

Mix onion with salt pork and beef which have been ground together by you or your butcher.

Soak the hard roll in the milk. Mix with the meats, breaking up the roll to distribute it thoroughly through the meat mixture.

Beat 4 eggs and add. Shape into balls.

Beat the remaining egg, mix with dry crumbs, and coat the meat balls with the mixture. Add salt and pepper to taste to each meat ball. Fry in hot butter, turning frequently to brown all over. Cook until done to taste.

Serves 6.

MEAT BALLS WITH SOUR CREAM

•

FRIKADELLER I SURFLØDE

4 pounds boneless beef chuck
Salt
Pepper
3 cups rye bread crumbs
4 cups light cream

Flour
¼ pound butter
½ cup olive oil
2 cups sour cream
2 cups dry red wine

Put chuck twice through a meat grinder. Combine with salt, pepper and bread crumbs. Add cream and mix lightly. Form into small balls. Roll in flour.

Melt butter, using large skillet. Add oil. Brown meat balls in fat mixture. Add sour cream and wine, stirring until well blended.

Serve from a tureen or chafing dish. Serves 7 to 8.

FILLET OF BEEF

•

OKSEFILET

4 pounds boneless sirloin or
  top round steak
½ pound butter
½ cup flour
1 cup beef stock
¾ cup champagne or still
  white wine

2 tablespoons thick tomato
  sauce
1 teaspoon salt
¼ pound mushrooms, sliced
2 tablespoons sherry
Pepper

Roast the fillet 1½ hours in a preheated 400° oven.

Melt 6 tablespoons of the butter in a frying pan. Add the flour, stirring until smooth and browned. Add the beef stock from the roasting pan, stirring until the sauce comes to a boil. Add the wine, tomato sauce and salt. Mix well. Cover and cook over low heat 45 minutes.

Melt the remaining butter in another pan. Sauté the sliced mushrooms 5 minutes, stirring occasionally. Add the sherry and pepper to taste.

Heap mushrooms and their cooking liquid over the beef. Slice it and serve with a separate bowl of the gravy.

Serves 6.

ROAST BEEF WITH BÉARNAISE SAUCE

•

OKSESTEG MED BEARNAISESAUCE

3½-pound piece of top round steak	Butter
Salt	1 fresh horseradish root, grated
Pepper	1 onion, chopped
	1 carrot, sliced

With a mallet pound the salt and pepper, to taste, into all sides of the beef. Place the roast, fattier side up, in a roasting pan with a little butter. Place the grated horseradish, onion and carrot on top of the meat. Dot with butter. Roast in a moderate oven (preheated to 325 degrees) for 1 hour and 10 minutes if you like beef rare — more, of course, if you prefer medium or well-done meat.

Serves 4. Serve with Béarnaise Sauce (*see below*) and crisp French-fried potatoes.

WARM BÉARNAISE SAUCE (VARM BEARNAISESAUCE)

4 tablespoons tarragon vinegar	¼ teaspoon pepper
1 teaspoon minced onion	3 tablespoons jellied meat stock,
¼ teaspoon white pepper	or jellied canned beef bouillon
½ teaspoon salt	½ teaspoon lemon juice
5 egg yolks	Chopped parsley
½ pound melted butter	

Mix vinegar, onion, pepper and salt and let boil until only ⅓ of the original quantity remains.

Remove from fire. Place pan over, but not in, hot water over low heat. Add egg yolks and butter alternately, a little at a time, beating after each addition.

Strain the sauce through a cheesecloth and season with the pepper, meat stock and lemon juice. When cool, add a little chopped parsley.

COLD BÉARNAISE SAUCE

1 teaspoon onion juice	¼ cup Béarnaise essence*
5 egg yolks	½ tablespoons chopped parsley
1 scant teaspoon salt	1¼ cups melted butter
¼ cup olive oil	1 small yellow onion, minced

* Béarnaise essence may be purchased at fancy grocery stores and some large super-markets.

Put onion juice in a glass mixing bowl. Mix with egg yolks and salt and add oil, a little at a time. Stir in the essence and the parsley. Mix well. Add the melted butter, a teaspoon at a time, beating well after each addition. Add the minced onion. Blend thoroughly.

BEEF POT ROAST IN SOUR CREAM

•

OKSESTEG I SURFLØDE

5-pound rump roast	½ cup water
2 scant teaspoons salt	1 cup sour cream
White pepper	¾ cup dry red wine
3 tablespoons butter	2 tablespoons flour
1 large onion, sliced	

Rub the roast well with salt and pepper. Brown it on both sides in the butter. Place the onion slices on top of the roast. Add the water, sour cream and wine.

Cover the pan and cook slowly either on top of the stove or in the oven for 3 hours or until tender, adding a little more wine if necessary.

Place the roast on a hot platter while you blend the flour into the liquid in the pan to make the gravy.

Serves 7 to 8.

CABBAGE WITH FORCEMEAT

•

FARSERET HVIDKÅL

1 large head of cabbage	1 teaspoon salt
1½ pounds forcemeat (see recipe which follows)	

Wash cabbage, drain and let stand inverted in cold water 1 hour or longer. Drain and rinse. Cut off outer leaves and save them. Scoop out the center of the cabbage, leaving enough of the exterior to make a strong wall. Pour hot water into the cabbage, drain, pour cold water into the head, drain, and fill with forcemeat.

Make a lid of the cabbage leaves you have saved. Tie them in place with a string. Place in a deep kettle. Add salt and enough boiling water to half cover the cabbage. Cover the kettle with a lid and boil gently for 3 hours.

To serve, remove the string and the lid of leaves and turn the cabbage onto a warm serving plate with the forcemeat down. Serve with melted butter or cream sauce. Serves 5 or 6.

FORCEMEAT (KØDFARS)

1½ pounds ground beef	Pinch of ground or grated nutmeg
1 teaspoon salt	2 cups hot milk
½ teaspoon pepper	2 cups cream
2 tablespoons cornstarch	

Mix the ground beef and the dry ingredients. Add the milk, a little at a time, and cook a few minutes over moderate heat. Add cream gradually, stirring after each addition. Remove from fire, cool, and stuff the cabbage.

CORNED BEEF

•

SPRÆNGT OKSEKØD

5 pounds corned beef	1 medium onion
6 whole black peppercorns	3 whole cloves
1 bay leaf	

After rinsing the meat under running water, cover with water in a kettle. Add the rest of the ingredients, cover and bring to the boiling point. Reduce the heat and let simmer until done, usually an hour to the pound.

Cabbage may be cooked in the juice after the meat has been removed. Tie the head of the cabbage so when done it will cut easily into good-sized wedges. (Cook cabbage until just barely tender.)

Just before serving, score the fat of the corned beef with a sharp knife. Spread well with a mixture of prepared mustard and brown sugar. Place under the broiler about 15 minutes, or until well glazed.

Serves 6 to 8. Add spice to your corned beef with:

HORSERADISH SAUCE (PEBERRODSSAUCE)

4 tablespoons sour cream	1 tablespoon vinegar
4 tablespoons horseradish (fresh!)	½ teaspoon salt
	Paprika (optional)

Whip the sour cream.

Blend the horseradish well with the vinegar and salt. Add a pinch of paprika if desired. Blend well with sour cream.

MEAT LOAF

•

OKSEFARS

3 pounds ground round steak	1 tablespoon chopped parsley
1 large onion, chopped	1 stalk celery, chopped
1 egg, beaten	1 teaspoon salt
½ cup cream	½ teaspoon white pepper
1 cup bread or cracker crumbs	2 teaspoons red wine

Mix ingredients in order given. Form into loaf shape.
Bake 1½ hours in a preheated 350° oven.
Serves 6.

MEAT PIE

•

KØDBUDDING

2 pounds top round steak	White pepper
1 pound cooked ham	½ cup meat stock
20 large mushrooms	½ cup sherry
3 tablespoons butter	½ cup cognac
2 tablespoons flour	Pastry (see recipe below)
Salt	

PASTRY

1½ cups flour	7 tablespoons shortening
½ teaspoon salt	3 to 4 tablespoons very cold water

Sift flour and salt together twice. Add shortening and cut into flour until particles are the size of peas. Gradually sprinkle cold water over the mixture. Work with a fork or fingers lightly until the dough forms a ball and no longer sticks to the sides of the mixing bowl. Roll dough on a lightly floured board to about ¼-inch thickness. Pat gently into shape about 1 inch larger in diameter than the casserole you wish to use for the meat pie.

FILLING FOR PIE

Cut the beef and ham in small serving pieces.

Wash mushrooms. Cut off and reserve the stems, but otherwise leave whole.

Sauté the ham in a frying pan in a little butter, and when well browned, place in a deep buttered casserole.

Cook the beef in the combination of butter and ham fat until browned and tender. Place beef on top of the ham in casserole.

Brown the mushroom tops in the fat left in the pan and distribute over beef. Sprinkle the mushroom *stems* with the flour, and season with salt and white pepper. Add the meat stock and simmer a few minutes, using the same frying pan in which other ingredients have been browned. Add the sherry and cognac, stirring well from the bottom to incorporate any tidbits which may be sticking to the pan in the rest of the mixture, and pour over the ingredients in the casserole.

Cover with the pastry. Crimp the edges on the rim of the casserole. Cut a few slits in the crust to allow the steam to escape.

Place in a preheated 450° oven and bake for 25 minutes, or until well browned.

Serves 6.

OLD RECIPE FOR DANISH STEW

·

STUVET OKSEKØD

3 tablespoons butter	¼ teaspoon white pepper
2 onions, chopped	¾ teaspoon baking powder
1 cup flour	½ teaspoon salt
2 cups beef broth or stock	1 tablespoon minced parsley
2½ pounds top or bottom round steak, cut into small squares	¼ teaspoon marjoram
	Pinch of pepper
2 tablespoons vinegar	3 tablespoons butter
1 teaspoon salt	2 tablespoons ice water

Melt the butter, add onions and brown 10 minutes over low heat. Add 3 tablespoons of the flour, stirring until smooth. Slowly add the broth or stock, stirring until the mixture comes to the boiling point.

Place the meat in a heavy skillet and sprinkle with the vinegar. Add the prepared sauce, 1 teaspoon salt, the ¼ teaspoon of pepper, and mix well. Cover and cook over low heat 2 hours.

Sift the baking powder, remaining flour and ½ teaspoon salt in a bowl. Add parsley, marjoram and pepper, mix well. Cut in the butter, add the ice water and toss lightly until a ball of dough is formed.

Shape into small balls and drop into the kettle of stew, replace the lid, and continue to cook over low heat 35 minutes more.

Arrange the meat on a platter with the dumplings around it. Pour the liquid from the skillet over all and serve. Serves 6.

HASH

•

HAKKET KØD

2 pounds boneless beef	Boiling water
½ pound salt pork	Salt
2 pounds raw potatoes, peeled	Pepper
1 onion, chopped fine	

Chop or grind the uncooked beef and salt pork together with the raw potatoes. (If you use a meat grinder, choose a coarse grind.)

Put all ingredients in a large, heavy iron frying pan. Cover with boiling water. Let simmer very slowly for 2 hours on top of the stove. The water should be very nearly absorbed, but enough should remain to leave the hash juicy. Serves 6.

BOILED BEEF WITH HORSERADISH

•

OKSEKØD MED PEBERROD

1 onion	¼ teaspoon pepper
1 carrot	4½ pounds boiling beef
1 bay leaf	1½ tablespoons flour
1 teaspoon salt	

Slice onion and carrot. With other ingredients except the flour, place with the boiling beef in a kettle with enough water to cover. Let simmer 4 hours on top of the stove until tender.

Remove fat from top of broth when cooled. Add flour to fat to make a smooth paste. Add 1 cup of the broth from the pan and cook, stirring, until thick. This is to be served as gravy for plain boiled potatoes. Slice the boiled beef and serve with:

HORSERADISH SAUCE (PEBERRODSSAUCE)

1 cup sour cream	Salt
1 tablespoon fresh horseradish	Pepper
1 teaspoon vinegar	

Mix all ingredients together, chill, and serve cold over cooled beef. Serves 6.

For an unusual mixture of hot and cold, accompany the beef with:

POTATO DUMPLINGS (KARTOFFELBOLLER)

4 large potatoes	½ cup sifted flour
1 teaspoon salt	½ cup dry bread crumbs
2 eggs, lightly beaten	½ cup butter, melted

Cook potatoes in their jackets until done. Peel and put them through a ricer, or mash them, while hot. Salt and let cool. Add eggs and mix well. Add the flour and work with the fingers until dough is smooth. If too moist, add a little more flour to make it firm enough to form a dozen or more dumplings, depending on their size.

Drop the dumplings into a kettle of boiling water or into boiling stock if you have some left from the liquid the beef was boiled in. Cover and let cook 15 minutes.

Brown the bread crumbs in the melted butter. Pour the buttered crumbs over the dumplings.

SOUR-CREAM SWISS STEAK

•

SCHWEIZERSTEG MED SURFLØDE

1 teaspoon salt	2 tablespoons chopped onion
¼ teaspoon pepper	3 tablespoons tomato purée
4 tablespoons flour	½ cup water
2 pounds Swiss steak	1 cup sour cream
3 tablespoons butter	

Mix salt and pepper with the flour and pound it into the steak. Brown the steak in the butter. Add onion, tomato purée and water.

Cover and simmer 1 hour over low heat, or bake 1 hour at 250 degrees in a preheated oven.

Add sour cream and mix well. Let simmer ½ hour longer.

Serves 4.

TENDERLOIN OF BEEF IN SOUR CREAM

•

OKSEMØRBRAD I SURFLØDE

2 pounds sirloin or top round fillet	2 tablespoons minced onion
1 teaspoon salt	¼ cup chopped celery
½ teaspoon pepper	¼ cup diced carrots
3 tablespoons butter	2 tablespoons minced parsley
1 tablespoon grated lemon rind	2 tablespoons flour
	1 cup sour cream

Rub fillets with salt and pepper. Melt butter, and when hot, add the fillets. Sprinkle with lemon rind. Mix vegetables and parsley together and spread them in a layer over the beef.

Roast ½ hour in a preheated 350° oven. Reduce oven to 225° and continue roasting 2 hours more.

Remove meat to a hot serving platter. Blend flour with liquid in roaster. Cook slowly on top of the stove until well blended. Add the sour cream, stirring until the sauce is thick and smooth. Season if you wish and serve over the meat.

Serves 4.

SOUR-CREAM POT ROAST

•

OKSESTEG I SURFLØDE

3 tablespoons butter	4 pounds beef chuck, bottom round steak, or other boneless cut of your choice for pot roasting
1 large onion, sliced	
4 anchovies, chopped	2 cups sour cream

Melt butter in roasting pan. Brown the onion lightly with the anchovies. Remove from pan and set aside.

Brown the roast on all sides over high heat to seal in the juices. Return onions and anchovies to roaster, pour the sour cream over all, cover and cook over low heat on top of the stove for 3 hours, basting often.

Wonderful surrounded with cooked, drained noodles and covered with hot Béarnaise (*page 219*) or Horseradish Sauce (*page 216*). Serves 6 to 8.

LIVER WITH HERBS
·

LEVERPOSTEJ MED KRYDDERIER

5 tablespoons butter	*¼ cup mixed herbs (thyme, mar-*
1½ pounds calves' liver	*joram, basil, rosemary)*
6 slices bacon	*Salt*
1 onion, minced	*Pepper*
2 tablespoons lemon juice	*¾ cup dry white wine*

Heat 2½ tablespoons of the butter in a heavy iron skillet, and when it begins to froth, brown the slices of liver quickly on both sides. Remove and place on an oven-proof platter.

Grill the bacon and place on top of the liver.

Melt the rest of the butter in the skillet. Add the remaining ingredients. Let come to a boil. Pour over the liver and bacon. Place the platter in a preheated 300° oven for 20 minutes. Serve at once.

Serves 3 to 4.

STEAK IN CHAMPAGNE
·

OKSESTEG I CHAMPAGNE

½ cup flour	*2 tablespoons butter*
Salt	*1 small onion, thinly sliced*
Pepper	*Champagne*
2 pounds top or bottom round	
steak, 1 inch thick	

Mix flour, salt and pepper. Pound the flour mixture into the steak. Cut meat into 2-inch-square pieces.

Lightly brown the butter in a heavy skillet. Brown the steak in it on both sides. Add the onion and continue to brown for a few minutes more. Add enough champagne to cover the meat. Put a lid on the skillet and cook over low heat for 1½ hours.

Serves 5 to 6.

MINCEMEAT

•

MINCERKØD

1 pound beef suet, ground	1 pound mixed candied peel,
1½ pounds raisins	chopped fine
1½ pounds currants	Juice and grated rind of 1 lemon
1½ pounds brown sugar	½ pound almonds, blanched and
1½ pounds apples, peeled and	chopped
chopped fine	¼ teaspoon cinnamon
1¼ cups brandy	¼ teaspoon nutmeg

Mix all ingredients thoroughly and place in a covered crock for 6 weeks for aging in a cool spot. Will keep months in a tightly covered crock or in sterilized, sealed Mason jars.

Makes 2½ quarts.

FORCEMEAT OF BEEF

•

FARSERET OKSEKØD

1 pound lean beef, cut in small	2 pounds raisins
pieces	1 pound brown sugar
1 cup water	1 cup molasses
2 teaspoons salt	1 tablespoon cinnamon
½ pound beef suet	1 teaspoon nutmeg
3 pounds tart apples, peeled and	1 teaspoon allspice
chopped	1½ cups brandy

Put the beef in a kettle with water and salt and cook slowly 1 hour, or until almost tender. Let cool. Reserve broth.

Put beef and suet through a food grinder. Return to kettle with broth. Add the rest of the ingredients except the brandy and let come to the boiling point. Lower the heat and simmer 2 hours, stirring often. Remove from heat and stir in brandy.

Cool and store in a covered crock in a cool place, or pack in jars and process in water bath 40 minutes. Makes about 2½ quarts.

STUFFED CALVES' HEARTS

·

FYLDTE KALVEHJERTER

2 calves' hearts (½ pound each)*	Butter
Stuffing (see recipe below)	½ cup water

Wash the hearts, slit to the center cavities. Remove gristle and blood vessels. Fill the cavities with stuffing. Sew up the slits. Brown well in butter.

Place in a baking pan, add the water and cover. Bake in a preheated 300° oven 1½ hours or until tender. Make a gravy, using the juices in the baking pan as a starter, to serve over the hearts.

Serves 4.

* A beef heart may be prepared the same way but must be cooked 4 hours.

STUFFING (FYLD)

⅓ cup butter	1 quart bread crumbs
¾ cup chopped celery	½ teaspoon salt
3 tablespoons chopped parsley	¼ teaspoon white pepper
2 tablespoons minced onion	

Melt butter in a skillet, add celery, parsley and onion. Cook until onion bits are transparent. Add to the bread crumbs with the seasonings. Combine thoroughly with a few quick strokes of the mixing spoon. Fill cavities of the hearts.

ROAST PHEASANT

·

FASANSTEG

2 pheasants	Pepper
4 tablespoons butter	2 cups white wine
Salt	

Dress the pheasants. Split down the back into halves. Fill each half with stuffing if you wish (see recipes which follow).

Melt the butter in a pan on top of the stove. Brown the birds in the butter until a golden brown. Season with salt and pepper to taste. Add the wine and let them simmer in the wine mixture until tender — about 2 to 3 hours in a preheated 350° oven. Serves 6 to 8.

STUFFING (FYLD TIL SMÅFUGLE)

1 pound butter	Salt
¼ cup cream	Pepper
4 cups bread crumbs	3 egg yolks
1 tablespoon flour	

Heat butter and cream to the boiling point. Stir in the crumbs, flour, salt and pepper to taste. Mix until well blended.

Beat in the egg yolks and stuff the pheasants.

STUFFING FOR PHEASANTS AND OTHER SMALL GAME BIRDS (FYLD FOR SMÅFUGLE)

½ pound beef	¼ teaspoon white pepper
Cooked giblets from game birds	2 tablespoons cream
1 onion	3 tablespoons red wine
½ teaspoon celery salt	

Boil the beef. Grind it together with the giblets and onion. Add the spices, cream and wine and mix thoroughly. Stuff the birds.

ROAST WILD DUCKS

·

ANDESTEG

3 wild ducks	Melted butter
Gin	½ cup red wine + 2 tablespoons
3 crab apples, pared and cored	per bird
3 tablespoons butter	4–6 ounces cognac
3 small onions, stuck with	1 tablespoon flour
3 cloves each	Salt
6 sprigs parsley	

Draw ducks (get directions from the hunter or his wife about this if you're not an expert) and clean each inside and out. Wipe them with gin. Place in each cavity an apple, 1 tablespoon of butter, 1 small onion studded with cloves, and 2 sprigs of parsley. Sew or skewer the openings, and rub the outside of each fowl with butter and pepper.

Roast the ducks in a fairly hot oven (preheated to 450 degrees) for 20 to 26 minutes. Baste with melted butter and 2 tablespoons of wine per bird.

Lower the heat to 350 degrees and roast until the joints move easily, indicating that the ducks are cooked. Remove from oven, pour cognac over birds, ignite, and let flame die.

Remove to warm platter or serving tray and carve.

To the juices in the roasting pan add ½ cup red wine, 1 tablespoon butter, flour and salt to taste. Heat the sauce for a few moments, stirring constantly.

Serve with wild rice tossed with mushrooms and almonds. Prosaic old turnips are a wonderful side dish with wild ducks. Serves 6.

ROAST GOOSE WITH APPLE DRESSING

•

STEGT GÅS FYLDT MED ÆBLER

14-pound goose	*2 tablespoons water*
2 teaspoons salt	*2 cups dry bread crumbs*
½ teaspoon white pepper	*1 small onion, chopped*
2 teaspoons caraway seeds	*⅛ teaspoon white pepper*
4 cups peeled, diced apples	*1 cup white wine*

Eight hours before roasting wash goose inside and out and remove any remaining pinfeathers. Dry well. Combine salt, pepper and caraway seeds and rub well into the skin and interior cavities.

Place diced apples in a saucepan with the water and cook over low heat until very soft. Mash the apples and add the bread crumbs, onion and pepper. Mix well. Stuff the goose with the dressing and fasten the opening with skewers, or sew with a string. Roast the fowl in a shallow pan in a preheated 350° oven. Skim off fat as it accumulates. When goose has cooked for 3 hours, pour the wine over it carefully. Continue roasting, basting often, for 3 hours more, or until the skin is brown and crisp.

ROAST GOOSE

•

STEGT GÅS

12- to 14-pound goose

DRESSING #1

8 slices toast
½ cup soft butter
1 teaspoon salt
½ teaspoon white pepper
1 teaspoon celery seeds

¼ teaspoon nutmeg
1 cup slivered almonds
1 small onion, minced
½ cup white wine

Crush toast with a rolling pin to reduce it to crumbs. Mix well with the remaining ingredients. Stuff goose and roast in a preheated 325° oven on a rack in an uncovered pan. Allow 25 minutes per pound, and prick skin of bird often while roasting to release fat.

POTATO AND ALMOND DRESSING #1 (KARTOFFEL- OG MANDELFYLD)

3 cups mashed potatoes
1 cup dry bread crumbs
Salt to taste
Pepper to taste

½ teaspoon sage
6 tablespoons butter
1 cup slivered almonds

Combine all ingredients and mix well. Stuff goose and roast as in preceding recipe until done.

PRUNE DRESSING (SVESKEFYLD TIL GÅSESTEG)

1 onion
Salt

Pepper

Wash, clean and wipe the goose inside and out, and rub with onion; discard the onion. Season with salt and pepper. Stuff as follows:

1 pound prunes, cooked and pitted
2 pounds apples, peeled, cored
  and quartered

1 pint dry white wine
2 tablespoons flour

Mix prunes and apples well and stuff the cavities of the goose. Sew with string or use skewers. Fasten neck skin to back with skewers. Loop cord around legs and tighten slightly. Place breast side down on rack of a roasting pan. Roast uncovered at 325 degrees in a preheated oven for 1 hour. Remove accumulated fat. Turn fowl breast side up. Add the wine. Roast until tender (*see preceding recipe for Roast Goose*). Prick skin often.

Place fowl on a heated platter. Remove skewers or string. Remove some of the dressing before carving to prevent slipping.

Add the flour to the liquid in the roaster, stirring until smooth. If necessary, add a little water and a cup of wine to make gravy of the right consistency.

Potato and Almond Dressing #2 (Kartoffel- og Mandelfyld)

2 cups warm mashed potatoes
1 cup bread crumbs
¼ teaspoon white pepper
4 tablespoons melted butter

1 tablespoon minced onion
1 cup almonds, ground
½ teaspoon salt

Mix ingredients in order given. Stuff the bird, and roast as directed in preceding recipes for Roast Goose.

Veal Dressing

1 pound veal
Goose giblets
1 onion, chopped
2 apples, peeled, cored and
    chopped

2 egg yolks
1 cup cream
1 cup soft bread crumbs
Salt
Pepper

Grind veal and giblets together in a meat grinder. Add onion and apples. Mix well. Add beaten egg yolks, cream, crumbs and seasoning. Mix thoroughly, stuff goose, and roast according to directions given in preceding recipes.

French Dressing for Goose (Fransk Gåsefyld)

2 pounds chestnuts
1 teaspoon sugar
Goose liver, sautéed briefly

4 tablespoons soft butter
Salt to taste
Pepper to taste

Either in a covered pan or in a cloth bag cook the chestnuts in a preheated hot oven (500°) until they burst. Peel them and chop them fine. Cook in a small amount of water with the sugar.

When tender add minced liver, butter, salt and pepper. Mix well and stuff the goose to be roasted as directed in foregoing recipes.

POTATO DRESSING (KARTOFFELMOS)

3½ pounds potatoes, peeled	2 eggs
⅔ cup celery, chopped	1 tablespoon poultry seasoning
2 small onions	1 teaspoon salt
½ cup butter	¼ teaspoon white pepper
4 cups dry bread crumbs	

Cook the potatoes until tender. Drain.

Mince or chop the celery and onions and brown in the butter. Remove from heat.

Put potatoes through a ricer (or an electric blender 1 cup at a time) and then into a bowl. Add the bread crumbs and mix well.

Beat the eggs until frothy. Add to the mixture with the seasonings. Spoon the stuffing into the cavity of the goose and skewer well.

This stuffing may be used for any fowl, and for meats as well, but if you use it for goose, try the following sauce to be served with it:

SAUCE

1 cup port wine	½ cup prepared brown mustard
Juice and grated rind of 2 lemons	Pinch of white pepper

Mix all ingredients. Heat in the top of a double boiler over hot water and serve at once.

STEWED CHICKEN

•

STEGT HØNE

1 stewing hen	1 medium-sized bunch parsley
½ pound soft butter	

Wash and dry chicken inside and out.

Chop parsley and cream it together with ¼ pound of the butter.

Stuff hen with this mixture.

Melt the remaining butter in a Dutch oven or a deep, heavy casserole. Sauté chicken, uncovered, until golden brown. Cover and simmer 3 hours, or until tender.

Remove chicken from pan. Add a little water to the drippings. Scrape the pan with a wooden spoon and stir to mix the thickened juices with the water. Serve this clear sauce over the chicken. Serves 4 to 5, depending on size of chicken.

CHICKEN WITH RICE

•

HØNE I RIS

4- to 5-pound stewing chicken   *6 cups salted water*

Cut chicken into serving pieces. Place in a deep, heavy skillet, add the salted water and simmer until about half done (approximately 1¼ hours). Put chicken in a large buttered casserole. Blend together the following ingredients:

2 cups stock from skillet	*¼ teaspoon nutmeg*
¼ cup flour	*⅛ teaspoon white pepper*
½ teaspoon salt	

Cook over a very slow fire until the consistency of medium cream sauce. Pour over chicken.

PREPARING THE RICE

1 cup rice	*⅔ cup chopped almonds*
1½ cups milk	*3 eggs, beaten*
½ teaspoon salt	*2 tablespoons dry bread crumbs,*
1 teaspoon sugar	*browned in*
1 teaspoon paprika	*2 tablespoons butter*
2½ tablespoons butter	*1 tablespoon minced parsley*

Put the rice in a heavy saucepan which can be covered. Add the milk and salt and let come to a boil. Turn the heat very low, cover and cook for 30 minutes, or until grains are nearly dry. Lift the lid from the pan as little as possible, and if you must stir, do it once only, gently, with a fork, to keep the rice flaky.

Mix sugar, paprika, butter and nuts and add to the rice slowly.

When rice has cooled, mix with the beaten eggs, saving 1½ tablespoons of the beaten eggs for the crust.

Place the rice mixture as a mound over the chicken. Cut a gash in the crust of rice to allow the steam to escape. Bake in a preheated moderate oven (350°) until the chicken is tender (about 1 hour). Brush with the reserved beaten egg mixture. Spread the buttered crumbs over the surface. Sprinkle with additional paprika and brown at 400 degrees. Sprinkle minced parsley over crust after removing casserole from oven.

Serves 9 to 10.

If you want gravy, remove a small quantity of liquid from the casserole *before* the rice is placed over the chicken, because the rice will absorb most of the liquid.

CHICKEN FRICASSEE

•

HØNSEFRIKASSÉ

2 3½- to 4-pound young chickens, cut into serving pieces	2 cups white wine
½ pound butter	1 pound mushrooms, sliced
12 tiny white onions	3 tablespoons flour
½ large stalk celery, chopped	4 egg yolks, beaten
Salt	½ cup light cream
Pepper	Minced parsley
	Chives

Place chicken pieces in roasting pan with ¼ pound of the butter, onions, celery and seasonings. Simmer over low heat on top of stove for 25 minutes. (If necessary, light two adjacent burners and place pan across both.) Add wine and mushrooms. Cover and let cook for 20 minutes more, or until chicken is tender.

Melt the remaining ¼ pound butter in another pan and stir in the flour, a little at a time. Blend until smooth, but do not allow to brown.

Place the chicken with onions, celery and mushrooms on a warm serving platter.

Add the broth to butter and flour a little at a time, mixing thoroughly. Stir constantly until it begins to boil, reduce heat to simmering point and add the beaten egg yolks mixed with the cream. Allow sauce to cook for a moment or two, stirring frequently. Remove from heat and add parsley and chives. Serves 7 to 8.

ROAST CHICKEN IN BRANDY
•
STEGT HØNE MED COGNAC

1 large roasting chicken, cut into
  serving pieces
Salt
White pepper

3 cups dry white wine
8 tablespoons butter
1 cup brandy

Salt and pepper chicken. Marinate in the dry white wine overnight.

Sauté the chicken pieces in the butter until golden brown. Place in a roaster with the butter and the marinade.

Cover and bake 50 minutes in a preheated 375° oven. Add more wine if necessary while baking.

Lower heat to 350 degrees. Roast until tender (length of time will depend on the age and condition of the chicken).

When ready to serve, place the cut-up fowl on a warm platter and pour the brandy over it. Ignite and bring to the table flaming. Use any leftover juices in the pan to quench the flames after your guests have properly admired the platter.

Allow at least ½ pound of fowl per person.

ROAST CHICKEN
•
STEGT KYLLING

5- to 6-pound roasting chicken
¼ pound butter
3 cups white wine
1½ cups cream

Salt
White pepper
½ cup blanched, slivered
  almonds

Cut chicken into serving pieces. Bake in butter in a shallow baking pan in a moderate oven (preheated to 375 degrees) until a golden brown. Turn off oven. Add wine and let marinate 1 hour.

Add the cream and season to taste. Heat oven to 300 degrees and continue cooking for another 30 minutes. Add almonds. Cook for another half hour, or until chicken is tender.

Allow at least ½ pound of fowl per person.

CHAMPAGNE CHICKEN

•

STEGT KYLLING MED CHAMPAGNE

6-pound roasting chicken	6 tablespoons butter
Salt	1 cup champagne
Pepper	1 cup cream
Stuffing of your choice	

Clean and wash the chicken inside and out. Mix salt and pepper to taste and rub over fowl. Stuff with your favorite dressing.

Melt the butter in a roasting pan and brown the fowl on top of the stove. Add champagne, cover and roast in a preheated 350° oven 20 minutes per pound, or until tender.

Remove chicken from roaster, add the cream to juices in the pan and cook, stirring frequently, for 10 minutes. Season with additional salt and pepper if necessary.

Carve the fowl and serve the sauce over individual portions. Serves 6 to 8.

SAUCES FOR MEATS AND FOWL

BRANDY SAUCE FOR A LARGE HAM

•

COGNACSAUCE TIL KOLD SKINKE

1 pint port wine	1 tablespoon cornstarch
1 pint ham stock	2 tablespoons cold water
1 cup thick tomato juice	½ pint brandy

Let wine, stock and tomato juice come to a boil. Add the cornstarch moistened with cold water and cook, stirring frequently, until smooth, thick and at the boiling point.

Add the brandy just before removing from heat.

CARDAMOM SAUCE

•

KARDEMOMMESAUCE

½ cup water
½ cup honey
¼ teaspoon ground cardamom

6 large mint leaves
¼ teaspoon salt
½ cup port wine

Blend the water and the honey with the cardamom seeds and place over very low heat. Simmer 5 minutes, stirring constantly.

Chop the mint leaves and add with the salt to the mixture. Simmer 2 minutes more. Remove from heat and let cool to room temperature.

When ready to serve, add the wine and mix well. If the sauce is too thick, add a little more wine and mix again.

Wonderful accompaniment for beef roasts or for barbecued beef.

BROWN SAUCE

•

BRUN SAUCE

4 tablespoons butter
4 tablespoons flour
3 cups meat stock or bouillon
3 tablespoons white vinegar

Salt
Pepper
3 tablespoons sherry

Melt butter over low heat. Stir in flour until smooth and lightly browned.

Add ½ of the meat stock, a little at a time, stirring well after each addition. Add rest of the stock with vinegar and boil slowly, stirring constantly. Add pepper and salt. Add sherry just before removing from heat.

Serve hot with beef.

BUTTERMILK COATING FOR CHICKEN

•

KÆRNEMÆLKSSAUCE TIL HØNE

¾ cup buttermilk
1 cup flour

½ teaspoon allspice
½ teasoon salt

Combine all ingredients and mix thoroughly.

Cut the chicken into serving pieces and dip each piece in the batter. Roll in crushed corn flakes or bread crumbs, and fry as you wish.

MUSHROOM SAUCE

·

CHAMPIGNONSSAUCE

¼ pound mushrooms, chopped
4 tablespoons butter
4 tablespoons flour
1½ cups milk

Salt
1 egg yolk, beaten
3 tablespoons sherry

Sauté mushrooms and stems in 2 tablespoons butter. When browned, remove from pan. Put the remaining butter into the pan. Lower heat and add the flour, stirring well to keep mixture from burning.

Add the milk gradually and mix well, cooking until smooth and thick. Just before removing from heat add salt, egg yolk and the mushrooms. Mix well and heat for 1 minute more over low heat.

Add the sherry just before removing from stove.

Serve with beef or chicken, or to add taste appeal to leftovers.

· 12 ·

SALADS

ANCHOVY SALAD

·

ANSJOSSALAT

18 anchovy fillets
8 pitted olives
2 sweet pickles
4 tablespoons smoked salmon
2 tablespoons olive oil
2 tablespoons vinegar

1 teaspoon prepared mustard
¼ teaspoon white pepper
½ cup stock
½ lemon
1 tomato

Rinse and wipe the anchovies and mash them. Cut olives in half. Slice the pickles thin. Cut salmon in thin strips.

Place the anchovy mash in the center of a serving platter and surround with olives, pickles and salmon.

Make a marinade of the oil, vinegar, mustard, pepper and stock and mix well. Pour over salad and garnish with thin slices of the lemon and tomato.

Serves 6.

HERRING SALAD #1

•

SILDESALAT

3 salt herrings
3 cups boiled, diced potatoes
  (do not overboil potatoes)
2½ cups cooked veal, cut into
  small pieces
1 large, firm dill pickle, cut into
  bite-size pieces
2½ cups tart apples, diced
2½ cups cooked, diced beets
Salt

Pepper
2 tablespoons minced onion
1 cup diced carrots, cooked
  until just tender
6 tablespoons vinegar
1 tablespoon sugar
1 cup whipping cream
2 hard-boiled eggs, sliced
1 hard-boiled egg, minced fine
Parsley

Wash herring. Cover with cold water and soak overnight. Skin and bone, using only the fillets. Dry and cut into small chunks. Prepare the salad 4 hours before serving.

Mix potatoes, fish, veal, pickle, apples and beets (reserve about ¼ of the beets for garnishing). Add salt and pepper to taste. Add onion and carrots and toss with a fork until lightly mixed.

Mix vinegar and sugar and pour over the salad.

Whip ½ of the cream and fold into the salad, mixing gently. Whip the rest of the cream and top the salad with it just as you are ready to serve.

Pack into a salad bowl. Chill 4 hours. Unmold on a chilled serving platter. Slice the 2 hard-boiled eggs over it. Garnish with remaining beets. Spread over the beets the minced hard-boiled egg. Decorate with sprigs of parsley.

Wonderful dish for a smørgåsbord. Serves 8.

HERRING SALAD #2

•

SILDESALAT

1 salt herring
3 cold boiled potatoes, diced
3 apples, pared and diced
Chopped parsley
2 tablespoons white vinegar

4 tablespoons olive oil
1 tablespoon sugar
1 teaspoon celery seeds
Pepper
Onion rings

Wash, clean and cut herring into thin strips. Mix with the potatoes and apples in a salad bowl. Blend in parsley.

Mix the vinegar, oil, sugar, celery seeds and pepper and pour over the salad.

Garnish with very thin onion rings. Chill until time to serve.

Serves 6.

LOBSTER AND VEGETABLE SALAD

•

HUMMER- OG GRØNTSAGSSALAT

6 carrots, cooked and diced

1 cauliflower, cooked and cut into
   chunks

2 cups lima beans, cooked

1 pound fresh peas, cooked

1 pound string beans, cooked

1 cup celery, diced

1 cup radishes, diced

1 cup cucumbers, peeled, seeded
   and diced

6 medium-sized firm tomatoes,
   peeled and seeded

3 hard-boiled eggs

½ teaspoon dry mustard

1 tablespoon white vinegar

1 tablespoon salt

¼ teaspoon white pepper

2 tablespoons olive oil

2 tablespoons plain gelatin

8 tablespoons hot water

½ cup cream

Prepare vegetables as directed. Mix together in a very large bowl and let chill until very cold.

Mince the hard-boiled eggs fine in a second bowl. Add the mustard, vinegar, salt and pepper. Beat well and add the olive oil.

Dissolve the gelatin in the hot water, let cool. Slowly add to the vinegar and oil mixture, beating well. Add the cream and blend well. Fold in the vegetables in the larger bowl. Chill until set. Unmold on a large serving platter. Top and garnish as follows:

4 1½-pound boiled lobsters
   chilled

1 pound cooked salmon

½ pound soft butter

3½ tablespoons cream, whipped

Salt

White pepper

1 pound boiled shrimp, chilled

Parsley

Radishes

Stuffed green olives

Remove meat from body, tail and claws of lobsters. Set aside legs for use at another time. Save the head and tail shells.

Skin, bone and put the cooked salmon through a meat grinder. Add butter and whipped cream and season with salt and pepper to taste. Cream these ingredients together thoroughly. Fill the empty lobster-tail shells with the salmon mixture and set aside for the moment.

This recipe must not only taste superb but look like a work of art. Your aim is to make it appear that the lobsters are swimming over the molded vegetables. To achieve this, turn the filled lobster tails, filled side down, over the mold. Where the tails would normally join the bodies of the lobsters, pile lobster meat to simulate as best you can the shape of the mid-section of a lobster. Add the empty head shells, empty side down, joining the lobster-meat bodies.

Peel the shrimp, place around the platter with sprigs of parsley, radishes and stuffed olives.

Serves a battalion.

HERRING SALAD #3

•

SILDESALAT

10 salt herrings	½ cup claret
Potatoes	2 tablespoons olive oil
Beets	2 tablespoons vinegar
Apples	Salt
Medium-sized sweet pickles	Pepper
2 tablespoons vinegar	Hard-boiled eggs
2 tablespoons olive oil	

Soak herrings in cold water 6 hours. Drain, and dry the fish well. Cut into bite-sized pieces.

Weigh the fish. Match their weight with a combination of potatoes, beets, apples and pickles, divided roughly into 4 equal portions. Boil potatoes and beets until done (reserving beet liquid). Peel and core apples. Cut into small cubes, along with vegetables and pickles. Place in a large salad bowl. Add herring bits.

Mix the first 2 tablespoons of vinegar and 2 tablespoons of olive oil, the claret and ½ the juice the beets were cooked in. (If you like sweet-sour salad dressings, put a little sugar in this liquid to taste.) Pour over salad and chill 12 hours.

Just before serving, mix the last 2 tablespoons of vinegar and 2 tablespoons of olive oil in the top of a double boiler over hot water and cook until somewhat thickened. Add salt and pepper to taste. Cool and pour over the salad. Garnish with hard-boiled eggs and parsley.

Serves 8 to 10.

SALMON AND VEGETABLE SALAD

•

LAKS- OG GRØNTSAGSSALAT

2 tomatoes	½ teaspoon salt
1 cucumber	¼ teaspoon white pepper
1 cup fresh peas, cooked	½ cup mayonnaise
2 teaspoons lemon juice	1½ cups cooked or canned salmon
1 teaspoon sugar	Parsley

Chill all ingredients.

Peel tomatoes and cut into wedges. Pare and cut cucumbers and mix with drained peas.

Mix lemon juice, sugar, salt and pepper and combine with the vegetables. Fold in mayonnaise and salmon. Put in a chilled salad bowl and serve on lettuce leaves. Top with a few sprigs of parsley.

Serves 4.

SALMON SALAD

•

LAKSSALAT

2 cups salmon, cooked	1 teaspoon lemon juice
1 cup sliced mushrooms	2 cups diced celery
2 tablespoons butter	Lettuce

Poach salmon in water to cover. Drain and save stock.

Sauté mushrooms in butter and add lemon juice just before removing from heat. Drain and add cooking liquid to fish stock.

Mix fish, mushrooms and celery together. Chill while you prepare the dressing.

DRESSING

4 tablespoons butter	3 egg yolks, beaten
4 tablespoons flour	2 tablespoons white wine
1 cup fish and mushroom stock	Salt
½ teaspoon sugar	White pepper
1 tablespoon white vinegar	Parsley

Melt the butter over low heat. Stir in the flour a little at a time until smooth. Add the stock gradually, stirring after each addition. Remove from heat and let cool somewhat. Add sugar and vinegar and mix well. Add egg yolks and stir until the mixture is smooth. Add the white wine, salt, pepper and a little minced parsley, mixing well.

Fold dressing gently into the chilled fish mixture.

Serve on a bed of lettuce leaves. Serves 6.

MACARONI SALAD
·
MAKARONISALAT

1 cup macaroni	½ teaspoon salt

Bring to a boil enough water to cover amply the macaroni. Add salt. Boil rapidly for 10 minutes. Reduce heat and boil slowly for 20 minutes more, adding more boiling water if necessary. Drain. Rinse with cold water. Chill.

Mix with following dressing:

DRESSING

1 cup whipping cream	1 teaspoon white vinegar
Salt	2 teaspoons fresh horseradish
1 teaspoon sugar	

Whip the cream stiff. Add salt to taste, sugar and vinegar, a few drops at a time. Mix well and add the horseradish. Fold into the chilled macaroni.

Serves 6.

BEAN SALAD

·

SALAT AF GRØNNE BØNNER

4 pounds green or wax beans
½ pound bacon, cut fine
1 onion, chopped fine
1 cup olive oil
1 teaspoon salt

1 tablespoon sugar
½ teaspoon white pepper
1 cup white vinegar
2 tablespoons hot water

Cook and drain the beans.

Fry the cut bacon until crisp and put in a bowl. Add the onion and oil and mix lightly. Add salt, sugar and pepper and toss lightly. Add vinegar and water.

Fold in the cooked beans until well coated. Chill in refrigerator for 1 hour before serving.

Serves 12 to 14.

NON-VEGETARIAN VEGETABLE SALAD

·

GRØNTSAGSSALAT

1 cup wax beans, cooked
1 cup green beans, cooked
1 small cauliflower, cooked
1 cup carrots, diced and cooked
3 tart apples, diced
3 dill pickles, cut into small pieces
1 pound cold boiled potatoes,
    diced
4 cups cooked meat, diced (use
    any combination of leftovers)

½ cup salad oil
1 cup white vinegar
¼ teaspoon dry mustard
½ cup radishes, diced
½ cup onions, sliced thin
1 cup endive, shredded
Salt
Pepper
Parsley, chopped
Lettuce

Combine all ingredients, being careful not to mash.

Chill and serve on lettuce leaves with additional dressing of your choice.

Serves 12.

RED CABBAGE SALAD

·

RØDKÅLSSALAT

1 head red cabbage	*1 lemon*
1 large tart apple	*Salt*
1 celery heart	*1 tablespoon sugar*
1 cup whipping cream	

Wash and drain cabbage well. Chop it, not too fine.

Peel the apple and dice it. Cut celery into short lengths.

Whip the cream stiff. Add lemon juice, salt and sugar. Mix all ingredients together and chill until serving time.

Serves 5 to 6.

COLESLAW

·

KÅLSALAT

3 cups cabbage, shredded or chopped	*½ teaspoon salt*
	¼ teaspoon white pepper
½ green pepper, chopped	*1 teaspoon celery seed*
½ red pepper, chopped	*1 tablespoon sugar*
½ teaspoon celery salt	*3 tablespoons white vinegar*
½ teaspoon onion salt	*6 tablespoons olive oil*

Place vegetables together in a salad bowl.

Combine all the seasonings and spices and add to the vegetables, tossing well. Add sugar, vinegar and oil and mix well.

Cover bowl and chill 1 hour.

Serves 6.

POTATO SALAD

·

KARTOFFELSALAT

Remember how good potato salad used to taste at Sunday-school picnics? Here's a recipe to turn nostalgic reminiscence into actuality.

8 slices of bacon
3 tablespoons flour
3 teaspoons chopped onion
⅔ cup vinegar
⅔ cup water
½ cup sugar

1 teaspoon salt
1 teaspoon dry mustard
Pinch of white pepper
4 pounds potatoes, boiled and
 chilled
½ cup minced parsley

Fry the bacon until crisp. Remove from pan, drain and crumble.

Add the flour and onion to the fat in the pan. Stir in the vinegar, water, sugar, salt and spices. Cook until medium thick. Cool.

Peel and dice potatoes. Sprinkle parsley and crumbled bacon over potatoes. Pour cooled dressing over all and mix gently to avoid mashing the potatoes.

Serves 8 to 10.

SOUR-CREAM POTATO SALAD

•

KARTOFFELSALAT MED SURFLØDE

8 cups cooked, diced potatoes
1 cup diced cucumber
1 tablespoon minced onion
¾ teaspoon celery seeds
1 teaspoon salt
½ teaspoon white pepper

3 hard-boiled eggs
1½ cups sour cream
1 cup mayonnaise
¼ cup vinegar
1 teaspoon dry mustard

Combine the potatoes, cucumber, onion, celery seeds, salt and pepper. Toss lightly.

Remove the egg yolks from the whites. Dice the whites and add to potato mixture.

Mash the yolks and combine with the sour cream, mayonnaise, vinegar and mustard. Add to the potato mix and toss very lightly.

Let stand 15 minutes before serving.

Garnish with chives or parsley or paprika or strips of pimiento — indeed, with anything of distinctive flavor and bright color.

SALAD DRESSINGS

SOUR-CREAM DRESSING

•

SURFLØDESAUCE

1 cup thick sour cream
1⅓ tablespoons sugar
1 tablespoon vinegar

1 tablespoon grated onion
2 teaspoons horseradish
1 teaspoon salt

Blend ingredients well. Chill thoroughly.
Wonderful over a mixture of several kinds of lettuce. Toss well.

OIL-AND-VINEGAR DRESSING

•

EDDIKE- OG OLIEMARINADE

2 tablespoons vinegar or lemon
   juice
5 tablespoons corn oil
1 tablespoon sugar

1 tablespoon tarragon
¼ teaspoon white pepper
½ teaspoon minced parsley

Mix ingredients well. Chill.
Delicious for potato, apple or fish salads.

MAYONNAISE DRESSING

•

MAYONNAISE

2 egg yolks
1½ teaspoons cold water
¼ teaspoon salt
1½ teaspoons vinegar

1 cup olive oil
¼ teaspoon paprika
Juice of 1 lemon

Beat the egg yolks with the water, salt and vinegar for about 30 seconds.

Beat the oil. Add the egg-yolk mixture to oil and beat at high speed with an electric mixer or in a blender for about 2 minutes, or until thick.

Add the other ingredients and beat until well blended.

VINEGAR DRESSING

·

EDDIKESAUCE

1 cup olive oil
1 cup vinegar
1 teaspoon salt

½ hard-boiled egg, minced
Parsley, chopped fine

Mix ingredients. Chill.
Stir or shake well before adding to salad.

POTATO SALAD DRESSING #1

·

SAUCE TIL KARTOFFELSALAT

3 tablespoons butter
2 tablespoons flour
½ teaspoon salt
1 teaspoon dry mustard
1 tablespoon sugar

½ teaspoon paprika
1½ cups milk
2 egg yolks, beaten
⅓ cup white vinegar

Melt butter.

Mix flour, salt, mustard, sugar and paprika, and blend with the butter. Add 1 cup of the milk.

Cook until medium thick, stirring frequently. Cool to lukewarm.

Mix remaining ½ cup milk with egg yolks. Stir into sauce. Add the vinegar and cook over low heat until thickened. Chill.

Good also as a sauce for fish, meat or cooked green vegetables.

POTATO SALAD DRESSING #2

·

SAUCE TIL KARTOFFELSALAT

½ teaspoon salt
¼ teaspoon white pepper
5 tablespoons olive oil
2 tablespoons white vinegar

2 tablespoons white wine
1 teaspoon fresh, grated
    horseradish
1 teaspoon sugar

Mix ingredients in order given. Chill.

LEMON DRESSING

•

CITRONSAUCE

1 cup olive oil

⅔ cup lemon juice

⅓ cup sugar

1 teaspoon salt

2 scant teaspoons paprika

1 teaspoon grated onion

Combine all ingredients in a jar. Shake until well blended. Chill. Shake well again before using.

Wonderful for fish salads.

DANISH DRESSING FOR COLESLAW

•

SAUCE TIL KÅLSALAT

1½ tablespoons butter

1 tablespoon flour

1 tablespoon sugar

½ teaspoon dry mustard

½ teaspoon salt

2 tablespoons white vinegar

2 tablespoons water, mixed with

1 egg, beaten

Combine all ingredients and cook over low heat until mixture begins to thicken slightly. Cool. If too thick, add enough cream to thin to desired consistency.

CINNAMON SAUCE

•

KANELSAUCE

3 egg yolks

2½ tablespoons sugar

½ tablespoon cornstarch

1 cup water

Pinch of salt

Juice of 1 lemon

¾ cup whipping cream

1½ teaspoons cinnamon

Beat egg yolks and sugar together.

Mix the cornstarch with the water and cook until thick and clear. Remove from heat. Stir into the egg mixture. Return to heat and cook, stirring, until thickened.

Add the salt and the lemon juice.

Whip the cream. Fold into the mixture with the cinnamon just before serving.

Delicious on fruit salad but also on such diverse dishes as puddings and pancakes.

· 13 ·

VEGETABLES

A DANISH COOK has many strings on her vegetable bow. She bakes them in "top hat" soufflés, puts them between light, fluffy pastry crusts, uses them as delicious sauces, or rolls them into envelopes with meats.

One reason why vegetables in Denmark are mouth-watering is that methods of cooking usually reserved for rich and rare ingredients are used there on the commonest varieties. This sophistication derives from the influence of the French during the early centuries when French chefs ruled Danish palace kitchens. Before long, recipes were being passed from palace maids to cottage mistresses. Vegetable cookery to this day in Denmark is a combination of court cooking and simple, garden-fresh fare supplied from rich and fertile farm lands.

To preserve the nutrients and fresh taste of their vegetables, the Danes use the basic quick-cooking methods which good cooks use all over the world. Their main method is the simplest possible — steaming in a perforated steamer set above a pot of boiling water. Good Danish cooks serve their vegetables as soon as they're done and never let them stand after turning off the heat.

The Danes have a variety of ways to make vegetables more interesting. If cauliflower is to be boiled, it is tied up whole in a net to preserve its whole-headed attractiveness. To turn it into a gourmet's dream, it is served with a sauce seasoned with minced ham, shrimps or tomatoes. Leeks, Danish style, make an unusual dish for those who are accustomed to using this vegetable chiefly for soups. The Danish cook first parboils leeks, then bakes and serves them with Hollandaise sauce.

Cinnamon enhances the sweetness of a vegetable like tender, young acorn squash. Nutmeg gives spinach an aromatic zip. There are few vegetables that do not get a sprinkling of caraway seeds, though they give their best and most special savor to potatoes. Danish cooks prefer fresh herbs, and for this reason they grow them in every available spot to be sure to have leaves handy to crush between two layers of cloth to put into the pot just before the vegetable has finished cooking.

The flair the Danes have for elevating the most familiar of vegetables to gourmet status is easily acquired if you flex your imagination.

VEGETABLE SOUFFLÉ

•

GRØNTSAGSFROMAGE

½ cup butter
⅔ cup flour
1 cup scalding hot milk
1 cup hot chicken broth
2 tablespoons grated Swiss or
    Parmesan cheese
5 egg yolks

Salt to taste
Sugar to taste
6 egg whites
2 tablespoons bread crumbs
¾ cup cooked, chopped
    vegetables

Spinach, carrots, cauliflower, broccoli, asparagus, mushrooms, cut green beans, peas, or lima beans are good bases for this soufflé.

Melt butter in a saucepan over low heat, and stir in the flour. Add hot milk and hot broth and stir until mixture thickens. Stir in grated cheese until melted. Remove mixture from heat and cool.

Add egg yolks, stirring in one at a time. Add salt and sugar.

Beat egg whites, not too stiffly, and fold into mixture.

Butter well a 2½-quart baking dish. Sprinkle bread crumbs so that they will adhere to bottom and sides of dish. Fill alternately with batter and vegetables, making sure that the top and bottom layers are of the soufflé batter.

Bake in a preheated 350° oven for 50 minutes.

Serve at once. Serves 6 to 8.

GREEN BEANS WITH MUSHROOMS

•

GRØNNE BØNNER

1 pound string beans	2 tablespoons flour
½ teaspoon sugar	2 cups light cream
½ teaspoon salt	Juice of 1 lemon
¼ teaspoon white pepper	Bread crumbs
½ pound mushrooms, sliced	¼ pound almonds, chopped
2 tablespoons butter	

Wash, break off ends and boil beans until tender. (Steam, if you prefer.) Season with sugar, salt and pepper while beans are cooking. Drain.

In a saucepan sauté the mushrooms until tender in the butter. When cooled somewhat add the flour and the cream. Cook over low heat, stirring often, until thickened. Remove from stove and add lemon juice.

Just before serving combine the beans with the mushroom sauce. Turn into a baking dish, sprinkle top with bread crumbs and almonds. Reheat and serve at once. Serves 6.

BUTTERED GINGER BEETS

•

RØDBEDER I INGEFÆRSAUCE

2½ cups cut-up beets	¼ cup vinegar
Pinch of salt	¼ cup water
1 teaspoon grated ginger root	3 tablespoons butter
½ cup sugar	Minced parsley
1½ teaspoons cornstarch	

Wash beets, boil in salted water and peel. Cut in bite-sized cubes. In a double boiler over hot water mix ginger, sugar, cornstarch, vinegar and water. Stir until smooth. Cook slowly to thicken, stirring frequently. Add cooked beets and butter.

Garnish with parsley and serve hot. Serves 6.

CABBAGE WITH WINE

•

HVIDKÅL I VINSAUCE

1 head cabbage	2 tablespoons brown sugar
1 onion	1½ teaspoons celery seeds
1 apple	½ teaspoon salt
2 tablespoons butter	1 cup dry white wine

Shred the cabbage fine. Grate onion and apple into the cabbage.

Cook in butter melted over low heat until vegetables are limp, shaking the pan now and then to prevent scorching.

Add the remaining ingredients. Mix well and let come to a boil. Reduce heat as low as possible and let simmer 15 minutes.

Serves 6.

HOT SLAW

•

VARM KÅLSTUVNING

1 head cabbage	2 teaspoons sugar
1 egg	¼ teaspoon white pepper
2 tablespoons flour	2 tablespoons butter
½ teaspoon salt	¾ cup milk
1 teaspoon dry mustard	¼ cup vinegar

Shred the cabbage.

Beat the egg in a bowl. Mix in the flour, salt, mustard, sugar and pepper until smooth.

Melt the butter in the top of a double boiler over boiling water and stir in egg mixture and milk. Slowly add the vinegar, beating constantly, and cook 5 minutes, or until sauce is thick.

Cook cabbage in salted water to cover for 6 minutes. Do not overcook. Cabbage should be crisp. Drain well.

Mix cabbage and sauce and serve hot. Serves 6.

RED CABBAGE

•

RØDKÅL

3 pounds red cabbage
¼ cup butter
4 tablespoons vinegar
½ cup water

2 tablespoons currant jelly
1 tablespoon sugar
1 teaspoon salt

Wash cabbage. Shred or quarter the head. Drain well.

Melt the butter in a saucepan. Put cabbage into melted butter and toss it around with a wooden spoon to coat it evenly. Add vinegar and water. Cover and cook over low heat until barely tender — 10 minutes if shredded; 15, if quartered.

Mix jelly, sugar and salt well and stir into the cabbage. Cook 5 minutes more to blend flavors thoroughly.

Prepared the day before and reheated just before it is served, this intriguing dish's flavor is improved. Serves 6.

CABBAGE ROLLS WITH GROUND MEAT

•

KÅLROULETTER

1 small onion, chopped fine
1 tablespoon butter
4-pound head of cabbage
¾ pound ground beef

¾ pound ground pork
1 cup cooked rice
Salt
Pepper

Sauté the onion in the butter.

Put cabbage whole in boiling water and let boil 10 minutes. Remove from water. Reserve liquid. Separate the leaves carefully.

Mix well the meats, rice, onion, salt and pepper to taste. Put 1 heaping tablespoon of the meat mixture on a bed of 2 or 3 leaves. Wrap and tie each roll well. Cook slowly in the water cabbage was cooked in.

When tender, coat the cabbage rolls in browned butter and serve hot. Serves 4 or 5.

GRANDMOTHER'S SWEET-SOUR CABBAGE

·

MORMORS HVIDKÅL

1 small onion, sliced	3 tablespoons white vinegar
3 tablespoons butter	1 tablespoon brown sugar
1 cup water	¼ teaspoon allspice
4 cups red cabbage, shredded	2 whole cloves
2 tart apples, cored, peeled and diced	

Brown onion lightly in the butter. Add remaining ingredients in order given.

Cook until cabbage is almost tender.

Serve immediately with a Butter Sauce (*page 267*). Serves 6.

BAKED CARROT RING

·

INDBAGTE GULERØDDER

2 tablespoons butter	1 teaspoon salt
2 tablespoons flour	¼ teaspoon pepper
½ cup light cream	3 eggs, separated
1 tablespoon grated Parmesan cheese	2 tablespoons bread crumbs
1 cup grated carrots	2 cups creamed peas or mushrooms

Melt butter in large saucepan. Add flour gradually and stir until smooth. Stir in alternately, a little at a time, the cream and the cheese. Add carrots, salt and pepper. Stir in the beaten egg yolks.

Beat egg whites until stiff and fold in.

Bake in a buttered ring mold coated with bread crumbs. Fill not more than ⅔ full. Set in a pan with enough hot water in it to come halfway up on the mold. Bake for about 50 minutes, or until firm, in a preheated 350° oven.

Unmold on a platter. Fill center of ring with tiny creamed peas or mushrooms.

Serves 6.

CAULIFLOWER WITH CHEESE

•

BLOMKÅLSGRATIN MED OST

1 large cauliflower
4 tablespoons butter
2 tablespoons flour
1½ cups milk
1 egg yolk, beaten

½ teaspoon sugar
2 tablespoons grated cheddar
 cheese
1 teaspoon salt
2 small rusks

Wash the cauliflower. Tie it tightly in a cheesecloth bag and cook until tender in boiling salted water. Drain and put in a baking dish.

Melt the butter, stir in the flour and blend well. Stir in the milk slowly, and when the sauce begins to thicken, stir in the egg yolk, sugar, cheese and salt. Cook and stir a few minutes longer to let the sauce get quite thick, then remove from the fire. Let it rest a few minutes.

Crush the rusks.

Pour the sauce over the cauliflower and sprinkle the top with the crushed rusk crumbs.

Place in a preheated 400° oven 15 minutes to brown.

Serves 6.

STUFFED EGGPLANT

•

FYLDTE GRATINEREDE AUBERGINER

2 large eggplants
2 onions
4 tomatoes
2 or 3 choice pieces of cooked
 chicken

1 teaspoon salt
½ teaspoon pepper
Butter
2 tablespoons fine bread crumbs
½ cup chopped parsley

Cut eggplants in half lengthwise and blanch 10 minutes in boiling water. Remove pulp, being careful not to break the skins.

Chop the onions, tomatoes and chicken very fine, and mix with some of the eggplant pulp. Add the salt and pepper, mixing well, and cook in a little butter in a frying pan, long enough to blend well. Combine with remaining eggplant pulp. Fill each half of the eggplant with the mixture, top with bread crumbs and bake in a preheated 350° oven for 20 minutes.

Before serving, sprinkle with chopped parsley. Serves 6.

BAKED LEEKS WITH HOLLANDAISE SAUCE

•

PORRER MED HOLLANDAISESAUCE

2 or 3 leeks per person   Hollandaise sauce (page 265)
1 tablespoon butter per person

Cut off the ends of the green tops. Wash leeks well. Cut into 2-inch lengths and parboil 2 or 3 minutes. Drain.

Lay the leeks in a baking dish. Dab each piece with butter and cook 10 minutes in a preheated 350° oven.

Serve in the leeks' own buttery juice with individual dishes of Hollandaise sauce for each person at the table.

FARM GIRL'S POTATOES

•

BONDEPIGES KARTOFLER

4 cups raw potatoes   ½ teaspoon salt
3 tablespoons minced onion   Pinch of white pepper
2 eggs, beaten   Deep fat for frying

Peel and grate the potatoes. Add onion, eggs, salt and pepper. Shape into balls and fry in deep fat. May also be baked or fried on a well-oiled griddle.

Serves 4.

CARAWAY POTATOES

•

KOMMENKARTOFLER

24 small new potatoes   ¼ pound butter
½ cup fresh chopped parsley   1 tablespoon caraway seeds
1 teaspoon fresh chopped dill

Boil potatoes until tender in salted water. Drain. Peel. Garnish with parsley and dill and serve doused with melted butter to which the caraway seeds have been added.

Serves 6.

POTATO SOUFFLÉ

•

KARTOFFELMOS

1½ medium-sized russet potatoes
per person to be served

Wash, peel and cut lengthwise into ¼-inch-thick slices all the potatoes you intend to use.

Have 2 kettles of deep fat and 2 deep-fat thermometers ready. The first kettle of fat should be heated to 230 degrees and kept at that temperature; the second, to 425 degrees.

Soak the potato slices in ice water for 5 minutes. Drain well and dry on paper towels.

Fry a few slices at a time for 5 minutes in the kettle of low-temperature fat. Transfer these to the kettle of hotter fat and cook until golden brown and as puffy as balloons. Drain, salt and serve immediately. Continue until all potato slices are cooked.

POTATO PUFFS

•

KARTOFFELBOLLER

2 pounds sweet or white potatoes   *1 cup brown sugar*
Salt   *¼ cup sesame seeds*
1 cup flour

Peel and boil potatoes. Drain and mash well. Season with salt to taste. Mix in the flour until the potatoes are of doughlike consistency.

With floured hands form the dough into small balls. Flatten them slightly, and on top of each place a teaspoon of brown sugar. Then form them into balls again.

Roll each ball in sesame seeds and fry in deep fat until a rich, dark brown.

Serves 6.

BAKED POTATO RING

·

BAGT KARTOFFELRAND

2 cups grated raw potatoes
½ cup melted butter
2 eggs, beaten
1 teaspoon grated onion

1 teaspoon salt
¼ teaspoon paprika
½ cup milk
½ cup grated sharp cheese

Combine grated raw potatoes with melted butter, beaten eggs, onion, salt and paprika, and mix well. Place in a well-buttered baking dish and pour the milk over mixture.

Bake 40 minutes in a preheated 350° oven. Remove from oven and sprinkle with grated cheese. Return to oven and bake until cheese has melted and browned.

Serves 6.

SPINACH PUDDING

·

SPINATBUDDING

2 pounds spinach
½ cup soft butter
8 egg yolks
¼ cup minced parsley
4 slices white bread, trimmed
Milk
¾ cup sour cream

Salt
Pepper
8 egg whites, beaten until stiff
2 cups dry bread crumbs
Melted butter
Lemon juice

Cook the spinach in a small amount of water just until tender. Drain and purée. Cream butter and add to the egg yolks, stirring well. Mix the puréed spinach with egg-yolk mixture and parsley.

Soak bread slices in milk and, using a sieve, press dry. Break up into small pieces and stir into spinach mixture. Add sour cream, salt and pepper to taste, and fold in the egg whites. As you fold, sift in the bread crumbs, reserving 2 tablespoons to coat a buttered mold.

Prepare 2-quart mold and pour in spinach mixture. Cover mold and set in a pan of water which comes halfway up the side of the mold. Steam for about 1¼ hours.

Turn out on a platter and serve hot with melted butter to which plenty of lemon juice has been added. Serves 6. Danish cooks often garnish the platter with small broiled artichokes.

SAUERKRAUT AND BEER

•

SURKÅL MED ØL

3 cups sauerkraut
3 cups flat beer
3 tablespoons butter

¼ teaspoon salt
⅛ teaspoon pepper
1 small onion (optional)

Partly drain the sauerkraut and marinate in ½ of the beer. Drain after it has marinated for 2 hours. Place in a skillet and pour the remaining beer over it. Add butter and salt and pepper. Cover and simmer slowly for 45 minutes.

If you like onions, nest a very small one in the center of the kraut while it is simmering.

Serves 4.

SQUASH WITH CINNAMON

•

FYLDTE GRÆSKAR MED KANEL

1 tender young squash per person
1 heaping tablespoon butter per
  squash

Salt
White pepper
Cinnamon

Use hard-skinned, firm squashes — acorn, summer, Hubbard, or almost any of the squash varieties available in winter. Steam squashes until tender. Cut in half. Scoop cooked squash out of the shells and mash well. Add all of the butter and salt and pepper to taste. Return to shells. Sprinkle cinnamon lightly over the top.

WHITE TURNIPS

•

FYLDTE ROER

6 large white turnips
1½ tablespoons butter

1 tablespoon bread crumbs

Wash, peel and cook turnips in salted water to cover until tender. Remove from heat, and when cool enough to handle, scoop out a small portion of the center and discard. Fill the openings with the stuffing for which the recipe is given below.

Brown 1½ tablespoons of butter in a saucepan to use for basting. Put stuffed turnips in a baking dish. Dribble with browned butter and top with bread crumbs.

Bake in a preheated 350° oven until brown, basting now and then. Serves 4.

Serve with bread thins toasted and spread with fresh sweet butter.

STUFFING

1 tablespoon butter	2 tablespoons blanched and
3 tablespoons bread crumbs	slivered almonds

Mix all ingredients together thoroughly.

SAUCES FOR VEGETABLES

HOLLANDAISE SAUCE

•

HOLLANDAISESAUCE

4 tablespoons water	5 egg yolks
2 teaspoons lemon juice or	1 teaspoon cold water
tarragon vinegar	1 pound butter, melted
Pinch of salt	3 teaspoons water

Combine water, vinegar and salt and cook in the top of a double boiler over hot water until liquid has been reduced to about ⅔ of the original quantity.

Beat the 5 egg yolks with the 1 teaspoon of cold water and add to the mixture. Beat well. Add the melted butter gradually, beating after each addition. Add the remaining 3 teaspoons of water, a few drops at a time.

Strain through a cheesecloth if you wish a fine-textured sauce.

SAUCE FOR ARTICHOKES

•

ARTISKOKSAUCE

4 tablespoons butter
4 tablespoons olive oil
12 anchovies

6 cloves garlic
Cream

Put oil and butter in a skillet. Add sliced and pounded anchovies and sliced garlic. Heat as hot as possible without burning the fats, stirring constantly. Remove from heat. Stir in as much cream as necessary to make a spread of fluffy consistency. Cool and use as a dip for chilled artichokes.

PARSLEY SAUCE

•

PERSILLESAUCE

2 tablespoons butter
2 tablespoons flour
Salt

Pepper
2 tablespoons minced parsley
1 cup milk

Melt the butter over low heat. Stir in the flour, salt, pepper and parsley, and mix until smooth.

Add the milk gradually, stirring occasionally. Allow sauce to cook for 15 minutes at a low temperature, stirring from time to time.

This is a pleasant sauce for any vegetable which lends itself to the creamed treatment or for combinations of leftover vegetables.

VEGETABLE SAUCE

•

GRØNTSAGSSAUCE

2 egg yolks
1½ cups sour cream
½ teaspoon sugar
1 tablespoon lemon juice

½ teaspoon salt
¼ teaspoon white pepper
¼ teaspoon paprika

Beat the egg yolks until lemon-colored and fluffy. Add other ingredients and place in the upper part of a double boiler. Cook over hot water, stirring until sauce thickens.

BUTTER SAUCE

•

SMØRSAUCE

¼ cup soft butter, creamed
¼ teaspoon salt
⅛ teaspoon white pepper

1 teaspoon chopped parsley
¾ tablespoon lemon juice

Place all ingredients except lemon juice in top of double boiler over hot water. Cook, stirring constantly, until creamy. Remove from heat and blend in lemon juice.

· 14 ·

PANCAKES, WAFFLES

AND DUMPLINGS

APPLE PANCAKES

·

ÆBLEPANDEKAGER

6 eggs
½ cup milk
1 cup flour
2 teaspoons sugar
½ teaspoon salt
½ cup cream

2 or 3 apples, peeled and sliced
Butter
Sugar
Cinnamon
Juice of 1 lemon

Beat the eggs lightly. Add the milk.

Combine the flour, sugar and salt. Stir the flour mixture into the egg mixture, stirring in the ½ cup of cream as you mix.

Fry the apple slices in butter in a skillet.

Cover the bottom of an oven-proof baking dish, or heavy skillet, with apples. Pour the batter over the slices and bake in a preheated 500° oven. When nearly done (20 to 25 minutes, or until the pancake looks like a cooked omelet), remove from oven and sprinkle here and there with a mixture of sugar and cinnamon to taste. Place dabs of butter on the pancake and return to oven until browned.

Just before serving, sprinkle with lemon juice, and cut into triangles. Serves 6.

BLACKBREAD PANCAKES

·

RUGMELSPANDEKAGER

2½ cups milk
½ teaspoon salt
½ cup butter
¼ cup sugar
½ cup sour cream
2 eggs, beaten

½ cake compressed yeast or
  ½ package dry yeast
1 tablespoon lukewarm water
5 cups sifted flour
1½ cups rye flour

Scald the milk and add the salt, butter, sugar and sour cream. Let cool.

Add the eggs and the yeast, which has been softened in the water. Add the flours and mix well.

Let rise 4 hours. Beat well and bake on an oiled griddle. Make small, thin cakes.

Serve at once with Huckleberry Sauce (page 281). Makes 36 3-inch pancakes.

BUCKWHEAT PANCAKES

·

BOGHVEDE-PANDEKAGER

3 tablespoons butter
2 eggs
1 cup buckwheat flour
1 cup white flour
1 teaspoon salt

2 tablespoons sugar
1 teaspoon baking soda
½ teaspoon baking powder
1½ cups milk

Melt the butter.

Beat the eggs well and mix with the butter.

Sift the flours with the other dry ingredients. Stir into egg and butter mixture. Add milk. Stir until smooth.

Bake on a hot, greased griddle.

Serve hot with Brandy Sauce (*page 280*). Makes 24 3-inch pancakes.

CORN MEAL PANCAKES

·

MAJSMELSPANDEKAGER

1½ cups corn meal
2½ cups white flour
4 teaspoons baking powder
¼ teaspoon salt
¼ cup sugar

¼ cup butter
2 eggs
½ cup light cream
1 cup cold water

Sift the corn meal, white flour, baking powder, salt and sugar together 3 or 4 times until the ingredients are very fine. Work in the butter in small chunks.

Beat the eggs. Add the cream and water and beat well for a few seconds. Add the cream mixture to the flour mixture, beating well.

Rub a heavy, hot skillet with a slice of bacon. Pour in the batter to a depth of about ¾ of an inch. Sprinkle with bits of bacon. Cover and cook about 4 minutes, or until bubbles appear all over the surface. Turn and cook on other side.

Makes about 18 4-inch pancakes.

DANISH PANCAKES

·

DANSKE PANDEKAGER

4 eggs
3 cups milk
2 cups sifted flour
1 cup milk
2 cups flour

1 teaspoon sugar
1½ teaspoons baking powder
½ teaspoon salt
½ pint whipping cream
Apricot jam

Beat eggs with 2 cups milk. Add other ingredients in order given, except whipping cream and jam.

Roll on a floured board into thin cakes about 6 inches across.

Fry in a lightly greased heavy skillet. Turn often until golden brown.

Whip cream. Serve over pancakes with jam.

Makes 16 to 18 pancakes.

GOURMET PANCAKES

•

FINE PANDEKAGER

4 eggs
¼ pound butter, melted
3 cups milk
2 cups sifted flour
1 teaspoon sugar

1½ teaspoons baking powder
½ teaspoon salt
1 cup heavy cream
Apricot jam

Mix all ingredients except heavy cream and jam in order given. Roll into thin pancakes about 6 inches in diameter. Fry in a well-heated heavy skillet until brown.

Whip cream and serve over pancakes with apricot jam.

POTATO PANCAKES

•

KARTOFFELPLETTER

2½ pounds potatoes
1 teaspoon salt
2 cups rye flour

2½ cups white flour
3 egg whites, beaten until frothy

Cook the potatoes in their jackets. Peel. Add salt and mash while warm. Work the flours into the mashed potatoes, a little at a time with egg whites. Knead the dough well.

Roll on a lightly floured board into thin round cakes.

Bake on both sides on a greased griddle over low heat until done. Watch them closely to keep them from burning.

Serve with melted butter and honey, or a cognac sauce (*page 281*).

Makes 16 to 18 pancakes.

RAISED WHOLE-WHEAT PANCAKES

•

PANDEKAGER AF USIGTET HVEDEMEL

1 cake compressed yeast or
   1 package dry yeast
2 cups lukewarm water
2 tablespoons molasses

1 cup milk, scalded and cooled
1½ teaspoons salt
1 cup sifted white flour
2 cups whole-wheat flour

Dissolve the yeast in the lukewarm water. Add the molasses. To this add scalded and cooled milk, salt and the sifted white flour. Blend.

Add the whole-wheat flour gradually, beating after each addition, until the batter is very smooth. Cover and let rise in a warm place for 1 hour.

Stir well. Bake on a hot, greased griddle.

Makes 16 4-inch pancakes. This dough may be set the night before if ¼ cake (or ¼ package) of yeast and ½ teaspoon of salt are added to the above recipe.

SOUR-DOUGH PANCAKES

•

SURDEJGSPANDEKAGER

SOUR-DOUGH STARTER

¼ package dry yeast	*1 scant cup flour*
¼ cup lukewarm water	

Dissolve yeast in the lukewarm water (about 100 degrees). Put the dissolved yeast in a good-sized bowl and add enough flour (¾ to 1 cup) to make a thin, runny batter. Place in a small crock and cover lightly with a tea towel.

Put in a warm place to sour. Each day for 5 days add ½ cup lukewarm water and just enough flour to keep the batter the same consistency as when you first mixed it. When the batter is sour to the taste it is ready to use for making pancakes. This should be in about 5 days but may take a little longer.

To make it easy to have these pancakes whenever you want them, without waiting 5 days for the starter to sour, set aside a small quantity of the starter each time you make pancakes. Add ½ cup lukewarm water to it and just enough flour for the runny batter mentioned above. Leave it in a warm place overnight, then store in your refrigerator until you wish to make pancakes. Add enough flour and water when you begin to make the pancakes to provide a sufficient quantity of starter for the number of cakes you wish to make.

SOUR-DOUGH PANCAKES

3 eggs
1 cup milk
2 cups sour-dough starter
1 tablespoon baking soda

2 teaspoons baking powder
2 teaspoons salt
¼ cup sugar
1¾ cups flour

Beat the eggs until light with the milk and the sour-dough starter.

Sift together the baking soda, baking powder, salt, sugar and flour. Combine the two mixtures and blend well.

Bake on a greased griddle or in an oiled skillet, browning on both sides. (If you wish to use an unoiled skillet or griddle, add ¼ cup of melted butter to the batter.) If you like very thin pancakes, add a little more milk to the batter.

Makes about 18 4-inch pancakes.

CREAM WAFFLES

•

FLØDEVAFLER

2 cups whipping cream
1⅓ cups sifted flour
4 tablespoons ice water

½ cup butter
Powdered sugar

Whip the cream until stiff. Fold in the flour, then the ice water. Chill 1 hour.

Melt the butter and stir into the batter.

Spoon a little batter into each section of a heated waffle iron and bake until brown.

Sprinkle with powdered sugar and serve hot. Serves 4.

GREAT-GRANDMOTHER'S WAFFLES

•

OLDEMORS VAFLER

½ cake fresh yeast or
  ½ package dry yeast
¼ cup warm water
4 cups sifted flour
1 cup cream
¼ cup butter

Pinch of salt
4 teaspoons sugar
8 eggs
½ glass brandy or cognac
Powdered sugar

Dissolve yeast in warm water. Blend in 1 cup sifted flour and set in a warm place to rise until doubled in bulk.

Heat cream to the boiling point. Add the butter.

To first mixture add the rest of the flour, salt and sugar.

Beat the eggs until frothy and lemon-colored. To them add the brandy or cognac, the cream and butter mixture and the yeast mixture. Blend together thoroughly. Let rest in a cool place for 2½ hours.

Fill a well-greased, hot waffle iron ⅔ full of batter. When waffle is crisp and golden brown, remove and sprinkle with powdered sugar.

If you have not relegated waffles to breakfast use only, top these with fresh fruits or fruit preserves and whipped cream and think in lunch, brunch or Sunday-supper terms.

SOUR-CREAM WAFFLES

•

SURFLØDE VAFLER

¼ cup butter
1 cup flour, sifted
2 tablespoons sugar
1 teaspoon baking soda
1 teaspoon ground cardamom

½ teaspoon salt
2 eggs, separated
1 cup sour cream
1 cup buttermilk

Melt the butter.

Sift together flour, sugar, baking soda, cardamom, salt; set aside.

Beat the egg yolks until lemon-colored and fluffy. Add melted butter slowly. Add the sour cream and buttermilk and beat until well blended. Add to the dry ingredients and mix until smooth.

Beat the egg whites until stiff and fold into the batter.

Serves 6.

COGNAC APPLE FRITTERS

•

COGNACÆBLESKIVER

4 apples
4 tablespoons cognac
1 egg, separated
½ cup milk
1 tablespoon sugar

1 cup flour
¼ teaspoon salt
1½ teaspoons baking powder
Powdered sugar

Peel, core and slice apples and place in a bowl. Pour cognac over them and cover tightly.

Beat the egg yolk and mix with the milk and sugar. Mix well.

Sift the flour into the egg-yolk mixture and add the salt and baking powder. Stir well.

Beat egg white until stiff. Fold into above mixture.

Dip the apple slices in the batter and fry in deep fat heated to 365 degrees for 2 to 4 minutes, or until golden brown on both sides. Dust with powdered sugar while warm.

Serves 6 to 8 people. To make these fritters even more delicious, serve them topped with Rum Sauce (*page 282*) or Apple Cream (*page 282*).

BRANDY OMELET

•

COGNAC-OMELET

6 eggs	*2 tablespoons butter*
¾ cup milk	*2 teaspoons sugar*
1 teaspoon sugar	*¼ cup brandy*
½ teaspoon salt	*1 orange*
¼ teaspoon white pepper	

Beat the eggs until foamy. Add the milk, the 1 teaspoon of sugar, salt and pepper and mix well.

Melt butter in a heavy skillet (preferably one used *only* for omelet making). Add the egg mixture and let cook over a low flame. As omelet cooks, lift the edges toward the center and tip the pan to cook all parts equally. Cook until firm but not dry.

Fold over and turn omelet onto a hot, buttered platter. Sprinkle with the 2 teaspoons of sugar and add the brandy which has been ignited. When the flame dies, garnish with orange sections or thin slices of orange.

Serves 4.

EGG DUMPLINGS

•

ÆGGEBOLLER

6 egg whites
4 egg yolks, beaten
2 tablespoons flour

3 tablespoons sugar
Salt
¼ cup butter

Beat the egg whites until stiff.

Stir remaining ingredients, except for the butter, together. Mix well. Fold the beaten egg whites into the mixture. Shape dough into small dumplings and place in a baking dish. Melt butter and pour over dumplings.

Bake 6 to 8 minutes in a preheated 350° oven.

These dumplings are especially good with chicken fricassee, but because they are light and fluffy, they may be used in many ways.

FLUFFY DUMPLINGS FOR FRICASSEE

•

FRIKASSÉBOLLER

2 eggs
1 cup milk
2¼ cups flour

4 teaspoons baking powder
1 teaspoon salt
¼ teaspoon nutmeg

Beat the eggs until light and fluffy. Add milk and mix well.

Sift the dry ingredients together and add to the egg mixture. Mix with as few strokes as possible.

Drop by teaspoonfuls into boiling broth. Turn the dumplings frequently so they will be well done on all sides, but do not cook longer than 10 minutes or they will be tough.

FLOUR DUMPLINGS

•

MELBOLLER

1½ cups flour
Pinch of white pepper
2 tablespoons melted butter

4 eggs, separated
Boiling stock or soup

Put flour and pepper in a bowl. Make a well in the center. Fill with the melted butter and beaten egg yolks. Work with a wooden spoon, gradually working in the flour.

Beat egg whites until stiff but not dry. Fold into flour mixture. The dough should be light but firm.

Shape into small balls and poach them in boiling stock or soup 10 minutes. When they have risen to the top of the liquid they are ready to serve.

MILK DUMPLINGS

•

MÆLKEBOLLER

1 quart milk	8 egg yolks, beaten
1 cup sugar	1 teaspoon vanilla
3½ tablespoons cornstarch	

Mix all ingredients well and put in a kettle to cook over low heat. Stir continuously until mixture thickens.

When thick, pour into a buttered pan about 2 inches deep. Let stand until cold. Invert pan and remove batter. Cut into diamond-shaped pieces and pile them back into the buttered pan.

Dot with butter and brown in a moderate oven (preheated to 350 degrees).

Serve in beef consommé, chicken broth, or other clear soups.

POTATO DUMPLINGS

•

KARTOFFELBOLLER

2 cups grated raw potatoes, measured after grating	1 teaspoon salt
	¼ teaspoon pepper
⅓ cup ground suet	¼ cup milk
3 eggs, beaten	3 cups flour

Blend ingredients in order given and drop by tablespoonfuls into hot broth or soup and boil 45 minutes.

Serve with meat or in soups. Makes 12 to 16 dumplings.

POTATO-CHEESE DUMPLINGS

•

KARTOFFELBOLLER

1 pound potatoes, peeled	*1 whole egg*
4 tablespoons butter	*1 egg yolk*
2 cups grated cheese	*Salt*
¾ cup flour	*Pepper*

Boil the potatoes and rub through a sieve or run through an electric blender while hot. Stir in the butter and cheese. Mix in the flour, egg and the egg yolk. Season to taste with salt and pepper.

Roll into small balls and poach in salted boiling water for 10 minutes. Drain and serve in almost any soup.

These make very acceptable family fare topped with warmed-up gravy leftovers.

STUFFED POTATO DUMPLINGS

•

FYLDTE KARTOFFELKUGLER

Dough

4 cups flour	*2 eggs*
¾ teaspoon salt	*4 tablespoons water*

Sift flour and salt into a bowl and make a well in the center. Place whole eggs and water in this well and mix until dry ingredients are moist. Knead until smooth. Cover the dough and let it rest while you make the filling; the dough will be less stiff after resting and will make the forming of dumplings easier.

Roll the dough on a floured board, thinner than for a piecrust, and cut into small pieces, about 3 inches square. Place a spoonful of the filling (see recipe below) on each square. Fold the dough over the filling to form a 3-cornered pocket. Seal the edges firmly.

Drop the dumplings into boiling broth or salted water and cook 15 minutes. Serve at once. Makes 16 dumplings.

(This recipe may be doubled and used as the jacket for a ham to be baked in the oven.)

FILLING

⅛ cup sweet onion, minced
¼ cup butter
1 cup small-curd, dry cottage
 cheese
2 cups cold mashed potatoes

1 egg
1 teaspoon celery salt
Salt
White pepper

Brown the onion in the butter. Combine with all other ingredients and mix until very smooth.

FRUIT DUMPLINGS

•

FRUGTBOLLER

2½ to 3 cups flour
3 teaspoons baking powder
½ teaspoon salt
2 eggs, beaten
1 cup milk

Peaches, black cherries, plums,
 or apricots
Flour
Melted butter
Cottage cheese
Sugar

Sift together flour, baking powder and salt.

Add the beaten eggs to the milk. Add to the flour mixture and blend well. Dough should be stiff enough to handle.

Wash and dry the fresh fruit you have selected. Remove pits. Roll fruit in enough additional flour to coat each piece thoroughly. Coat your hands with flour and cover each piece of fruit completely with a ¼-inch layer of dough. Pinch the edges firmly together.

Drop dumplings into rapidly boiling salted water. Cover and let cook until fruit is tender when pricked with a toothpick — 15 to 20 minutes.

Serve dumplings with melted butter, cottage cheese and a sprinkling of sugar. Makes 12 dumplings.

PLUM DUMPLINGS

•

BLOMMEBOLLER

3 pounds potatoes	2 pounds ripe plums
5 cups flour	Sugar cubes
4 tablespoons sugar	¾ cup bread crumbs
2 eggs, beaten	3 tablespoons melted butter
Pinch of salt	Sugar
4 tablespoons melted butter	Cinnamon

Cook and peel the potatoes. Mash in a large bowl. Add the flour, sugar, eggs, salt and melted butter and mix well to make a dough.

Roll out quite thin and cut into rounds the diameter of a teacup.

Remove pits from the plums and fill each cavity with a sugar cube. Place 1 filled plum in each round of dough and pinch edges together.

Cook in lightly salted boiling water about 10 minutes. While the dumplings are cooking, mix the bread crumbs with the melted butter. When dumplings are cooked, drain and roll in bread-crumb mixture and then in sugar and cinnamon.

These are a delicious accompaniment to either roast beef or roast pork.

SAUCES FOR PANCAKES AND WAFFLES

BRANDY SAUCE #1

•

COGNACSAUCE

1 cup soft butter	½ cup brandy
3 cups brown sugar	2 eggs
½ cup lemon juice	Pinch of salt
1 teaspoon grated lemon rind	

Mix all ingredients and cook in the top of a double boiler over hot water. Beat until thick, about 7 minutes.

Makes 3 cups of sauce. This old Danish recipe may also be used over fruit cakes and other desserts.

BRANDY SAUCE #2

•

COGNACSAUCE

3 egg yolks
½ cup sugar

¾ cup white wine
1 tablespoon cognac
or other brandy

Beat egg yolks and sugar together in the top of a double boiler over hot water until thick and creamy. Add the wine and cook a little longer until further thickened. Stir in the cognac and serve hot.

Particularly good over potato pancakes, but may be used for any pancakes or waffles.

HUCKLEBERRY SAUCE

•

BLÅBÆRSAUCE

2 cups sugar
2 tablespoons cornstarch

1 cup boiling water
2 cups huckleberry or blueberry
juice

Mix sugar and cornstarch. Add the boiling water slowly and let boil, stirring, for 5 minutes.

Cool, then stir in the juice and chill before reheating to serve over pancakes or waffles.

CARAMEL SAUCE

•

KARAMELSAUCE

1 cup water
1 cup sugar

¼ cup cream
½ teaspoon maple sugar or extract

Cook water and sugar until they become syrupy.

Remove from fire and add the cream and maple sugar or extract and stir until smooth.

Serve hot or cold.

RUM SAUCE

•

ROMSAUCE

2 eggs   1 cup heavy cream
1 cup powdered sugar   4 teaspoons rum

Beat the eggs until lemon-colored and frothy. Add the powdered sugar gradually, beating continually until all is used.

Whip cream and add with the rum to the above mixture, folding in gently at first and then beating well.

APPLE CREAM

•

ÆBLECREME

1 egg white   ½ teaspoon cinnamon
2 cups thick applesauce   ½ teaspoon nutmeg
½ cup heavy cream

Beat egg white until stiff. Fold in applesauce. Whip cream and fold in. Sprinkle cinnamon and nutmeg over the mixture.

· 15 ·

PIES, PUDDINGS

AND OTHER SWEETS

THE DESSERT traditions of Denmark differ from ours in many ways. Generations ago pies were unknown, though today housewives both in Denmark and the United States have contributed much to the art. Torten and sponge cakes were more popular than our frosted sweet layer cakes. Fruit soups were often served as desserts, just as some gourmet restaurants do today. Clabbered milk, almond, fruit, rum and rice puddings were favorites at the family table. Tiny pancakes and æbleskiver baked in special pans and served with whipped cream and fruit preserves have a universal place throughout the Scandinavian countries.

Fresh fruits are always served as dessert during the summer months at the peak of their beautiful color and mouth-watering taste, unadorned except for a dab of whipped cream sprinkled with a mixture of powdered sugar and cinnamon.

FRUIT TARTS

•

FRUGTLINSER

2½ cups flour	12 tablespoons soft butter
½ teaspoon salt	6 tablespoons ice water

Sift flour and salt. Add butter, working it in with your fingers. Moisten with ice water.

Wrap in a thin, clean towel or napkin. Place in refrigerator while preparing the filling, as follows:

FILLING

1 cup almonds, ground	1 tablespoon butter
1 cup raisins, ground	1 egg, beaten
Juice and grated rind of 1 lemon	1 teaspoon vanilla
1 tablespoon boiling water	2 tablespoons very fine cracker
1 cup sugar	crumbs

Place the nuts and raisins in a bowl with lemon juice and grated rind. Stir in the boiling water, sugar and butter. Add the egg and mix well. Add vanilla and cracker crumbs. Blend all ingredients together thoroughly.

MAKING THE TARTS

Roll the pastry dough to ¼ inch thick, or less, on a buttered board. Cut into 4-inch squares and place a tablespoonful of the filling on each square. Fold over to make a triangle. Pinch the edges of each together with a fork dipped in flour. Prick the top of each tart with the fork.

Bake 20 to 22 minutes in a preheated 450° oven, or until lightly browned. Sprinkle with powdered sugar while still warm.

Makes 16 to 18 tarts.

EGGNOG PIE

•

ÆGGEROMTÆRTER

6 eggs, separated	1½ cups light cream, chilled well
¼ cup sugar	1 tablespoon plain gelatin
3 tablespoons rum	5 tablespoons sugar
1 teaspoon vanilla	Nutmeg

Beat the egg yolks well. Add the ¼ cup sugar, rum and vanilla and beat until well blended. Add the cream and beat until the mixture is well blended.

Beat the egg whites until stiff peaks form. Gently fold into the yolk mixture.

Add the gelatin which has been soaked in 1 tablespoon of cold water, folding in gently. Pour into a baked pie shell (see recipe which follows). Sprinkle with a mixture of sugar and grated nutmeg.

Chill 3 hours before serving.

Pie Shell

1 cup shortening
¼ cup boiling water
3 cups flour

½ teaspoon baking powder
¼ teaspoon salt

Break up shortening in a bowl. Pour the boiling water over it and beat until smooth.

Sift flour, baking powder and salt into it and mix well. Roll out at once on floured board and line a pie tin. Turn edge under and flute. Prick bottom and sides with fork. Bake in a preheated 475° oven 8 to 10 minutes.

(This pastry may be chilled if not to be used immediately. Roll *after* chilling.)

SOUR-CREAM NUT PIE

•

NØDDETÆRTER MED FLØDECREME

2 eggs
1 cup sugar
1 cup sour cream
1 teaspoon cornstarch

½ teaspoon lemon extract
¼ teaspoon cinnamon
¼ teaspoon ground cloves
1 cup nut meats

Beat the eggs well. Add the remaining ingredients, except the nuts, and mix well.

Pour mixture into an unbaked pie shell (*see above*) which has been lined with ground nut meats.

Bake 5 minutes in a preheated 450° oven. Lower heat to 325 degrees and bake 40 minutes more, or until firm.

SOUR-CREAM PRUNE PIE

·

SVESKETÆRTER MED FLØDECREME

1 cup dried prunes, soaked 3 hours in cold water	½ cup sugar
4 eggs, separated	¼ teaspoon nutmeg
½ cup sour cream	1 teaspoon cinnamon
½ teaspoon lemon extract	Pinch of salt
	Whipping cream (optional)

Pit the prunes. Pull into chunks.

Beat the egg yolks until thick and lemon-colored. Add remaining ingredients, except egg whites and whipping cream, and mix well.

Beat egg whites until stiff. Fold into above mixture. Pour into an unbaked pie shell and bake until firm in a preheated 375° oven.

Serve topped with whipped cream if desired.

PUFF PASTRY

·

BLADDEJG ELLER BUTTERDEJG

1 cup unsalted butter	½ cup ice water
2 cups flour, sifted 3 times	¼ cup cognac

Chill all ingredients. If unsalted butter is not available, wash the butter well in ice water. Reserve 1 tablespoon of the butter. Shape the remaining butter into a flat cake 1 inch thick.

Blend the 1 tablespoon of butter into the flour and moisten to a stiff dough with the ice water and cognac. Knead it on a lightly floured board until smooth and elastic, about 2 minutes. Cover and let rest a few minutes.

Roll into a rectangle about ¼ inch thick, using as little flour on the board and the rolling pin as possible. Place the butter in the center of the lower half of the pastry, sprinkling lightly with flour. Fold upper half over. Press edges firmly together. Fold ends over, pressing tightly. Let stand 5 minutes. Roll very lightly to the original shape and thickness. Fold again.

Pastry must be chilled well before each rolling. Try wrapping pastry in a towel and plunging it into a pan of cracked ice. Handle dough as little and as quickly as possible.

Line baking sheet or sheets with double thickness of waxed paper. Cut pastry in desired shapes. Bake in a preheated 425° oven about 15 minutes. Fill or top with your choice of the recipes in this section, or in Chapter 1, or with a favorite of your own.

CREAM PUFFS

•

FYLDTE VANDBAKKELSER

1 cup butter	*¼ teaspoon salt*
2 cups water	*8 eggs*
2 cups flour	

Place butter and water in a saucepan and bring to a boil. Add the flour and the salt. Lower the heat and beat the mixture until it forms a ball and slides away from the sides of the pan. Remove from heat.

Add the eggs one at a time, beating hard after each addition until the dough is very smooth. Drop from a spoon on a greased baking sheet about 2 inches apart.

Bake 20 minutes in a preheated 400° oven. Then lower heat to 350° and bake 25 minutes more. Makes about 30 medium-sized shells.

When puffs have cooled, cut off the tops and fill as follows:

CUSTARD

1½ cups light cream	*½ teaspoon salt*
4½ cups milk	*6 eggs*
1½ cups sugar	*1½ cups whipping cream*
1 cup flour	*Vanilla*

Combine milk and cream in top of a double boiler and warm over low heat.

Sift the dry ingredients together. Add the milk and cream to them slowly, stirring constantly. Return this mixture to top of double boiler and boil until thick, stirring to keep smooth and to prevent scorching.

Beat the eggs until frothy. Add the cooked mixture to them. Return again to the top of the double boiler and cook a few minutes longer, stirring continually.

Let cool. Whip the heavy cream and fold into the mixture. Add vanilla. Fill the puffs, cover with their tops and serve.

ROSETTES

•

ROSETBAKKELSER

1 cup flour	¼ teaspoon salt
1 cup milk	2 eggs
1 teaspoon sugar	

Mix flour and milk and beat until smooth. Add sugar and salt. Break eggs into the mixture and stir gently until thoroughly mixed.

Rosettes (which must be made in special irons — available in the housewares departments of large department stores or restaurant supply houses) must be deep-fried. Heat fat in a small, deep pan, somewhat larger than the head of the rosette iron, containing about 2½ inches of cooking oil. Dip iron first into hot fat, then into batter, without letting batter run over top of iron. Transfer batter-filled iron to the fat; submerge it totally for 25 to 35 seconds. Remove rosettes from pan, reheat pan, and repeat process until all batter is used.

Drain on paper towels and roll in sugar.

Makes 24 rosettes.

JELLY FRITTERS

•

GELÉBEIGNETS

2 cups milk	½ cup sugar
1 cake compressed yeast or	3 eggs, lightly beaten
1 package dry yeast	Flour
4½ cups flour	Jam or jelly
½ cup butter, melted	Granulated sugar

Scald milk and cool to lukewarm. Pour ¼ cup milk over yeast and let stand while beating rest of milk with 2¼ cups of the flour to make a smooth dough. Add dissolved yeast and beat well. Put in a warm place to rise.

When risen to half again its original size add melted butter, sugar and beaten eggs, and stir in remaining flour. Mix thoroughly with a wooden spoon. If dough seems limp, add a little more flour.

Roll dough ½ inch thick on a floured board and cut into rounds with a cookie cutter. On half of the cookies pile some jelly or jam. Cover each with a plain round and press them together well. Put on floured board and let rise until doubled in bulk.

Fry in deep fat heated to 370 degrees until brown on each side. Turn only once. Do not crowd while frying.

Drain on paper towels and roll lightly in granulated sugar.

Makes 12 large fritters.

DANISH DUMPLINGS

•

ÆBLESKIVER

Æbleskiver are the famous Danish dessert dumplings that are a cross between a dumpling, a doughnut and a fritter. They should be cooked in special pans, but well-buttered popover or muffin tins will do. (See *page 14* for some sources of supply for æbleskiver pans, but remember that they weigh 7 pounds and that shipping costs will thus be high. Look for them in the housewares department of your local department store or hardware store before you order them by mail.)

1 cup thick sour cream	*1 teaspoon baking soda*
⅔ cup milk	*½ teaspoon ground cardamom*
3 egg yolks, beaten	*¾ teaspoon salt*
2 tablespoons melted butter	*3 egg whites*
2 cups sifted flour	*⅛ pound butter*
2 tablespoons sugar	*Powdered sugar*

Combine and mix well the sour cream, milk, egg yolks and melted butter.

Sift the dry ingredients together. Make a well in the center. Pour liquid mixture all at once into the well, stirring until thoroughly blended.

Beat the egg whites until rounded peaks are formed. Spread the batter *over* the beaten egg whites and fold together gently.

Set the æbleskiver or muffin pan over low heat on top of the stove and test the pan by dropping a few drops of cold water into one of the wells. If the drops dance around in small beads, the pan is ready to use. Grease the little wells in the pan thoroughly with melted butter. Pour the batter into the wells, filling about ½ full.

With a fork, turn the æbleskiver frequently to brown evenly, but do not pierce. *After* they have browned, insert a toothpick in the center of one or two of the æbleskiver. If the toothpick comes out clean, they are ready. Sprinkle with powdered sugar immediately after removing from the wells.

Makes 24 to 28 æbleskiver. Delicious accompanied by tart jam and a good cup of coffee.

RAISED ÆBLESKIVER WITH CURRANTS

1 cake compressed yeast or	1 cup light cream
1 package dry yeast	2 cups sifted flour
¼ cup lukewarm water	4 eggs
1 tablespoon sugar	1 teaspoon nutmeg
½ teaspoon salt	Currants
1 cup milk	

Dissolve the yeast in the lukewarm water. Add sugar and salt.

Heat the milk and cream until lukewarm. Add the flour and the dissolved yeast.

Add the eggs, one at a time, beating well after each addition. Add the nutmeg and blend well. Cover lightly and allow the dough to rise 2 hours in a warm place.

Brush the skiver pan well with butter and heat. Place 1 tablespoon of batter and 1 teaspoon of currants in each well, pressing the currants down. Bake 3 minutes in the pan on top of the stove, turning to brown on both sides. Roll or dust with powdered sugar when taken from the pan.

Serve at once with Caramel Sauce (*page 281*) or other sauce of your choice.

ÆBLESKIVER WITH APPLESAUCE

3 eggs, separated	2 cups flour
2 teaspoons sugar	1 teaspoon baking soda
½ teaspoon salt	1 teaspoon baking powder
2 cups buttermilk	Applesauce

Beat egg yolks. Add sugar, salt and buttermilk.

Sift flour, soda and baking powder together. Add to egg yolk and sugar mixture.

Beat egg whites until stiff and fold into batter.

Place a small amount of fat or oil in the wells of the skiver pan and fill them ⅔ full of the batter. Place a teaspoon of applesauce on top of the batter, then barely cover with a dab of dough. Cook until bubbly. Turn carefully and bake on the other side.

Serve hot with jam or jelly or roll in powdered sugar.

ALMOND PUDDING

·

MANDELBUDDING

1 scant tablespoon cornstarch, or	½ cup milk
1 tablespoon unflavored gelatin	3 eggs, separated
¼ cup cold water	½ teaspoon vanilla extract
1½ cups hot cream	Pinch of salt
½ cup sugar	½ cup ground almonds

Soak cornstarch or gelatin in the cold water until softened. Stir it into the cream. Add ⅓ cup of the sugar and the milk. Cook, stirring continuously, over low heat until hot. Do not allow to boil.

Beat the egg yolks and remaining sugar until frothy. If eggs are extra large, add an additional tablespoon of sugar. Pour a little of the hot mixture over the egg yolks, then stir all into the milk mixture. Let cook about 2 minutes over low heat, stirring often to prevent scorching. Remove from heat. Let cool until thick. Add the vanilla.

Whip egg whites with a wire whisk and add, together with the salt. Blend well. Fold in the ground almonds. Chill.

Pour cold fruit juice over each serving and top with whipped cream. Or spoon vanilla sauce over pudding in sherbet glasses.

Serves 4 to 6.

APPLE PUDDING

·

ÆBLEBUDDING

8 large cooking apples	3 tablespoons flour
¼ cup sugar	3 tablespoons sugar
2 tablespoons butter	1 cup cream
⅓ cup water	Cinnamon
3 eggs	Whipping cream

Pare, core and slice the apples.

Make a syrup of the sugar, butter and water. Cook the apples in the syrup until tender. Place in a buttered baking dish.

Beat the eggs until creamy. Add the flour and sugar and mix well. Add the cream slowly and pour mixture over the apples.

Bake in a moderate oven (preheated to 350°) for 50 minutes, or until it is set. Cover the baking dish with waxed paper while cooking to prevent browning too much.

Served topped with whipped cream and a little cinnamon. Serves 8.

BAKED APPLE PORCUPINE

•

INDBAGTE ÆBLER

1 cup sugar	1 tablespoon Cointreau
1 cup water	Juice and grated rind of 1 lemon
1 dozen firm baking apples, peeled, cored and halved	1 cup blanched almonds
	3 egg whites
Salt	½ cup powdered sugar
1 cup apricot jam or marmalade	

Heat the sugar in water until sugar is dissolved. Place 12 apple halves in this syrup and cook them gently until tender but *not* soft. Remove the apples carefully and set aside. Put remaining apple halves in the syrup and allow these to cook as with first batch.

The syrup by now will have become thick. Pour it through a sieve and add just a pinch of salt.

Mix half of the apricot jam or marmalade with the liqueur and fill the apple halves with it. Stir the rest of the marmalade into the boiled apple syrup with the juice and grated rind of the lemon.

Place the apple halves in the form of a mound on a heatproof serving platter, round side up. Fill the spaces between the apples with the juice mixture and smooth over.

Slice the almonds and set aside.

Beat the egg whites until they hold a stiff peak. Fold in the powdered sugar. Spread this mixture over the mound. Dust the top of the mound with additional powdered sugar. Stick the almond halves here and there on the mound to make them look as much as possible like porcupine quills.

Put platter in a 350° oven which has been preheated for 15 minutes, and bake 15 minutes until lightly browned. Watch carefully. Almonds will burn quickly.

CARROT PUDDING

•

GULERODBUDDING

1 teaspoon baking soda	1 teaspoon salt
1 cup grated raw potatoes	½ teaspoon white pepper
1 cup grated raw carrots	1 egg
1 cup sugar	2 tablespoons melted butter
1 cup flour	½ teaspoon cinnamon
1 cup raisins	½ teaspoon nutmeg

Add the soda to the potatoes and mix well. Then mix the remaining ingredients in the order given, and combine with potatoes.

Put in a buttered baking dish and steam 2 hours in a moderate oven (preheated to 350°), placing the baking dish in a pan of water to prevent scorching on the bottom.

Remove from oven. Let cool 5 minutes. Remove pudding from baking dish by inverting over serving platter.

Serves 6 to 8.

CHRISTMAS PUDDING

•

JULEBUDDING

4½ cups suet, chopped or ground fine	½ teaspoon nutmeg
1 pound sugar	1½ teaspoons salt
1 pound small seedless white raisins	1 pound dry bread crumbs, crushed fine
¼ pound candied lemon peel, chopped	4 cups sifted flour
¼ pound candied orange peel, chopped	1 pound eggs, weighed in their shells
1 teaspoon mixed ground spices (cinnamon, cloves, allspice, etc.)	½ pint milk
	4 tablespoons brandy

Mix all dry ingredients and blend well.

Beat the eggs until light and frothy. Add the milk and brandy to the beaten eggs. Moisten the dry ingredients with this liquid and let it stand in a cool place 12 hours.

Put the batter in buttered baking pans, filling each about ¾ full. Cover with aluminum foil. Tie a cloth tightly around each pan and boil in water for 8 hours.

Will keep for weeks. Reheat 2 hours before serving. Top with your favorite sauce.

This recipe will make about 9 pounds of pudding, so make sure you have plenty of pans of the size you want ready before you begin.

FLOATING ISLAND

•

BUDDING

12 egg whites	1 teaspoon vanilla extract
1¼ cups sugar	1 quart milk

Beat the egg whites until frothy but not stiff. Fold the sugar and vanilla gently into the beaten egg whites.

Scald the milk in a large kettle, and when it reaches the boiling point, drop portions of the beaten egg whites into it, cooking about 1 minute on each side. Remove these egg dumplings onto a clean towel as they are cooked and until the sauce is made, as follows:

VANILLA CUSTARD SAUCE

1 cup sugar	1 teaspoon vanilla extract
6 egg yolks, beaten frothy	

Cool milk in kettle to lukewarm.

Mix the sugar with the egg yolks and add to the mixture in the kettle. Cook slowly until the sauce coats a spoon. Add vanilla, cool, strain and pour into a large tureen. Float the egg-white dumplings on top.

Serves 10 to 12.

PRUNE MERINGUE PUDDING

•

FRUGTBUDDING

2½ cups milk, scalded
¼ cup sugar
¼ teaspoon salt
½ cup farina
1 tablespoon butter
¼ teaspoon nutmeg

1 cup cooked, pitted and
    chopped prunes
2 eggs, separated
¼ cup sugar for meringue
¼ teaspoon salt for meringue
½ teaspoon vanilla extract

Stir sugar, salt and farina slowly into scalded milk. Cook until thick, stirring constantly.

Add butter, nutmeg, prunes and the egg yolks, which you have beaten well. Turn mixture into a buttered baking dish.

Beat the egg whites until stiff and fold in the sugar, salt and vanilla. Spread this mixture over the batter and bake in a preheated 325° oven 15 minutes, or until the meringue is a delicate brown.

Serves 6.

MOLASSES PUDDING

•

SIRUPBUDDING

1 cup soft butter
1 cup molasses
1 cup hot water

1 teaspoon baking soda
3 cups flour
1 cup raisins

Cream the butter, add molasses and mix. Add the hot water and stir well.

Sift the soda and flour together and beat well into the butter mixture. Fold in the raisins.

Place the batter in a greased steaming can and steam 3 hours. (Empty baking-powder tins with tightly fitting lids make good steaming cans. Fill ⅔ full. Place on a rack in a heavy kettle with an inch of boiling water in the bottom. Cover the kettle.)

Serve warm or cold with a sauce. Serves 8.

CHRISTMAS RICE PUDDING

•

JULERISENGRØD

6 cups milk	1 whole almond
1 cup rice	Cinnamon
3 tablespoons sugar	Sugar
½ teaspoon salt	Cream

Put milk, rice, sugar and salt into the top of a double boiler. Cover and cook 2½ to 3 hours over water until rice is soft and thick. Remove lid for the last 10 minutes of cooking.

Put an almond in the rice pudding just before serving. According to old Danish legend, whoever finds the almond at Christmas will have a series of lucky adventures.

Sprinkle the pudding with cinnamon and sugar and accompany with a pitcher of cream.

Serves 6 to 8.

RHUBARB TAPIOCA PUDDING

•

RABARBERBUDDING MED TAPIOCA

⅓ cup pearl tapioca	3 cups raw rhubarb, cut up
2½ cups boiling water	1 cup sugar
Pinch of salt	¼ teaspoon nutmeg, scant

Cover tapioca with cold water and soak overnight or until tapioca has absorbed all the water. Add the boiling water and salt and cook until the mixture comes to the boiling point. Put over water in the top of a double boiler and cook until it becomes transparent.

Place rhubarb in a well-buttered casserole or baking dish, cover with sugar and nutmeg, pour tapioca over and bake 25 to 30 minutes in a preheated 350° oven. Serves 6.

Serve hot or cold with lemon sauce, as follows:

LEMON SAUCE

1 cup sugar	2 cups boiling water
2 tablespoons soft butter	Juice and grated rind of 1 lemon
2 tablespoons flour	

Mix sugar, butter and flour until well blended. Slowly add the boiling water and cook about 15 minutes over very low heat or in the top of a double boiler over hot water. Add the lemon juice and rind and blend well.

RHUBARB PUDDING

·

RABARBERBUDDING

1 pound fresh rhubarb	¾ cup whipping cream
2 quarts water	1 egg yolk, beaten
Sugar to taste	Cinnamon (optional)
1½ tablespoons cornstarch	Ground nuts (optional)

Wash and cut the fresh rhubarb into small pieces. Cook in the 2 quarts of water until soft and mushy. Put the mixture through a sieve. Sweeten to taste.

Blend the cornstarch with a little cold water and stir gently into the pudding. Cook until clear and slightly thickened.

Whip the cream and fold in the egg yolk.

Beat the thickened pudding into the cream mixture and serve at once with any sauce you like, or top with whipped cream with a dash of cinnamon and a few ground nuts sprinkled over it.

Serves 6 to 8.

RUM CREAM MOLD

·

ROMFROMAGE

1½ tablespoons unflavored gelatin, or 1 tablespoon cornstarch	¼ cup sugar
	¼ teaspoon salt
3 tablespoons cold milk	2 tablespoons light rum
1½ cups cream	½ cup heavy cream
1 cup milk	Ground almonds
4 egg yolks	

Dissolve the gelatin or cornstarch in the cold milk. Set aside.

Scald the cream and the 1 cup of milk.

Beat the egg yolks with the sugar and salt. Take a few spoons of the hot cream mixture and slowly add to the egg mixture. Slowly add the rest of the cream mixture.

Place in the top of a double boiler to cook, stirring until it begins to thicken. Lower the heat and cook until the mixture coats the spoon. Remove from heat and allow to cool somewhat.

Add slowly the gelatin or cornstarch and stir well. Add the rum, blending well. Pour the mixture into a wet mold and chill for 2 hours.

When ready to serve, unmold, place dots of whipped cream over it and sprinkle with ground almonds.

Serves 6 to 8.

STRAWBERRY AND RHUBARB COMPOTE
•
JORDBÆR- OG RABARBERKOMPOT

1 quart strawberries	*1 teaspoon cornstarch*
2½ cups cut rhubarb	*1 tablespoon cold water*
1⅝ cups water	*Cream*
4½ cups sugar	

Wash the fruit. Cook the rhubarb in the water with the sugar over low heat until soft. When soft, lift the rhubarb out of the juice and then boil the strawberries in the juice for 2 minutes. Take out strawberries.

Arrange rhubarb and strawberries in layers in a bowl.

Stir the cornstarch with the cold water until smooth. Stir into the hot juice and let boil 2 minutes, stirring constantly. Pour over the fruit.

Serve hot or cold with cream. Serves 6 to 8.

FROZEN WHIPPED CREAM
•
FROSSEN FLØDE

3 cups whipping cream	*1 teaspoon vanilla extract*
3 tablespoons sugar	*Crushed fresh berries*

Whip the cream until stiff, and sweeten with the sugar. Add vanilla.

Turn in an ice-cream freezer until frozen, then pack in equal parts of ice and salt for 1 to 2 hours, or put into mold in freezing compartment of your refrigerator until serving time.

When ready to serve, add crushed fruit or berries for a topping. Serves 8 to 12.

CARAMEL CUSTARD

•

KARAMELBUDDING

12 eggs, separated
1 cup sugar
1 quart light cream

2 teaspoons vanilla
Brown sugar

Beat 6 egg whites and 12 egg yolks with the sugar for 15 minutes at low speed with an electric beater. Add the cream and vanilla. Heat to the boiling point. Let cool.

Melt enough brown sugar in a little water to line the bottom of a baking dish. Pour the batter over this and bake in a pan of hot water 1½ hours, or until set, in a preheated 250° oven.

Whip the other 6 egg whites with a little sugar until stiff but not dry. Spread over the dish of custard. Raise oven heat to 425°. Return baking dish to oven for 8 to 10 minutes, or until meringue is golden brown.

PEASANT GIRL WITH VEIL

•

BONDEPIGE MED SLØR

1¼ pounds tart apples
1 soupbowlful of grated, dry rye
   bread
2 tablespoons sugar

½ teaspoon salt
1 teaspoon butter
Chocolate
Whipping cream

Peel, core and slice the apples. Cook until soft, almost a pulp.

Mix the rye bread crumbs, sugar and salt. Add butter and cook over low heat until mixture is almost dry. Stir frequently to prevent scorching. Put a layer of this mixture in a greased baking dish; cover with a layer of apples. Continue alternating layers until all ingredients are used.

Sprinkle with grated chocolate. Bake in a preheated 350° oven 15 minutes.

Serve with a generous helping of whipped cream. Serves 4 or 5.

SAUCES FOR PUDDINGS AND OTHER DESSERTS

VANILLA SAUCE

•

VANILLESAUCE

4 egg yolks
½ cup sugar
1 teaspoon cornstarch

Pinch of salt
2 cups cream, scalded
1 teaspoon vanilla extract

Beat the egg yolks, sugar, cornstarch and salt until thick and lemon-colored. Slowly add the cream and cook in the top of a double boiler over hot water until thick. Beat well and blend in the vanilla.

WHITE WINE DESSERT SAUCE

•

VINSAUCE

3 egg yolks
½ cup sugar

¾ cup white wine

Beat the egg yolks well. Add the sugar and beat again. Cook in the top of a double boiler over hot water until thick.

Remove from heat and stir in the wine. Replace over lower part of double boiler and cook for a moment more.

BRANDY SAUCE #1

•

COGNACSAUCE

2 eggs, separated
2 cups powdered sugar

4 tablespoons brandy
½ pint whipping cream

Beat the egg yolks well. Add the sugar and beat. Add the brandy and beat again.

Whip the egg whites until stiff and fold in. Whip the cream and fold in gently but thoroughly. If you wish, sprinkle a little nutmeg on top.

BRANDY SAUCE #2

•

COGNACSAUCE

1 cup sugar
6 egg yolks
4 tablespoons dry white wine

1 teaspoon vanilla extract
6 tablespoons brandy

Mix sugar, egg yolks and white wine.

Cook over boiling water in the top of a double boiler, beating until thick.

Remove from heat. Add vanilla and brandy and mix well.

LEMON SAUCE

•

CITRONSAUCE

1 cup sugar
½ cup white wine
½ cup water

Grated rind and juice of 1 lemon
6 egg yolks

Mix sugar, wine, water and grated lemon rind. Beat egg yolks lightly and add with juice of lemon.

Simmer, stirring frequently, until the sauce begins to thicken.

Excellent over plain cake or bland custards which need an emphatic topping.

LIQUEUR SAUCE

•

LIKØRSAUCE

¾ cup water
4½ tablespoons sugar
1 teaspoon cornstarch
1½ tablespoons cold water

½ cup liqueur (Cointreau, anisette, crème de menthe or other flavor of your choice)

Mix water and sugar and cook to a thin syrup in the top of a double boiler placed directly over low heat.

Mix cornstarch with the cold water and stir into the syrup. Cook until clear. Place over hot water in lower part of double boiler to keep warm until you wish to serve it. Fold in the liqueur and blend well.

Serve over steamed puddings, ice cream or custards.

RED WINE DESSERT SAUCE

•

RØDVINSAUCE

1 cup red wine
½ cup cherry juice from cooked or canned cherries
1 tablespoon cornstarch

5 tablespoons water
1 tablespoon cognac
Almonds, ground or chopped (optional)

Put wine and cherry juice in saucepan.

Make a paste of cornstarch and water.

Heat wine and juice to boiling point and add moistened cornstarch to them. Stir until the mixture comes to a boil again. Let boil 1 or 2 minutes.

Remove from flame and add cognac. Chopped or ground almonds may be added.

Delicious over ice cream or custards.

CHERRY BRANDY SAUCE

•

COGNACSAUCE

1 pound sour red cherries
3 cups water
1 small stick cinnamon

2 tablespoons cornstarch
1 cup sugar
4 tablespoons brandy

Wash and pit cherries. Cook in water to cover with cinnamon stick 1 hour.

Discard cinnamon stick. Put cherries through a sieve and bring the juice to the boiling point.

Soften the cornstarch with a little cold water, mix with the sugar and stir into the hot juice. Cook 12 minutes, stirring constantly. Remove from heat and stir in brandy.

Serve cold on puddings, fruit cakes or other cakes.

NUTMEG SAUCE

•

SAUCE MED MUSKATNØD

1 cup sugar
⅜ teaspoon ground nutmeg
3 tablespoons flour
Pinch of salt

2 cups boiling water
1 tablespoon vinegar
1 tablespoon butter

Mix sugar, nutmeg, flour and salt and stir into the boiling water. Cook until thickened, stirring constantly.

Remove from fire and add vinegar and butter, mixing well.

Serve over bread or cottage pudding.

CHOCOLATE SAUCE

•

CHOKOLADESAUCE

8 tablespoons semi-sweet or milk
    chocolate "bits"
2 cups milk
1 egg yolk

1 tablespoon powdered sugar
1 teaspoon cornstarch
½ tablespoon cognac

Stir chocolate and milk in the top of double boiler over hot water until well mixed.

Beat the egg yolk and sugar together.

Mix the cornstarch with a little of the hot chocolate mixture. Mix well and stir into the yolk and sugar. Add this to the mixture in top of double boiler and let come to the boiling point.

Remove from heat and add the cognac. Beat and let rest a few moments. Serve warm or cold over any dessert for which a rich chocolate flavor is desired.

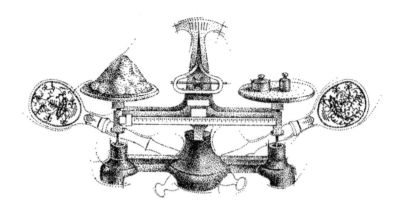

· 16 ·

CANDIES

CANDYMAKING was taught in many homes in Denmark as one of the most useful of womanly arts. The mother who made good confectionery acquired a reputation for being a gracious hostess.

You need the following to make gourmet candy: a marble slab; a shallow box about 3 inches deep lined with zinc or metal with similar properties; a couple of candy scrapers or children's toy hoes; a strong spatula with a hardwood handle; a double boiler; a thin, long-bladed, flexible palette knife; a scale; fancy molds; wooden spoons of many sizes; a measuring cup; a pair of tongs for dipping, and a candy thermometer.

Sugar should be confectioners' XXX for the finest of candy and the uncooked varieties. Grade A is not as fine but may be used for cooked candies of lesser grade than fondant.

ANISE CANDY

•

ANISKONFEKT

3 cups white sugar
1 cup light syrup
½ cup water

3 tablespoons vinegar
1 teaspoon oil of anise
1 teaspoon red food coloring

Boil sugar, syrup, water and vinegar to the hard-crack stage, 300 degrees, without stirring. Remove from the fire and quickly stir in the oil of anise and the red coloring.

Pour at once into a greased shallow pan about 10 by 8 inches. When the surface of the mixture is firm enough to hold the impression of a lightly drawn line, mark into 1-inch squares, or smaller, with a silver knife. When cold, break along the lines.

Will make about 80 squares of candy.

CHRISTMAS CANDY

•

JULEKONFEKT

2 cups raisins
1 cup blanched almonds, slivered
  or whole

½ pound semi-sweet or milk
  chocolate, melted

Rinse the raisins in hot water, drain and dry thoroughly.

Add raisins and almonds to half the melted chocolate. Mix well.

Cover cookie sheets with waxed paper. Pour mixture onto pans. Let cool for five minutes.

Spread remaining chocolate over the mixture. Let harden a few minutes. Cut into desired shapes.

DANISH CANDY

•

KARAMELLER

3 cups light brown sugar
¾ cup water
¼ teaspoon salt

2 egg whites
1 teaspoon vanilla

Dissolve the sugar in the water. Cook without stirring to 255 degrees (the hard-ball stage).

While the syrup is cooking, add the salt to the egg whites and then beat them until frothy.

Remove the syrup from the flame when it forms a hard ball and pour gradually over the egg whites, beating constantly. Add the vanilla. Continue beating until candy cools and will hold its shape. Drop by spoonfuls onto a buttered pan and mark into squares.

FONDANT

·

SUKKERKONFEKT

Frequent testing of the syrup is of paramount importance to the success of this. To prepare the fondant which is the creamy foundation for bonbons and exquisite creams, the syrup must be removed from the flame at the soft-ball stage—238 degrees. Do not stir the syrup while it is cooking. *Do* stir sugar and water together until the sugar is completely dissolved before cooking.

If the syrup should grain, add a few drops of boiling water until the grains are dissolved.

Here's what you need:

6 cups fine confectioners' sugar   *¼ teaspoon cream of tartar*
2 cups water

Boil rapidly together over a quick flame to the soft-ball stage. Remove from heat. Let cool to lukewarm before proceeding to use any of the recipes which follow (or others of your choice) for bonbons or creams. Yields about 1½ pounds of fondant.

Uncooked Fondant

1 egg white, beaten until frothy   *1 pound confectioners' sugar*
Equal amount of water

Mix egg white and water together. Whip in sugar a small amount at a time until you have a paste which will stand in a stiff peak and hold any shape you mold it into with your fingers.

Color and flavor this as you wish or in accordance with the directions in your favorite recipe. Makes about 2 pounds. Use all the fondant because it will harden rather quickly. This recipe may be substituted, as a center, for cooked fondant whenever you wish.

CHOCOLATE CREAMS

•

CHOKOLADEPRALINE

Fondant	*Paraffin*
1 pound bitter, semi-sweet, or	*Butter*
milk chocolate	*Vanilla*

Mold fondant into balls or other shapes with your fingers and let stand overnight on a marble slab, or on waxed paper, until thoroughly hardened. The longer they harden, the better.

Melt the chocolate very slowly in the top of a double boiler. When melted, add to it a lump of paraffin about the size of a walnut and a lump of butter half the size of the paraffin. Add a few drops of vanilla.

Keep the water in the lower part of the double boiler boiling to make sure the chocolate remains melted. Dip the fondant balls with tongs into the chocolate. Slip them onto waxed paper at once.

ALMOND CREAMS

•

MANDELKONFEKT

Fondant	*1 cup or more ground almonds*

Mold the fondant into fancy shapes and press finely ground almonds deep into the top and sides.

WALNUT CREAMS

•

VALNØDDEKONFEKT

Fondant	*English walnut halves*

Mold the fondant in any size and shape of your choice. Place half a nut meat on top of each piece.

OLD·FASHIONED HARD CANDY

•

BOLSJER

1 cup water	*¾ cup white syrup*
2 cups sugar	*½ teaspoon oil of anise*

Mix water, sugar and syrup and boil until a few drops of the mixture form hard, brittle threads when dropped into cold water (230–234°).

Remove from flame and add the oil of anise. Pour into well-greased pans. Mark into squares when the candy begins to cool, and break off as soon as possible.

Our Christmas tree was always trimmed with lovely, handmade ornaments — strings of popcorn, shiny apples, and fruits and vegetables made of marzipan with a string through each to hang on a branch, and decorated eggs. If you feel that sculpture in marzipan is not one of your talents, candy molds in various shapes are available at specialty stores all over the United States.

Here are 3 recipes for marzipan particularly well suited to decorative use but so good to eat you may find your Christmas ornaments mysteriously disappearing off the tree.

UNCOOKED MARZIPAN

•

MARCIPAN

½ cup confectioners' sugar	*2 egg whites*
½ cup granulated sugar	*Almond, or lemon, extract to taste*
2 cups almonds, ground	*Food coloring*

Sift the confectioners' and granulated sugars together. Add the ground almonds and mix well.

Beat the egg whites until frothy and blend into them the sugar and almond mixture. Add the extract and coloring.

Knead on a marble slab or table top until smooth. Add a little more sugar if necessary to form a stiff paste. Allow mixture to stand for a few hours. Then press small pieces into molds, or shape with your fingers as your skill and fancy dictate. Use the entire recipe at once. The mixture can't be saved for later shaping.

COOKED MARZIPAN

•

KOGT MARCIPAN

3 cups fine granulated sugar
1 cup water
5 cups almonds, ground

Almond, or lemon, extract to taste
Food coloring

Dissolve the sugar and water in a saucepan and add the ground almonds. Cook, stirring constantly, until the mixture comes away from the sides of the pan.

Remove from fire and turn out on a marble slab or spotlessly clean table top. Knead until smooth, adding the extract and coloring a few drops at a time while mixture is still warm.

Mold into any desired shapes.

MARZIPAN TO BE STORED FOR LATER USE

4 cups almonds, ground
1¼ pounds fondant (page 306)
4 cups sugar
2 cups water

1 tablespoon white syrup
Flavoring extract to taste
Food coloring

Rub almonds into the fondant with a wooden spoon.

Put sugar and water in a pan and heat slowly until sugar is dissolved. Add the syrup and let come to a boil, without stirring, until it forms a hard ball when tested in cold water. Add the fondant-almond blend at once and stir until it begins to harden.

Turn out on marble slab and knead until smooth. Add flavoring and food coloring while warm.

This marzipan will keep well if wrapped in waxed paper and a clean, soft cloth and stored in an airtight can in your refrigerator or freezer.

Here is a marzipan more suited to eating than decoration:

MARZIPAN WITH ALMOND PASTE

Almond Paste (Mandelcreme)

2 cups blanched almonds
½ cup confectioners' sugar
½ cup granulated sugar

Few drops of vanilla
Ice water

Put almonds through a nut grinder. Measure.

Combine all ingredients with enough ice water to form a stiff paste. Pound with a wooden mallet until the grain of the nuts has become very smooth and thoroughly blended. The paste is now ready to use in marzipan.

MARZIPAN (MARCIPAN)

1 pound almond paste (page 309)	6 cups powdered sugar
1/3 cup light syrup	Flavoring
1½ cups marshmallow topping	Food coloring

Mix almond paste, syrup and marshmallow topping in a bowl and mix well. Add the sugar, a little at a time, until the mixture holds its shape. Let stand overnight. Add desired flavoring extract and knead the marzipan well, adding a little more sugar if necessary to make it retain its shape.

Break off chunks and form into shapes and sizes of your pleasure, using different colorings to suit the objects you're simulating. Roll in powdered sugar. Let stand until dry.

ALMOND PASTE CANDY

•

MANDELKONFEKT

1 pound blanched almonds	¼ teaspoon salt
4 egg whites	2½ cups confectioners' sugar

Grind almonds 2 or 3 times.

Beat egg whites with salt until foamy but not too stiff. Stir in the sugar gradually so it is well blended. Add the ground almonds, mix and knead well until creamy and smooth. If the paste seems too stiff, add a few drops of lemon juice, one drop at a time until paste seems right to form into shapes. If it gets too thin, add more sugar.

Pack the mixture in a container with a cover and let rest in a cool place for at least 2 days to ripen. Shape into balls or other forms and roll in powdered sugar. It may also be rolled into small jelly-roll shapes and sliced.

Let stand overnight to form a crust if you would like to paint your shapes with food colorings to resemble strawberries, bananas, oranges, apricots, carrots, potatoes, etc. Use your own imagination to improvise stems and leaves when you need them.

POWDERED SUGAR CANDY

•

SUKKERKONFEKT

4 large potatoes, cooked and
    mashed
4 pounds powdered sugar

Food coloring (optional)
½ cup crushed pecans
1 tablespoon vanilla

Beat as much of the powdered sugar as is required to make a stiff mixture into the mashed potatoes while they are very hot.
    Add any food coloring desired. Add pecans and vanilla.
    Roll into small balls.
    This confection stays fresh and flavorful for a long time.

COCONUT CANDY

•

KOKOSNØDKONFEKT

1 cup white sugar
1 cup brown sugar
1 cup white syrup
1 cup sour cream

1 cup shredded coconut
1 teaspoon vanilla
2 tablespoons butter

Put the sugars, syrup and sour cream in a saucepan and stir until well mixed. Bring to a boil. Boil to a firm-ball stage (245°).
    Remove from fire and stir in the coconut, vanilla and butter. Pour the mixture into a buttered pan, mark into squares before it cools, and wrap squares individually in waxed paper when cold.

OLD DANISH RECIPE FOR CANDIED FRUITS

•

KANDISEREDE FRUGTER

3½ pounds granulated sugar   *1 pint* soft *water*

Make a syrup by boiling the water and the sugar 3 to 5 minutes.

Remove from fire. Immerse the fruit in the saucepan of syrup for about 2 hours. Strain off the syrup, which may be used for other candies or frostings.

Spread fruit on a flat pan or cookie sheet. Place in a warm oven with the door of the oven open and the heat turned off. When moisture has dried off the fruit, the sugar will have crystallized. Remove and store.

Any of the following fruits can be crystallized in this manner: grapes, plums, cherries, sections of oranges and lemons, grapefruit, tangerines, or pineapple.

INDEX

DANISH INDEX OF RECIPES

INDEX

[A recipe index in Danish will be found on page 331.]

Æbleskiver:
  raised, with currants, 290
  with applesauce, 290
Almond:
  bread, 21
  buns, 57
  butter balls, 102
  cake, 78-79
  cider frosting, 85
  cinnamon rolls, 59
  creams, 307
  filling, 113, 130
  icebox cookies, 114
  macaroons, 102
  paste, 95
  pastry ring, 62
  -potato dressing, 232, 233
  prune bread, 53
  pudding, 291
  rusks, 42
  slices, 63
  torte, 96
  torte, Bertine's, 98
  wine cookies, 104
Almond paste, 95
  candy, 310-11
  marzipan with, 309-10
Almonds, fish fillets with, 195
  sand cookies with, 127
Ammonia cookies, 103
Anchovies, potatoes and, scalloped, 168
Anchovy:
  paste, 140
  salad, 241
  spread, 143
Anise:
  candy, 305
  cookies, 101
  loaf, 21
Anniversary cake, 79
Apple:
  coffee cake, 71-72
  cream, 282
  dressing, roast goose with, 231
  fritters, cognac, 274
  pancakes, 268-69

porcupine, baked, 292
pudding, 291
soup, 183
Applesauce:
  æbleskiver with, 290
  cake, 79
Apricot buttermilk bread, 44
Apricot glaze, 135
Aspic:
  eel in, with creamed horseradish, 163
  fish in, 162
  meat, 166
  veal in, 165

Baked:
  apple porcupine, 292
  carrot ring, 259
  ham in wine, 211
  leeks with Hollandaise sauce, 261
  potato ring, 263
Baking utensils and equipment, mail-order sources for, 14
Barley soup, 178
Basic sweet dough, 43
Bean salad, 247
Béarnaise sauce, 219
Beef:
  boiled, with horseradish, 224
  corned, 221-22
  fillet of, 218
  forcemeat, 228
    cabbage with, 220
  hash, 224
  pot roast in sour cream, 220, 226
  roast, with Béarnaise sauce, 219
  steak, *see* Steak
  tenderloin in sour cream, 226
Beer:
  bread, 23
  bread, with fruit, 51
  cake, chocolate, 84
  cake from Kolding, 81
  cooking roasts with, 214
  fish cooked in, 196
  ham in, 213
  meat loaf, 208

DANISH INDEX OF RECIPES